ANTISUYO

THE SEARCH FOR THE LOST CITIES OF THE AMAZON

GENE SAVOY

SIMON AND SCHUSTER · NEW YORK

PUBLISHED BY SIMON AND SCHUSTER
ROCKEFELLER CENTER, 630 FIFTH AVENUE
NEW YORK, NEW YORK 10020

FIRST PRINTING

SBN 671-20220-0
LIBRARY OF CONGRESS CATALOG CARD NUMBER: 74-84132
DESIGNED BY EVE METZ
MANUFACTURED IN THE UNITED STATES OF AMERICA
PRINTED BY HALLIDAY LITHOGRAPH CO., HANOVER, MASS.
BOUND BY AMERICAN BOOK-STRATFORD PRESS, NEW YORK

This volume is dedicated to the memory of
Max Uhle, Antonio Raimondi, Julio C. Tello and Hiram Bingham
who cut the first trails.

and

To the people of Peru
without whose collaboration and kind assistance
the explorations—and this book—
could not have been realized.

ACKNOWLEDGMENTS

The author wishes to express his gratitude to all the many persons who contributed to the explorations and to the compilation of this book. Particular thanks are extended to the former President of the Republic of Peru, Fernando Belaúnde Terry, the Minister of Government, the Ministry of Education, the Guardia Civil y Policía, the Patronato Nacional de Arqueología, Servicio Aéreo Fotográfico Nacional (SAN), a division of the Peruvian Air Force, and especially to Benjamín Roca Muelle, ex-president of the Peruvian Tourist Corporation, for the valuable assistance given the expeditions. I also wish to thank the Prefects of the Departments of La Libertad, Cuzco and Amazonas for their help, and to acknowledge the invaluable aid given by the Centro de Estudios Arqueológicos de Chachapoyas, particularly to Father Carlos Gates Chavez, Arturo Zuviate and Germán Santillán. I am also indebted to my many friends at the National University of Trujillo, the Department of Archaeology and the Museum staff, to Eulogio Garrido, Virgilio Vanini de los Rios, Dr. Francisco Iriarte Brenner, Constante Traverso Lombardi and Guillermo Ganoza Vargas. Also to my many friends and colleagues in Lima who contributed to my research, these include: Emilio Harth-Terré, Gary Vescelius, Henry Reichlen, Hans Horkheimer, María de Diez Canseco, and many others.

Thanks are also extended to Dr. George O'Neill, professor of Anthropology at the City College of New York, for reading the original manuscript; and to Dr. Emilio Romero and César García Rossell of the Geographical Society of Lima; to Father Avencio Villarejo and the monks of the St. Augustine Monastery of Lima who gave me the use of the library. To all commercial firms and institutions who helped with my expeditions special thanks are extended, in particular to our special friends, Isaac and José Varón of the Savoy Hotel, Anselmo Fukuda and the Nikon people of Japan, Faucett Airlines, Robert Kicklighter of LAN Chile and Lou García of Braniff Inter-

7

national. I owe a debt of thanks to Carl Landegger, who arranged for carbon-14 tests of artifacts from the Chachapoyas ruins.

I must also give thanks to Julie D'Alton, Brooke Newman and Michael Korda of Simon and Schuster, who gave invaluable editorial criticism and helped shape the manuscript for the press. I am also grateful to C. N. Griffis and Dean Johnsos for their suggestions on the early chapters, and to my literary agent, Bertha Klausner. I owe much to Oscar Egusquiza for his technical assistance in helping make final photographs. I am grateful to my present secretary, Sylvia Ontaneda B., and to my former secretary Marysia Ryszarda Stasiaczek, both of whom typed the manuscript. To all members of the Andean Explorers Club, particularly to Jaime Casapia, Ivan Ortiz and to my former field assistant, Douglas Sharon, and to the many that must go unnamed: my muleteers, cargo-bearers, machetemen, guides, hunters and friends who accompanied me during my years of explorations; and to those who aided our movements while in the interior, special thanks which words cannot express are here given. Without them my work could not have been realized.

CONTENTS

PREFACE

This book is the story of my adventures as an explorer, taken from my notes written over a period of twelve years. I kept a daily account of my explorations, thoughts and observations, in the hope that one day they would be published. To some it may not read like an adventure, but adventure seldom happens the way we think it does.

I am not a professional scientist. I taught myself what I know about archaeology, anthropology and history from reading, study and practical field experience. I simply call myself an explorer and let it go at that. No one explores without a motivation and mine was a love of science and mythology. Call it love of adventure—or manhood wanting to express itself. I became an explorer because of the unpredictable and tremendous challenge confronting me. I was bored and disenchanted with an age when our technology is conquering outer space and turning our civilization into a mechanized mass society, where the individual is lost in the craze for material gain. I felt that South America was the last real frontier, the Dark Continent untamed. There, a man could get his feet on the ground. There, was an opportunity to make a contribution to man's knowledge. My fervent wish is that the reader (who undoubtedly has a spark of the fire of wanderlust inside as I did) will find my book as interesting to read as it was to live, and will perhaps feel the urge to take the same road I took. There are still many lost cities waiting to be discovered by anyone rebellious enough to start looking for them.

Gene Savoy

Andean Explorers Club
Lima, Peru
August 15, 1969

PART I

THE EARLY EXPLORATIONS

1957-63

1 · South America Calls

MEN DREAM of adventure and I am no exception. I cannot remember not wanting to be an explorer. I hated school when I was a boy. I would sit in the classroom listening to our history teacher describe the Fall of the Roman Empire, stressing names, dates and places, and I would gaze abstractedly out the window, wandering back in time and wishing I could visit the ancient temples and dusty gardens to see for myself what it was all like. I longed to break away and fly to strange and wondrous places. The best part of school was vacation time when my father would take me on trips to the north woods of Oregon and Washington. When we weren't hunting or fishing he would show me the haunts of wild animals. Sitting for hours we would watch deer, pumas, wildcats and black bears. Sometimes we would do nothing but follow a dung beetle as it trailed over dead leaves and pine cones. In this way my father taught me patience and how to observe. He used to say that a man is only as good in the woods as his power to be aware of everything, no matter how small or insignificant.

As I grew older, we would go out to the Indian reservation and talk with the old men of the camp. I learned to look up to them as an old and wise race who knew the woods better than anyone. My great grandmother was part Cherokee Indian, and although my ancestors were predominately French and English, the fact that I was one sixty-fourth Cherokee was powerfully romantic to a young boy. The notion of running away to the reservation entered my head more than once during school. It was natural, then, for me to form an early interest in the history, legends and folklore of North American Indians.

In 1947, after two years in the Naval Air Service during World War II, I entered the University of Portland. Even then I was haunted by dreams of travel and adventure and I dropped out before graduating to become publisher and editor of a lumberman's trade journal and later a weekly newspaper. My work took me up and down the Pacific Coast from California to

15

Canada and left me spare time to pursue my interest in Indian life. I was a member of the Oregon Archaeological Society and often joined in on weekend digs where we were overjoyed if we found a few bits of broken bone or a few arrowheads after a hard day's screening. But I grew tired of excavation and took up archaeological photography because it gave me the freedom to roam about, which was more to my nature.

Later I founded and presided over an explorers' club in Portland which attracted an ardent following. We would meet at the club headquarters and talk for hours about mounting an expedition to Mexico and discovering a Mayan city in the Yucatán jungles, or finding a lost Inca city in Peru. But we never did it. We were all young businessmen trying to get ahead in the world. One or two of us managed to get away on a two-week vacation to Mexico once a year; but that was as close to the grand expedition as we ever got. Mostly we contented ourselves with spelunking caves, climbing mountains or looking for the proverbial arrowheads.

More time passed and there were periods when it looked as if I were going to become a financial success in publishing. In 1956 the blow came. I woke up one morning to discover I had lost my company, holdings, home, money. Not long after, my wife and I decided to terminate our marriage.

After I recovered from the initial shock of financial failure I began to experience a marvelous sense of independence. I was absolutely free to do exactly as I wanted. One day I jumped into my old panel truck equipped with bed, stove, books and camping gear and drove down to California where I spent three months in the Sierra Nevada planning my new life. I weighed the possibilities of returning to the university to study archaeology and anthropology but gave it up because of my age. Almost thirty and enflamed with restlessness, an education seemed tame in the light of what I really wanted to do. "Why not strike out and go to Mexico or South America and explore for lost cities as you've always wanted to do?" I asked myself. As a journalist and photographer, perhaps I could write and illustrate articles on a free-lance basis, picking up on the job what had to be learned about archaeology and anthropology. The more I thought about it, the more intriguing the idea became. I was determined to go but I wasn't sure just how to manage it.

Through a curious chain of events the opportunity came the following year. Earlier I had given a lecture to a group of dedicated amateur archaeologists and explorers and my ideas had been picked up by a news reporter and ran across the U.S. by one of the big wire services. I had shown my motion-picture film of stone carvings, petroglyphs and pictographs etched on boulders along the Columbia River Valley between Oregon and Washington (soon to be inundated by flood waters of The Dalles Dam then under construction), and from other parts of the Pacific Northwest up to and including British Columbia, Canada. I described what I believed to be similarities in design between the picture writings and carvings of the Maya civilization of Mesoamerica and the Chavín culture, a high civilization which archaeologists say existed in the northern Andes of Peru sometime between 1800 and 400 B.C. I offered the hypothesis that there may have been contact between North and South America at one time. I speculated that there could have been trade between the Americas by land and sea routes. The discoverer of the Chavín culture speculated that its origins might be found in the tropical rain forest east of the Andes. This seemed like a logical deduction. Many early civilizations in the world flowered in tropical regions and it was reasonable to assume that remains of ancient high civilizations in the Americas might exist in the jungles of South America.

The idea intrigued me. Perhaps the remains of ancient civilizations could be found in the Amazon Rain Forest. An old anthropologist friend and teacher at the University of Portland was fascinated by my ideas. He pointed out that the Mayan civilization was native to the tropics but in scientific conservatism doubted that I would find evidence of older cultures in the tropics as it seemed likely that the southern cultures had their origins in the Andes. Yet, he encouraged me to go ahead with my plans to explore by saying that while the most notable archaeological sites in South America are found along the coast and highlands, there is some evidence to suggest long habitation in the jungles. Excavations along the Amazon and lesser tributaries of Brazil, Peru, Colombia, Ecuador and Venezuela have uncovered pottery fragments of high workmanship, but no great cities of high civilizations have been found in jungle regions, except for a few sites on the eastern slopes of the Andes. "Find those cities," he said, "and you may revolutionize current ideas on the matter."

As a result of the news story, an American archaeologist scheduled to leave for South America to participate in a botanical expedition wrote me a letter bearing a Mexican postmark dated March 29, 1957. He was departing for Peru, had read about my interest in pre-Columbian cultures and asked if I would like to join on as cameraman and chief photographer. While the main purpose of the jungle expedition was to gather plants and herbs with possible medical properties, he intended to conduct some archaeological investigation on his own. He offered nothing more than the privilege of filming the expedition and the right to use the film as I liked. I was to pay my own passage to Peru and return. If acceptable I was to wire my answer to the American Embassy in Lima before the middle of April. It took me exactly five minutes to make up my mind. I telegraphed giving the time and date of arrival.

I boarded a plane in Los Angeles the night of April 12, but upon arrival in Lima discovered that problems had developed. The financial backers—a drug firm interested in the commercial possibilities of any plants that might be used for medical cures—had decided that they could not meet the last-minute demands of the leaders who had asked for additional funds. So the expedition was off.

Borrowing funds from family and friends, I flew to Trujillo, Peru's third city, to plan an expedition of my own. A young Canadian by the name of Douglas Sharon took interest in my ideas. Short, thin and wiry, of Scottish descent, with sandy-blond hair, clear blue eyes and a row of even, white teeth, he was animated by a warm disposition that made him easy to work with. He joined in my work as my assistant. This was the beginning of a close association which was to last a good number of years and carry us through many an adventure together.

I traveled to Lima in 1957 and visited the publisher of the *Peruvian Times*, a weekly English language news magazine. Explaining that I was a free-lance journalist-photographer turned explorer, I asked if they would consider publishing a series of illustrated articles on my field trips. Both Donald Griffis and his father, C. N. Griffis, an old-time publisher with half a century of reporting in South America, agreed to run a series. The pay wasn't astronomical, but it was pay. With a publisher I began to feel secure.

Upon my return to Trujillo, I found myself in a pleasurably unexpected situation. Lunching one day with friends from a local English construction company that was building the nearby port of Salaverry for the Peruvian government, I was introduced to an attractive, blue-eyed blonde by the name of Dolly Clarke Cabada. To my delight she, like so many women from well-to-do Peruvian families, spoke English. I never thought I would marry again, but months later I proposed.

That July I decided to film the desert since I had several thousand feet of 16mm film that had to be used. Going over to the National University of Trujillo to seek assistance, I met Don José Eulogio Garrido, Director of the National Archaeological Museum who offered to give me whatever technical assistance I required. He offered a jeep with driver and field assistant and the use of the museum staff. Later an airplane was provided for aerial survey work.

Garrido, an old man who was an authority on north coast civilizations of times past, took pains to explain something about the great Chimu civilization, which appears to have been built over the remains of the Mochica culture, and whose center was at the magnificent mud-walled city of Chanchan close to Trujillo which covers an area of eleven square miles. Before their conquest by the Incas in A.D. 1466, the Chimu Empire flourished for over three centuries spreading north to Ecuador and south to Lima. A great trading people, the Chimu sent large balsa fleets by sea to Ecuador and beyond. Several archaeologists had noted Chimu influence in the north and I had noted the similarity of Chimu motifs with those of the Mayans of

Mesoamerica. Chimu had reached a high level of advancement long before the imperial armies of the Inca overthrew their culture. Their mud temples were paneled with gold and the city walls painted brilliant colors. Artificial gardens were created in precious metals; whole trees, flowers, plants, fruits, vegetables, birds and animals fashioned in gold and silver. The stone works of the Incas seem insignificant in comparison to these mighty works.

After a long and difficult war, the Incas plundered the fabulously wealthy treasury of Chimu which included some of the finest art pieces ever produced in ancient Peru, and sent the Chimu goldsmiths and craftsmen to Cuzco to work in the Inca capital. With the conquest of the Chimu Kingdom, the Incas absorbed into their empire what is believed to have been the largest and most powerful regime they had ever defeated. Observing the magnificent remains of adobe temples, pyramids and city layouts scattered about the sandy deserts of north and central Peru, it is obvious what the victory must have meant to them.

When I visited the great metropolitan complex of Chanchan for the first time, I was amazed at its high walls of packed clay and gravel, the complex interiors and the highly artistic and sensitive wall frieze which decorates the great maze of adobe structures. The majestic Huacas of the Sun and Moon in the nearby Moche Valley are no less imposing. Built of millions of sun-dried bricks and originally painted with murals, these imposing step-pyramids, which were built by an older people called the Mochicas or Moche who were absorbed by a highland race long before the coming of Chimu, stand in the desert wastes like the artificial mountains they are. One is reminded of the ziggurats of ancient Babylonia, but of course the Peruvian pyramids are of much later origin.

When the Spaniards came they looted these and other ruins of their remaining gold and silver, and melted down the sacred metal into ingots for transport to Spain. In this way the majority of Chimu and Mochica art work was lost to the world. However, many private collections and public museums in Peru and around the world have managed to preserve thousands of richly decorated ceramic vases, gold ornaments and colorful textiles which tell us how sophisticated these coastal people were.

Searching through the archives I came upon a copy of an old Spanish manuscript by Miguel Cavello Balboa that told of Naymlap, a Lambayeque chief (a culture to the north sometimes identified with Chimu), having come by sea on a great fleet of ships that strengthened my own ideas about cultural exchanges between old civilizations by means of the sea.

Gleaning what I could from a number of old texts, I turned my attention to a study of Mochica-Chimu artifacts in the museum and private collections in the community. It was clear to me that the profusion of serpents, monkeys and jaguars illustrated on pottery and textiles bore traces of an undoubted contact with the jungle. The evidence of parrot feathers used in feather-weaving strengthened this hypothesis. If the Chimu had arrived from the sea, had they migrated south from the jungles of Honduras, Guatemala or Mexico? Or had the older Mochicas bequeathed this jungle iconography to the newcomers? If so, had they too come from the sea having made contact with tropical regions before arriving in Peru? Or had they reached the Peruvian coast from the jungles east of the Andes? There was little, if any, real archaeological evidence to support any of these theories. But I felt pretty certain that the Mochicas and the Chimu had been a seafaring people; this was evidenced by the large variety of ceramic representations showing reed balsa boats and multi-decked galleys. Old texts were illustrated with ships made of totora or reed and balsa-log rafts used to haul cargo up and down the coast before the coming of the conquistadores. Their use of pearls, conch shells and a variety of other objects indicated they had traded with or had contact with foreign shores.

Even more important was the evidence that suggested these people were very familiar with—indeed, may have had their origin in—the jungles; a concept which was generally opposed in archaeological circles. As far as I could make out from my talks with scholars, no city-type dwellings of any ancient Peruvian high civilization had been found beyond the eastern Cordilleras. Chavín, Kuelap, Huánuco and Marañón sites are found on the eastern slopes of the Andes, but these are isolated and remote. The accumulated findings demonstrated that older cultures were restricted to the coast and highlands (any contact with the jungle was thought to be minimal). This concept seemed to be supported both in Peru and abroad. The evidence which supported my growing conviction was mostly hypothetical and based on my visual examination of vase and textile representations which showed sea and jungle scenes—generally thought to be mythological illustrations— but from what I could gather the Mochica and Chimu were a very practical people and depicted daily events in art work. I felt I had a stroke of good luck and stumbled on to my first real lead. The question now was finding the missing pieces to this fascinating puzzle.

In June 1958, I left Peru for an extended trip to Mexico with Dolly, who by this time was becoming interested in my explorations. We were married and spent six months visiting all the ruins of Yucatán, where I fulfilled an old desire to study the Mayan ruins firsthand. Our trip was interrupted when Dolly became pregnant. Complications arose and we journeyed to Florida for competent medical treatment. She gave birth to a fine healthy boy, though premature. In 1960 we went to live in Mexico, first at Veracruz, then Jalapa, so I could continue my research of ancient Mexican cultures. Early 1961 saw us once again back in Peru with the intention of settling down permanently. I was by this time firmly convinced from my studies— and by some inner, intuitive power—that the high and low jungles of eastern Peru contained vestiges of forgotten civilizations.

I compared the Aztecs of Mexico with the Incas of Peru, both highland cultures, so it would appear, who came upon the scene at a comparatively late period in history. The older and more advanced culture of Mexico had been the Mayas, a tropical people. Was it not possible that Peru, too, had had its own earlier jungle civilization that might be favorably compared to the Mayas? I was staking everything on my assumption being correct and was determined to explore full-time in order to prove it—or at least to satisfy my own curiosity.

2 · Disaster

UPON OUR RETURN to Peru I organized the Andean Explorers Club as an informal, non-profit group of archaeological enthusiasts and explorers. We decided to hunt for archaeological remains in out-of-the-way places, document our work by camera and make our findings available to scientific institutions, museums and specialists, both in Peru and abroad. We were able to enlist about one hundred members, fortunately including a few financial backers. I was elected President and Chief Explorer; Douglas Sharon, Field Secretary; Oscar Egusquiza, Peruvian photographer, our chief laboratory technician; and Mirko Ristivojevich, a Yugoslavian, aviator. A number of local and foreign archaeologists promised to help us analyze our findings. The main purpose of the Club, in addition to serving as a vehicle for full- and part-time explorers who could take to the field in search of unreported archaeological remains, was to popularize our work through magazine and newspaper articles, photographic exhibitions and motion-picture showings. Everyone was enthusiastic about my plan to launch an attack on the eastern jungles in search of city ruins and I spent the first few months researching such a project.

The late Julio C. Tello, the Peruvian archaeologist who gave the world of archaeology the Chavín culture, thought to be Peru's oldest at the time, had studied this high civilization that flourished in northern Peru three thousand years ago and documented his findings. He theorized that this mysterious people, who attained a remarkable level of advancement on the eastern slopes of the Andes, originated in the eastern forests. This was in opposition to the German archaeologist-anthropologist, Max Uhle, the first to classify Peruvian cultures, who supposed that the older cultures had their origin in Mexico or Central America and probably came to Peru by sea. Tello had observed that the farther east one explores, the older the cultures encountered. To my knowledge no one had ever investigated this unusual theory. It gave support to my own thinking and I decided to use Tello's theories as a base for an exploration project across the Marañón River. If one is to explore the jungle one cannot start cutting a swath through the vegetation, machete in hand, in hopes of bumping into an overgrown city. It isn't that simple. The jungles are too vast and wild for that. Tello's ideas could be used as a road that could be followed. At least I hoped they could.

So it was that I finally decided to start looking for jungle remains. My plan was to move my family to the heart of the Chavín Empire and to study the remains of these ancient people.

We leased a picturesque two-story house in Yungay, a small town in the beautiful Callejón de Huaylas. The region is often called the Switzerland of Peru because of the spectacular snowcapped Cordillera Blanca whose jagged, saw-toothed pinnacles form the world's longest chain of high mountains. They average 18,000 to 20,000 feet in altitude—with the exception of the famous Huascarán Mountain which towers 22,198 feet—and dwarf the alps. Mountain climbers come from all over the world to scale these challenging peaks.

I would use Yungay as a highland base of explorations in the Ancash region and the upper Marañón, dividing my time between Trujillo and the sierra. Many Chavín sites, including the magnificent temple ruins of Chavín de Huantar, were nearby. The whole area was littered with archaeological remains and I found traces of roads that ran in an easterly direction. With great anticipation, I began preparations for exploring these highland arterials. I felt strongly that they would lead into the jungle and, if this should prove to be true, there was a strong possibility of finding evidence that might strengthen Tello's theory that the Chavín culture originated east of the Marañón River. I found this a terrifically exciting prospect.

Suddenly, my plans were unexpectedly and drastically changed—this time by a catastrophe which almost crushed my spirit of adventure forever.

Early one day, Dolly and I drove to Ranrahirca, a small village of white-washed cottages with red tile roofs near Yungay, to purchase building materials. A small town of twenty-five hundred persons, Ranrahirca was situated in a fertile valley which had its origin near the Huascarán. Another fifteen hundred people lived in villages farther up the valley. It was the major fruit-producing center for the whole area. We had thought about living there, since it offered a marvelous view of the Huascarán, but chose Yungay instead. Though heavily populated, these valleys never felt safe to me because of their long and bitter history of avalanches. The residential section of Huarás had been wiped out several years before with the loss of nearly five thousand people. It was one of Peru's great catastrophes. Similar avalanches had struck this valley in 1912, according to stories told by the old men of the village, and Yungay had been completely destroyed in 1872, before it was moved to its present location behind the safety of a large mountain.

We returned home and Dolly left for Huarás, capital of the department

23

of Ancash, to do some shopping. Later in the day she visited friends at the resort hotel at Monterrey with our two sons, and when our smaller son, Jamil, accidentally got his feet wet in the garden, she immediately started for home. That early departure probably saved her life.

About this time, while I was writing, I heard a loud, roaring sound. It came like distant thunder from the direction of the Huascarán. I remember looking up from my typewriter, but I didn't see anything unusual. I thought perhaps some snow and ice had fallen from one of the glaciers. This wasn't uncommon; spring and summer thaws weaken the accumulation of snow and ice on the Andean heights. I went back to my work. At that moment, my wife and children were ten minutes from Ranrahirca.

The inhabitants of the village were celebrating the final day of the Fiesta of the Christ Child. The market was filled with many visitors; bands filled the mountain air with music, bursting skyrockets left puffs of white smoke against the blue sky. Processions of colorfully dressed people wound their way through the narrow streets carrying baskets of flower offerings to the Infant Jesus. Everyone was in a gay, festive mood. No one had the slightest idea of the terrible tragedy which was about to take place.

I heard Dolly drive up and sent the house boys out to help with the packages. A strange stillness had fallen over the village in spite of the street noise. The birds had stopped singing and the soft breeze that had been blowing most of the day subsided. Not a leaf rustled. It was twenty minutes after six. My wife had no more than put everything away and changed Jamil's shoes and stockings when Douglas Sharon's younger brother, Robert, ran in to report that an avalanche had swept over Ranrahirca. The community was reported to be completely wiped out.

A short time later a group of men came to the house and asked us to join a search party. We went down to the scene of the avalanche and were faced with a great wall of mud, stones, huge chunks of ice and snow thirty feet high, half a mile wide. It completely covered what had been a pleasant village a few hours before—a staggering sight.

We set to work looking for survivors. Late that night some of us returned to Yungay and other stayed on to look for friends and families. Very few were found alive. Ranrahirca was gone. We knew several thousands had perished and that January 10, 1962, would go down as one of the world's worst avalanche disasters.

At dawn, four of us started a new search for survivors. We learned that a second avalanche had struck at two o'clock in the morning and had carried off many rescuers working by lantern light. Two hours later a third and final flow swept over the valley. Some said that the famous church of the Lord of Miracles with its beautiful silver images and paintings, in the center of the village, had withstood the first avalanche. Survivors by the hundreds had flocked to it to call upon the Lord to save them but were swept away in the second flood of snow, mud, ice and rock that carried away what remained of the village.

One usually pictures an avalanche as a huge mass of white, puffy snow, but this one wasn't that pretty. Nearly three million tons of glacier and rock had dropped off the face of the Huascarán and plummeted straight down a steep gorge. It had ten times the force of a bursting dam. It cut down everything like a grinding stone. Small villages and their inhabitants were carried away before it struck Ranrahirca. Like a giant tidal wave, it drove into the mountainside across the Santa River with a terrific roar and continued down the Santa destroying bridges as it went until it finally spent itself in the Pacific Ocean a hundred miles away.

Dawn brought a gray, sad, misty morning. Everyone looked for the Huascarán; but dark clouds hid it from view. Somebody said the whole mountain had fallen down. Survivors who had fled to the safety of the hilltops during the night began to come down to the floor of the valley now that it was growing light. They had heard the first rumblings of the avalanche and thinking it was the end of the world, had rushed uphill.

A wrinkle-faced old man was sitting on the ground under a large, brown poncho. He was cursing the Huascarán with shaking fist. "Villain!" he ranted. "Killer of women and children! Come out and face me like a man! Why do you hide behind clouds? Assassin! Coward! I am waiting for you!" To these people the mountain was a living thing.

"They are all gone," stammered a young man with tears in his eyes, "all gone. I alone am alive!" He came over to speak with us. He had lost seventy-two kinfolk: wife, children, mother, father, brothers, sisters, aunts, cousins—everyone. He had searched all night without finding a living soul. He accompanied us for a while as we made our way along the edge of the avalanche flow until he fell in with a group of people.

Farther along we came across a farmhouse. The landslide had taken away about a third of the south side nearest the flow, and mud was seeping inside through the doors. Outside on the porch sat a wizened old man. His daughter was at the front door, trying to sweep away the mud which was coming in like a thick, heavy carpet. He made no attempt to help.

"It is worse than Huarás. Worse than Huarás," he kept saying over and over again, while looking up toward the Huascarán. He was referring to an earlier avalanche which had struck Huarás some years before.

"Old man," I said, "the mud is filling your house. Help your daughter."

"I won't touch the mud," he answered sternly. "It has killed my people!"

"But you are alive and you must fight the mud," said one of the men.

"It is a defilement to touch it," he answered. "A terrible defilement." I found myself unable to answer.

He turned and looked at me, spoke in a voice heavy with melancholy.

"Is it not a terrible thing to see Ranrahirca die?"

25

"Yes," I agreed, "a terrible thing."

Yanama Chico had been a tiny village of nine hundred people located above Ranrahirca in the lofty crags of the Cordillera. Not one of its two hundred houses remained standing. Schacsha with its four hundred inhabitants had disappeared also. So had Uchucoto—and others. They had vanished without a trace. Sadly, we returned to the lower valley over the trail on which we had come. Occasionally we met small groups of anguished survivors clustered together, quietly surveying the silent, deathlike canyon which only a few hours before had been a raging deluge.

Later we learned that no less than four thousand and possibly as many as five thousand persons had been swept to their deaths in the catastrophe. The tragedy had come at dinnertime with people at home. The fiesta had brought family and friends from all over the valley to visit relatives, which made the loss far greater than it would have been ordinarily. The census reports would never tell the true story. Of that, I was certain.

The community had asked my wife and me to help solicit aid and assistance from Lima. The road to Huarás was out and a bridge beyond Caras had been washed away; we were isolated except by air. Yungay's water supply was cut and there was no running water for sewage disposal. The city fathers were afraid of a possible epidemic of typhoid and typhus. I had been up to look at the water source and felt there was real danger from pollution from human corpses and animal carcasses. We would need a water filter, so I took specimens of drinking water to Lima for analysis.

Ten days passed before we were able to arrange for an airplane back to Yungay with help from the Peruvian Air Force. A deadly pall hung over the town. I expected to see the community swarming with activity, as it had been the day we left, but it was nearly deserted. The press had slipped out as suddenly as it had gone in. A few medical doctors arrived to help with special cases. The Peruvian Army had everything under military control. Food was being airlifted because the roads were still cut. It was as though the village had died. The public fountain was empty, the plaza was deserted. The tall royal palms stood like tombstones. We passed a funeral procession on the way to the cemetery. Bold black crosses were etched on doorways, a sign that people were dying. A riderless mare with shaggy mane and glazed eyes grazed on tufts of grass growing out of the cobblestone street near our home. It gave out a foreboding neigh that sent a shiver down our spines, and then moved off at a trot.

When the villagers learned we were in town, they came to see us. I explained what I had been able to achieve in Lima, but they said that nothing was being done about the water filter. Many children were down with fever. Even our son Jamil was not feeling well, and his condition grew worse. The doctor warned us that a rough journey in the bouncy, two-motored army plane and the 20,000-foot flight over the Andes might be fatal and so I decided to leave him with my wife and try to bring back a specialist. Determined to find medical help for my son and a new filter for our village, I left by plane for Trujillo.

I had spoken to the American Ambassador by telephone and he informed me that the American people were willing to give Yungay a water filter if it could be flown in and approved by the Peruvian government. I planned to fly to Lima the next day. That night Douglas, who had braved a cold, long trail to Huarás, got through to me on the telephone. Jamil had passed away. I spent the rest of the night desperately trying to make arrangements to fly back to Yungay. Early the next morning I was flown by special army plane through the courtesy and understanding of a sympathetic general of the Peruvian Army. It was the longest flight of my life.

3 · Exploring the Great Walls of Peru

February 1962

AFTER THE AVALANCHE we returned to our coastal headquarters at Trujillo. I had considered returning to the States; yet, an adventurous heart is not easily changed, not even by pain and loss. So I decided to carry on with my work.

One day in February I called Mirko Ristivojevich, the Club pilot, with whom I had made many aerial surveys along the coast and suggested that we go exploring by air.

From the air above the flat, sandy desert, the jigsaw puzzle of ancient settlements suddenly falls into place. On the ground, they appear to be a meaningless hodgepodge of assorted mud walls, broken buildings, stepped-pyramids and pitted, bone-strewn fields. From the air these outlines take on a far more important appearance. The temple grounds and surrounding urban settlements, irrigation works, roads and hilltop fortifications blend together into a meaningful pattern.

We drew up a flight plan that brought us directly over the delta of the Santa River at an altitude of about 3,000 feet. To the east we could make out the snowy crests of the Huascarán only sixty miles away. It was hard to believe that Yungay was so close, and yet so completely alien to the coastal plains spread out below. Far below, the rushing waters of the Santa tumbled down from the Callejón de Huaylas to empty into the Pacific. Several islands rose up out of the sea like icebergs, their rocky pinnacles topped with white guano. Lines of foaming waves broke up on the sandy beaches.

The strip of desert coast at this point gives way to the rolling foothills of the Andes, gradually rising up to form the Cordillera Negra which, though snowless, average 10,000 to 15,000 feet above sea level and beyond that, the snowy heights of the Cordillera Blanca, a chain of the Western Andes, gives birth to the mother of all rivers, the Amazon. These mountains slope off to the east where the high jungles of the Peruvian *montaña* begin and they in turn drop down to form a tangled green sea of jungle that spreads all the way to the Atlantic coast 3,000 miles away. By flying due east up over the Andes we would come out over the jungle in an hour or so.

Ancient peoples had been attracted to this fabulously rich land as far back as 10,000 years or more. Evidence of old occupations, crumbled away and buried under deep layers of sand and earth, have been carefully dug up by archaeologists, but the vestiges of more recent occupations such as the Mochica, Chimu, Paracas, Nazca, among others along the coast and highlands, are everywhere. Surprisingly, a large number remain archaeologically unstudied and unreported. It seems odd that an ancient land contained within only three times the size of California should possess so many unknown sites, but Peru is so incredibly varied—worlds within worlds and no connecting roads—that archaeological exploration is now just beginning.

I observed the complex of ruins stretching over the desert below; many were all but covered by sand blown by sea winds. Garrido had brought my attention to the existence of the so-called Great Wall of Peru which, like the larger and famous wall of China, was believed to have been thrown up by the Chimu as a barricade against invasion. The stone and adobe brick construction had first been spotted from the air in 1931 by the Shippee-Johnson Aerial Photographic Expedition while making a routine flight over the Santa Valley, the largest river of the coast which empties into the Pacific south of Trujillo and just north of Chimbote, a large fishing and iron center.

Julio C. Tello, the famous Peruvian authority, and two Americans had examined a portion of the wall a few years later (which confused the picture even more, because, in Tello's opinion, the wall was pre-Chimu), but the greater part of this strange barrier had not been thoroughly explored nor photographed; nor had the great stone structures been examined on the south bank of the river across from the wall. The Shippee-Johnson Expedition had spotted fourteen such structures and assumed these rectangular, circular and square buildings to be fortresses. Garrido said that as far as he was concerned the Great Wall and the structures on the opposite bank were unexplored and as much a mystery today as they had been twenty-five years before.

This sounded like a tremendously interesting subject for photographic exploration and in July 1957, we put together the Great Wall of Peru Expedition under the auspices of the museum and the university at Trujillo. I took command as field leader, assisted by Sharon and a museum assistant, Pedro Puerta. Garrido served as archaeologist. A jeep with driver and an airplane and pilot were placed at our disposal.

Mirko had been orbiting and studying the ruins scattered below, and I pointed out traces of the Great Wall. It had been discovered thirty years earlier and although parts of it were undoubtedly uncovered during ground explorations, aerial survey had put these pieces together to make a synthesis of the whole.

I suggested to Mirko that we explore the wall further. He nodded approval and made a wide sweep above the ocean that brought us to the delta where we picked up the wall again. It ran over the desert parallel with the river and disappeared into the hills to the east. Suddenly our plane was buffeted up and down in the treacherous drafts which are created by the strong winds sweeping down from the highlands. Mirko brought the plane down to 1,500 feet and the plane smoothed out.

The coastal section of the Great Wall is made of adobe brick and a mixture of mud and stone shaped like an inverted "V" and runs across the desert at angles. It eventually cuts back up over the hills where it serpentines over the mountainous terrain. At this point, where the wall runs through extensive stretches of isolated areas, the ancient builders used piled stone in place of the adobe brick. If the wall had actually been built for defense, naturally a stronger material would have been preferable for greater protection in strategic places.

On the other hand, our ground explorations had located sections constructed from adobe farther up river, but these were either fragmentary or secondary walls or the outer walls of temple and pyramid layouts. The best section of wall was found a little west of the hacienda Tanguche and was built of piled stone cemented with mud. It stood 8 to 10 feet high on the average, but in some places it was 14 to 15 feet; it gave the appearance of having been much higher at one time before the centuries of time began to topple it.

We flew on past fragmentary walls and scattered ruins including pyramids, temple layouts, large stone buildings and defending walls at the summits.

We reached Suchimancillo, crossed over to Tablones on the south bank of the Santa and barreled up a dry canyon where we could see massive fortresses perched atop the surrounding hills. The sound of our engine sent a terrible reverberation bouncing off the dry, rocky heights. Mirko banked the plane and swept past a string of circular constructions with square turrets jutting out on all sides. We banked and skimmed over a dusty plateau. A double-walled, turreted building of stone block stood at the far end flanked by two slopes. (Plate 1.) He headed for it and shot past the 15-foot walls like a rocket, zooming up and gaining altitude. (Plate 2.)

[PLATE 1] *Aerial photograph of rectangular stone building, possibly a fortress, with seven protruding turrets and an inner wall lined with rooms. Structure is situated on plateau of Santa Valley.*

The Great Wall and the stone forms had remained a mystery for over thirty years. Who built them? What were they used for? This was something that hadn't been answered.

Parts of the lower ground had been excavated and had revealed the Santa culture but the high hilltops surrounding the region were untouched by archaeologists; they were situated atop craggy elevations that rose as high as 3,000 feet above the valley floor. I knew how difficult it was to explore them because I tackled these heights in 1957–58. I had been astounded by the size and variety of the cyclopean structures. They were circular, rectangular, oval and pear-shaped with salient angles. Stone walls measured up to 18 feet high, 6 feet or more thick, and anywhere from one to several city blocks in length. Some of the stones used in construction were the size of a small automobile and weighed many tons. It is possible that some sections of these walls may originally have stood 30 to 40 feet high, judging from the thousands of tons of building blocks that have since fallen down the sides of the hills.

Our circuitous flight pattern brought us over a mountain range upland from Tablones in the Chuquicara Valley on the rail route to Huallance. We sighted several oval-shaped citadels with concentric walls, then dropped lower down the valley in the upper regions of Vinzos. All along the mountain ranges and spurs we saw similar constructions as those in the Tablones area. These structures were U-shaped, rectangular and elliptical. One was formed like a pentagon with defending walls. Another had what looked like a moat with escarpments around it.

From the air, we counted thirty-four strongholds crowning the heights—twenty more than had previously been known—and the following day we sighted eight more.

Two historians, Pedro Cieza de León, the Spaniard, and Garcilaso de la Vega, the son of an Inca princess and a Spanish conquistador, wrote that the Santa Valley was the most beautiful and most heavily populated on the whole Peruvian coast before the Spanish Conquest. Garcilaso tells us in his *Royal Commentaries of the Inca*, that the Great Lord of Chimu resisted the Inca Tupac Yupanqui who led a great army against them. A long and terrible war was supposed to have been fought in this valley and it was not until the Inca brought up 20,000 fresh troops and offered favorable peace terms that the Lord Chimu brought the war (believed to be the costliest the Incas had waged up to that time) to a close. The Santa massif looked indeed like a Peruvian Maginot Line.

Nowhere in all Peru—indeed, in all America—does one find such sophisticated and well-designed defensive fortifications. Here was real proof that seemed to support Garcilaso's claim that the Chimu had fortified this valley for their great war with the Incas. Up to this time there had been no actual archaeological proof to support this famous Peruvian historian.

The new finds in the Santa Valley had rekindled my enthusiasm. Back at Coishco that afternoon we decided to explore all the river valleys on the north coast within the known Chimu kingdom with the idea that we might locate other walls like that of the Santa. A few days later we began an aerial exploration program that spanned a year's time.

One sunny morning, we were pleasantly surprised to discover a second Great Wall in the Nepeña Valley. (Plate 3.) It originated near the coast with a group of walls that coursed inland over the rolling hills and finally narrowed to a single wall that ran across the coastal desert among spurs of the Andes, where it was lost in the uplands beyond Moro. Although many expert archaeologists had excavated ruins in this valley, none had noted the existence of the wall. We spotted secondary walls which cut through urban layouts suggesting that the main wall might have been built over an older settlement. It runs for many miles along the north bank of the river, but for the most part is in a poor state of repair.

Some days later, with even greater surprise, we discovered a third Great Wall in the Casma Valley, south of Nepeña. We followed the wall along the north bank of the Santa River until we lost it in the upper heights. The only noteworthy fortress structure we observed from the air was the well-known Chancaillo fortress situated atop a 600-foot spur. It is composed of three concentric walls built of rough stone blocks, the outer one measuring

[PLATE 3] *Great Wall of Nepeña River Valley. Aerial photograph shows wall and old road coursing along low slopes of the western Andes near Pacific coast.*

twelve feet thick and nearly a thousand paces in circumference. It was similar to those found in the Santa Valley, except there were no turrets.

We cruised over an ancient route that led from the Casma Valley to Huarás sighting many stone constructions in the highlands between this and the Nepeña Valley. Many were overgrown with grass and wood growth. Dropping back down to the coastal strip we continued our survey of the fertile valleys where we located fragmentary walls in the Sechin and Viru regions, all archaeologically known for their spectacular temple and pyramid layouts. We pored over numerous vertical photographic plates of the north coast taken by high-flying Peruvian Air Force planes and with the aid of lenses traced lines and dots which answered the description of fortifications, walls and roads. Going in at low altitude in the Chimbote-Lacarmarca, Chao, Huarmey, Culebra, Supe and Huara river basins we took hundreds of oblique air photographs in an effort to put the pieces together of this gigantic jigsaw puzzle. While we identified a large number of walls and buildings in these valleys, they did not equal those found in the Santa, Casma and Nepeña regions.

In the latter half of 1962, we followed up our aerial explorations on the ground. All the resident members of the Explorers Club joined in, including Douglas, Oscar Egusquiza, our Peruvian photographic laboratory technician, Mirko and myself. We scrambled up the sizzling, rocky, mountain heights under a dazzling sun to double-check our aerial survey work.

The structures were even more imposing on the ground than they had been from the air. Nearly all of them were invisible from the floor of the valley which explains why they had not been reported by archaeologists. Once on the ramparts, we could see all the way to the snowy Cordillera Blanca and the Pacific Ocean without being seen from below. We spent one whole day on these arid, blazing wastes under a condor-filled sky with only an occasional cactus for shade, beating off clouds of stinging sand flies that swarmed about our heads, hiking to the summits of granite precipices which crawled with poisonous scorpions and asps. Too tired to make the descent to the valley, we often spent the night on these heights, moving inside the great walled enclosures to escape the cold night wind that sweeps over the mountains of Peru.

Unlike the adobe compounds of Chanchan and the stone constructions found in the Casma and the Nepeña valleys, those of the Santa boasted parapets which suggest defensive works, a presumed line of Chimu fortifications. Our studies of pottery shards showed Mochica-Chimu influence. We found traces of other ancient cultures that had either developed in the valley or had penetrated it. Chavín pottery fragments told us that these highland people had used the Santa as an outlet to the coast. The Tiahuanaco-Huari crusade had left their imprints in this valley, as had the cultures from the

Callejón de Huaylas and Marañón regions. We found many Inca and Spanish artifacts.

Who had built these mountain citadels? Had they actually been intended as fortifications? Archaeologists came in at our request and made cursory ground studies, but they could not answer the questions. Just as Garcilaso had believed, it was my opinion that these buildings had been used by the Chimu people against the encroaching Incas. Quite possibly they had originally been constructed by an earlier culture and used by other peoples who had occupied this valley, but the Chimu could have developed them to their greatest level as fortifications. Our new findings were particularly intriguing. They suggested that this ancient gateway from the highlands to the coast had at one time been the epicenter of a vast network of urban and military buildings linked with other valleys to the north and south. Only further explorations would offer explanations.

4 · Pre-Inca Highways

ONE MARCH DAY in 1963 we took off from Tambor Real to make a scouting
trip over the coastal strip. We had noticed an unusually wide roadway some
days before while making a leisurely flight over the Santa Valley and decided
to nose around to see where it went. Far too wide to be Inca—which followed
a standard fifteen- to twenty-four-foot width—we suspected we had stumbled
upon one of the older Mochica-Chimu inter-valley roads.

A half hour droned by and we climbed to 10,000 feet in order to take
a series of vertical shots. We had removed the door from my side of the plane
and I found myself shivering in a cold draft that whistled in through the
gaping doorway. Mirko flew a 360-degree circle while I worked my hand-held
camera getting a dozen good photographs. With that we cut the motor and
ghosted down to 1,000 feet where I could get some oblique photos.

Picking up the road, we drifted north, making side sweeps over the flat
desert. Numerous secondary roads cut back and forth on the sandy wastes
like lines of a giant crossword puzzle. They angled off in crazy directions,
some toward the highlands, but we kept our eyes glued to the bigger highway.
At one time the road must have crossed the upper Santa either by means of
a suspension bridge made from cables of vegetable fibers, or more likely over
a floating balsa bridge of bundles of totora-reed pontoons used in Inca and
pre-Inca times, because the old road continued on the other side running in
a southerly direction. Difficult to follow in some places due to drifting sands,
it stood out clearly where strong winds cut across the sterile stretches of sandy
plains. Advancing over the wild, open country past Lacarmarca into the
Nepeña Valley, the inland coast road followed the natural desert corridors
bursting out into the San Jacinto region—a large, ancient urban center.

We flew back and forth, keeping the road under the cowling of the aircraft, taking photographs before continuing south again. From what I could
tell, we had located an important inter-valley highway unreported up to that
time. Fragments of it might have been known, but the big highway we had
been following was a continuous roadway linking up the coastal valleys. Far

inland, it was a different system than those previously known on the western seaboard. The Incas built their roads in a straight line, but this larger one followed the natural course of the terrain. It swept past valleys and dry gorges ever advancing over the flatlands in a graceful manner. If it continued into Casma Valley, it would more than likely prove to be the key arterial of the Mochica or the Chimu nations who had dominated these valleys for several centuries before the latter was absorbed by the Incas. A road system such as this would have been useful to the Mochica-Chimu, who controlled these valleys. However, it was altogether possible that the Tiahuanaco or the earlier Chavín may have built penetration roads from the highlands while connecting these important valleys. Their influence was certainly felt on the coast. We had discovered this during our ground probes with archaeologists.

In the Sechín Desert, a wide stretch of arid yellow-ochre sand north of the Casma Valley, we caught sight of a number of secondary roads angling off in all directions. But the larger inter-valley road dominated the scene. The modern asphalt road connecting the communities of Casma and Huarás stood out on the desert like a black ribbon. It cut through the ancient arterial, which dwarfed the more recent construction, just where it forked out into three, distinct branches. (Map I.) Each was walled in by a rough, stone boundary about three feet in height. Two roads ran down the coast, one heading toward Yautan, the other toward Casma. The third coursed up in the direction of Huarás . . . something that led me to consider it a possible connection between the highlands and the coast in ancient times.

For several minutes we flew over the old highway that snaked along the floor of the desert. (Plate 4.) It measured some 100 feet in width (confirmed later during ground reconnaissance). In some places it had been washed away by flash floods which result from the torrential rains that fall on these normally arid places every forty or fifty years. Otherwise the road was easy to trace. Soon we came across a rectangular tambo (way station) located close to the old highway system. Made of stone, it consisted of nearly fifty small rooms or storage bins. Off to one side we sighted a large enclosure, possibly used as a corral for the large llama herds which the ancient Mochicas used to transport cargo up and down the desert strip, in much the same way as the camel was used in Arabia. Some distance beyond this the 100-foot-wide road flared out of the desert into a large, ancient urban section in the Casma Valley. This mighty road may possibly have had some connection with the very old pyramid-temple layouts of Moxeke and Pallca and the buildings at Cerro Sechín, among a number of other large settlements in this immediate vicinity. Not far away, another unusually large road junction lay imprinted on the rocky ground below.

We photographed the road junctions and then crisscrossed the wind-swept desert trying to pick up further traces. We swung up a valley and saw bits of road wall and a maze of cross-lines. The roads followed the natural

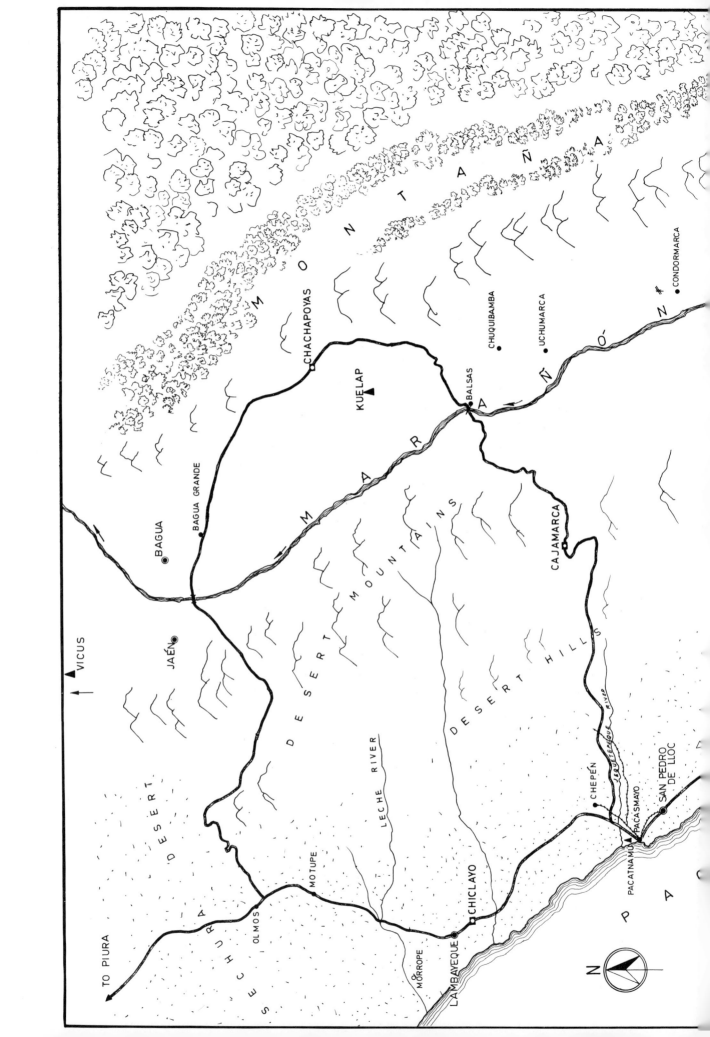

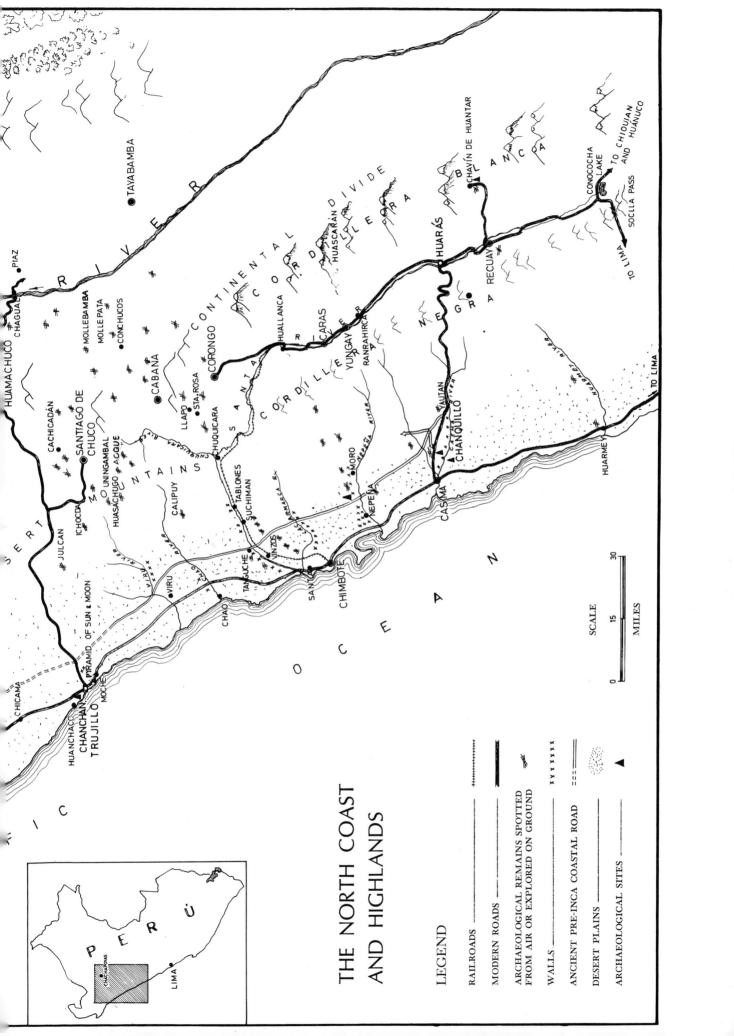

THE NORTH COAST
AND HIGHLANDS

LEGEND

RAILROADS

MODERN ROADS

ARCHAEOLOGICAL REMAINS SPOTTED
FROM AIR OR EXPLORED ON GROUND

WALLS

ANCIENT PRE-INCA COASTAL ROAD

DESERT PLAINS

ARCHAEOLOGICAL SITES

SCALE

0   15   30

MILES

PERÚ

LIMA

CHICAMA
HUANCHACO
CHANCHAN
TRUJILLO
MOCHE
PYRAMID OF SUN & MOON

CHAO
VIRU
VIRU RIVER
TANGUCHE
SANTA
CHIMBOTE

JULCAN
ICHOCDA
HUASACHUGO ACQUE
UNINGAMBAL
CALIPUY
SUCHIMAN
TABLONES
VINZOS
NEPEÑA
CASMA

CACHICADÁN
SANTIAGO DE
CHUCO
MOUNTAINS

LLAPO
STA. ROSA
CABANA
CHUQUICARA

MOLLEBAMBA
MOLLE PATA
CONCHUCOS

TAVABAMBA

PIAZ
CHAGUAL

HUAMACHUCO

RIVER

CONTINENTAL DIVIDE
CORONGO
HUALLANCA
CARAS
YUNGAY
RANRAHIRCA
MORO
AUTAN
CHANQUILLO

SANTA RIVER
CHUQUICARA RIVER
TABLACHACA RIVER
NEPEÑA RIVER
CASMA RIVER

CORDILLERA

CORDILLERA BLANCA
HUASCARÁN

CORDILLERA NEGRA
HUARÁS
RECUAY

CHAVÍN DE HUANTAR
CONOCOCHA
LAKE
SOCLLA PASS
TO CHIQUIAN
AND HUÁNUCO

TO LIMA

HUARMEY
HUARMEY RIVER

DESERT

PACIFIC OCEAN

CHACHAPOYAS

course of valley routes but we couldn't put the pieces together. They were part of a valley road system long since destroyed by age and erosion.

The entire Sechín Valley appeared to consist of a maze of desert road-ways and major intersections. I couldn't account for such a large number in this desolate region, except that the valley was a strategic gateway from Huarás to Casma. This suggests that the coast and highlands had been linked by means of great super roadways before the coming of the Incas. This would indicate that the Incas absorbed many of the older roads into their famous "Royal Road" system. Short of gas, we headed for Tambor Real.

The following day we resumed our road hunting. We found that the huge roadway ran north up through the Chao and Viru valleys to a mountain range near Moche. The road ended there, but we picked up a smaller road that zigzagged up the mountain spurs. On the other side we encountered a

40

good many road patterns, most of which had been previously traced. These roads were much narrower, averaging about 30 feet. The widest system was a known road which measured more than seventy feet across and ran for a short distance above Chanchan. We had a difficult time picking up our roadway due to the continually drifting sand dunes, some of the largest in the world, which obliterated the road. We managed to track it up to Chicama where we lost it again. From that point we made several flights that took us up and down the coast north to Pacasmayo and the ancient desert cities of Pacatnamú and Lambayeque and we lost every trace of the highway until the Sechura Desert region where it again appeared, some two hundred and fifty miles from the Casma Valley. We had explored a desert stretch equal in length to that of ancient Egypt.

Our explorations drew page one headlines in the Lima press and several archaeologists became interested in more details, particularly Doctor Hans Horkheimer, a German authority and long resident of Peru. He was terribly excited about the walls and fortresses in the north, but even more so about the "wide pre-Inca roads of the coast." Victor von Hagen and Allen Holmberg thought the large Sechín intersections were probably ceremonial highways. Others said the roads, walls and hilltop structures were strictly for military purposes.

The news stories also attracted the interest of several laymen, which turned out to be a stroke of luck. A former companion from my earlier explorations, Rafael Flores Rosell, dropped in at our field headquarters in Trujillo. A pilot with an interest in the accounts of our aerial explorations, he asked if we had seen an old road in the upper Viru Valley. We hadn't. He told us that it staircased up the sides of the Cordillera Negra where it leveled off at around 11,000 feet, in the vicinity of Uningambal. It passed through a good number of archaeologically unknown ancient stone ruins of the highlands of Santiago de Chuco, two or three of which could safely be regarded as ancient cities of some unknown civilization. He suggested we inspect them from the air.

Mirko and I borrowed a plane from a friend and took off to explore the ruins Rafael had described. According to radio reports the cloudy weather was lifting in the highlands. Mirko and I had flown twenty minutes through the thick blanket of curling fog. Suddenly it thinned out and we came out into the bright, morning sunlight. The peaks of the lowland Andes jutted out of the white mists like phantom pyramids on a powdery desert. Searching carefully we picked up the sinuous road Rafael had told us about in upper Viru and followed it to the grasslands of Santiago de Chuco.

Fat cattle dotted the countryside grazing lazily on dew-covered grass, unconcerned about the high-flying object that moved overhead in the thin air. On the summit of a wooded hillock known as Acque, at about 12,000 feet altitude, we spotted a group of buildings. It was easy to tell this had been

[PLATE 5] *Stone wall with niches, windows and doorways at tumbling highland city of Acque, north sierra.*

an ancient city of considerable size at one time. Its walls still stood a respectable 25 feet high. (Plate 5.) We orbited a few minutes, then swung north in the direction of the hacienda Uningambal, a mammoth estate which spread out over 250,000 acres of these remote Andean ranges. We passed over many scattered ruins, but the most impressive was a little-known site situated at Huasachugo, a chain of the three high hills just a few hours by mule from the hacienda. It was a complete city, with doors and windows inset along rectangular and circular-shaped stone walls, and plazas and courtyards. The architecture was similar to that found throughout the area and included many circular buildings.

A little northwest we caught sight of another large area of ruins spread out on the hilltops of Sulcha near the tiny pueblo of Carabamba. To the east we picked up still another city in the Coronas-Calamarca region. We could see the Huasachugo ruins far to the southwest and traces of a road linking them. Farther east other interesting ruins came into view in the Icchal-Llaras-Huacamarca zone, northwest of the highland village of Santiago de Chuco. Most were badly destroyed, but many were still imposing when seen from the air. After a brief inspection of hilltop ruins in the eastern Mollebamba-Mollebambita area, we dropped southward, sighting broken ruins along the summits of the mountain chains culminating in Calipuy. Finally we brought our aerial inspection to a close by passing over the old fortified areas of Caban, Ancos and Santa Rosa, coming out in the Chuquicara Valley and thence to the Santa Valley. We wondered who had built these "forgotten cities of the northern Andes." They did not seem to be of Inca design and were undoubtedly erected by a people who ruled over this mountainous domain before the all-absorbing Incas overwhelmed them. Who these people were, and where they came from will remain a mystery until the area is studied. Even then we may never know the answers. That the area is rich in copper, gold, silver and other minerals may explain their presence in this otherwise bleak, sad land of rolling mountain chains.

One day while in Trujillo, Rafael told me he had seen ancient roads on the other side of the Marañón River. A friend of his, Teodorico Ganoza, a hunter and outdoorsman, had followed one of these roads down from the high Andes into the eastern jungles. He had been anxious to find a route to the port of Juanjuí, situated on the Hallaga River, and had given vague references to ruins existing between the latter river and the Marañón. I did not learn their exact location, except that they were east of the highland pueblos of Patáz and Pias. Rafael warned me it would be difficult to penetrate this area because there were many cattle rustlers in the highlands who were known to kill intruders without hesitation. Also, there were dealers in narcotics who sought out the hot, lush ground down in the *montaña* where they illegally raised opium-producing poppy flowers. He speculated that they may have accidentally stumbled upon ruins during their quest for land but would hesitate to make this knowledge public for fear of their illicit crops being discovered. These ruins had been rumored to exist for many years, he explained. However, he cautioned, more than a few explorers had been killed trying to reach this sanctuary for one reason or another.

A short time later I learned that government road engineers had made an expedition from the highlands east of the Marañón down through the *montaña* to Juanjuí looking for a route for a proposed highway. It had taken them forty days to make the trek and two men had been killed. They had heard of the existence of archaeological remains along the way, but had not searched for them. Old hunters and explorers in the small communities of Bolívar, Calemar and Juanjuí claimed that there were ruins strewn about the *montaña* and told of an old colonial village, long since abandoned, built by Franciscan friars at a place named Pajatén. I arranged to obtain a photostatic copy of the official government map of the expedition. "*Ruinas de Pajatén*" had been marked on a river of the same name, though the engineers had never actually been there. Checking into my English edition of Garcilaso's *Royal Commentaries of the Inca*, I was amazed to discover that the

43

old historian gave reference to an ancient people who had ruled over a vast jungle empire in this region.

The Incas built a military road from Huánuco, some four hundred miles south, into the heart of this region. Not much was known about the road. Modern historians gave reference to its existence—Victor von Hagen had traveled over parts of it during his Inca Road Expedition. It seemed to me that this might be the same road referred to by Rafael. The entire length of the zone appeared to be a mystery, so we decided to take a look and drop down to "Pajatén country."

Our twin-motored aircraft labored over the Continental Divide and the scene changed drastically. We flew over the high mountain passes of the Cordillera Blanca and came out over the barren uplands of the eastern Andes. Below, the Marañón River looked like a molten ribbon of silver, running in a deep gorge. The immense gap below looked large enough to hold a dozen Grand Canyons.

After crossing the Continental Divide we looked for signs of roads. Within a few minutes we caught sight of what looked like a mule trail coursing over the open puna country south to north; but upon closer examination with our binoculars we found it to be an ancient highway. We followed it for some distance, picking up groups of ruined buildings—some large and imposing—along the mountain spurs. But big menacing clouds blocked our northward flight and we dropped back to the south. We were surprised to find a smaller road going in an easterly direction leading off the main north-south road. It was a raised causeway, six to eight feet wide. This was the first of its kind I had seen in Peru. Built of roughly-dressed stone, about two to four feet high, it ran over the marshlands for several miles until it eventually disappeared in the upper jungles to the east.

We took a course down a nameless river valley through shreds of clouds, straining our eyes for telltale signs of the road. But it was no use trying to see under the dense vegetation. We pushed on over the dipping forested hill country for several minutes and then decided to turn back because of heavy cloud cover. We hadn't noticed it as we were flying eastward, but the return trip brought a long, white cliff into view, not more than five minutes' flying time from where we last caught sight of the branch road dropping into the jungle.

I had been told to look for one of these *peñas*, since ruins had been seen at its base by hunters heading into the *montaña*. We wheeled above the geological formation of sandstone, studying it with binoculars. It rose up out of the green forest like a white monument, some 10,000 feet in height, nearly a mile long, 500 feet above the highest jungle. Suddenly I noticed a plateau covered with luxuriant growth at the base of the promontory. It was several hundred yards long and flat. "There could be ruins down there!" I exclaimed. Mirko banked the plane, and we both stared out the window. Several overgrown

44

levels staircased the upper hill. "Trees don't normally grow like that," I said, peering into my glasses. This was a perfect setting for a citadel on the order of Machu Picchu. Mirko kept circling and we could see the deep valley farther to the west that probably brought the old road down to the base of the mountain. Roads lead to ruins! I kept my eyes glued on the view below. I recalled Tupac Yupanqui's account of having crossed the Marañón sometime around A.D. 1480 with an Inca army. He climbed a mountain range and descended into the jungles where he made war against the Chacha people of the Chachapoyas (Chiachiapoias) Kingdom. He commented on their temples built up against overhanging cliffs such as the one we were now observing. Had we found an old temple of the Chachapoyas? It was difficult to tell. But we had good evidence that suggested a road led into the valley. Excitedly I began planning a ground expedition that would traverse the road and cut its way through the jungle to this fascinating temple site. Three long years would pass before such an expedition could come into being.

We made a final circuit over the area taking photographs through cumulus cloud masses. We ran into a rain squall and the sky fell under a gloomy pall. We sheered away from the cliff and headed west. Huge formations of cumulus drifted by. Ahead they were building into thunderheads. The turbulent air bucked the plane violently and the visibility dropped. We were forced to use more throttle to get above the great walls of vapor. Had we flown through them we would have been tossed around like a paper boat in a whirlpool. The spinning propellers whipped up the powdery veils into tiny corkscrews of nebula as we pulled up through the edges of the muck, the plane shuddering against the cold, dense air pockets.

Then we were enveloped in a milky mass. We strained our eyes for a gap in the clouds. The engines roaring at full power began to overheat. The peaks of the jagged Andes were all around us, some 3,000 feet above our altitude. According to the compass they lay thirty air miles to the south of us. But one could never be sure of compass readings on these ranges with their heavy deposits of minerals. Numerous airplane wrecks litter these parts, victims of overcast and wrong compass readings. We flew on blindly for a quarter of an hour. Sweat began to trickle down my back and I felt sick.

Suddenly the mists thinned and we popped out into the sunlight with the craggy, zigzag heights of the Andes all around us. We had managed to get over the Continental Divide through a pass.

Mirko turned to me and grinned, put the plane in a little crazy dance and throttled back the engines. For the first time in what seemed like a century, I drew a deep breath. The oil temperature returned to normal and we began the long descent back to the warm, golden coastal strip.

5 · Tomb Robbers
Guard Their Secrets

ONE OF PERU'S greatest problems is the unlawful practice of tomb robbery. Almost every household possesses a few huacos, the well-known colorful and decorative anthropomorphic baked-clay pottery ceramics that come out of the ground in seemingly endless numbers. The wealthier families have collections that number into the thousands of pieces, including gold and silver ornaments set with semiprecious stones, and other valuable objects. Nearly all of these artifacts are dug up illegally. To date, government steps to control unlawful diggings and smuggling of antiquities have been painfully ineffectual.

In such places as Trujillo—whose economy depends upon the large sugarcane producing haciendas surrounding it—one finds great quantities of these ancient objects sold in public markets. It is not uncommon to see dealers hawking their ill-gotten wares on street corners. Residents and tourists pick them up at prices everyone can afford to pay. Built squarely in the middle of the Mochica-Chimu Empire, Trujillo is surrounded with ancient ruins. Many of these sites are situated on hacienda property which is theoretically protected by the state archaeological department. But as it is, thousands of underpaid hacienda workers, living in a land of inflation and soaring prices, supplement their incomes by breaking into tombs and pyramids.

It is not difficult to sell these objects, especially if they are made of gold and silver. Some tomb robbers do so well they turn professional. Several have made their fortunes by striking an unusually rich haul. The majority, however, simply eke out a living, and a poor one at that. There is never a shortage of buyers. Even those who cannot afford the prices will pay for pieces as a status symbol. The most wealthy and reliable buyers are known to almost everyone. *Huaqueros*, as they are known in Spanish, are busy selling at all hours of the day and night. When a rare object turns up the word spreads quickly and diggers start hunting for other pieces like it which may bring a more handsome price.

One night Rafael, who knew my interest in locating ancient ruins unreported to archaeologists, told me about a casual acquaintance of his—a *huaquero*—who had been bragging about his discovery of a fabulously rich area of ruins in the desert ruins of Sechura. From what he said, it was an immense city of conically-shaped sun-dried bricks, half buried by sand. They had started digging at the site and stumbled upon huge caches of artifacts buried deep under the ground. They soon gave up trying to dig by hand and brought in a tractor. From what I was able to learn, the finds had been so stupendous they had made a full-scale project out of it with several tractors and hired workmen operating around the clock. I was appalled to learn that they were leveling pyramids and temples to the ground. Terribly excited about the prospects of locating what might prove to be a desert city of great importance, I asked Rafael to introduce me to the grave robber. He made a telephone call to some friends and a half hour later they arrived by car. We decided to "drop in" on the unsuspecting tomb robber for a friendly little chat and a round of drinks. We picked up a bottle of *pisco*, the Peruvian white brandy, and drove out to his home. There were four of us. One of the men had thought of bringing his guitar, which proved to be a wise decision.

Our man must have been preparing to retire, for we pounded on the door a good five minutes before he finally appeared in his shirttail. "What is it, what do you want?"

"We only came by for a *copa*," came the sly reply.

"But it is late, I have had enough to drink. I will see you tomorrow." The door started to close but one of the men jammed it with his foot. "How can you refuse to drink with your friends? Do you want the gringo to think we are inhospitable?"

Then the man with the guitar began to play and sing. The others chorused in, "*En Trujillo nació Dios . . . la Virgin María en Chocope . . .*" (God was born in Trujillo and the Virgin Mary in Chocope.) There isn't a Trujillano alive who can resist music, friends and singing for long. They continued singing, taunting him with their songs. Someone opened the bottle and poured out a drink offering him the glass, singing, "*Tomate una copa, una copa de vino . . . tomate una copa, una copa de vino . . .*" (Drink this glass, this glass of wine . . .) Soon we were all singing.

It was well past midnight, the hour of the *serenata* in Peru, and our man succumbed to his amigos by taking the first drink, saving a small portion which he threw on the ground, an ancient custom in this land of song and wine.

"*Ya se la tomó . . . ya se la tomó . . .*" (He has already drunk it . . . etc.)

47

They began to pass the glass around chorusing, "*Ya ahora le toca al vecino*
. . ." (Now it is the neighbor's turn.) Soon everyone was inside the house and
our host was singing merrily away, relaxed, drunk.

"Show the gringo what you have inside the other room," someone said,
winking in my direction. Everyone soon agreed that I should be allowed
to see it. He disappeared into a side room and a few minutes later returned
with a few selected anthropomorphic pottery vessels which brought "ohs"
and "ahs" from everyone in the room. Seeing our great satisfaction at these
original objects, he showed us more artifacts. After a while he began to take
pleasure in his little game, shuttling back and forth from the side room,
piling object upon object on the floor in glee. There were sensitive, finely-
worked pottery vessels of what I believed to be of Mochica-Chimu manu-
facture, including a large assortment of pottery figurines, ornaments, textiles
and implements of copper, bronze, and silver. Some of these pieces were made
of two and three types of metal. He displayed face masks, figurines and
armloads of delicate beads exquisitely fashioned in gold, silver, turquoise,
pearl and coral. After several minutes' absence he reappeared decked out in
a golden breastplate and gold helmet brandishing a lance, looking like a
knight in shining armor—or a court jester—for he was playing a set of pipes
of Pan and doing a little jig like the Pied Piper. He motioned for us to follow
him into the storeroom. There we saw literally hundreds of pounds of priceless antiquities, some set with semi-precious stones, stacked on the floor along
with a large number of silvered and gold-gilt scales of armor attached to
beautiful quilted cotton textiles, and helmets, lance heads, pikes, javelins and
battle-axes. He offered me a few pieces which I refused. "Go ahead and take
them, we're trucking this stuff to Lima by the ton," he said. Picking up a
ceramic flute, he whistled a tune and danced around the room again. After
a while he sank to the floor exhausted and giddy from too much alcohol and
exertion.

Garcilaso de la Vega and Pedro Cieza de León, among others, do their
best to tell us what the conquistadores must have seen. It surpassed anything
yet encountered in the Indies. They had been told in Panama that the Land
of Gold lay to the south. The first men who landed at Tumbes returned
to the ships with fantastic accounts of the riches they had seen. If Pizarro had
had reservations about these reports they were soon dispelled when he saw for
himself the great adobe and stone-worked sun temples covered inside and out
with sheets of solid gold. Even the gates, doors and beams were graced with
precious metal. Thrones, chairs and benches lining the walls were also of
gold and set with emeralds and precious stones, so arranged to reflect the rays
of the rising and setting sun. These temples were filled with golden ornaments, sun disks and images. Gold and silver life-size statues of men, women
and children stood frozen in courtyards. Water fed by golden pipes splashed
over metal baths and fountains paneled with gold and silver. Golden en-

closures housed a wonderland garden where even the soil was of gold dust planted with silver stalks and golden ears of corn, flowers, plants, fruit trees, insects, birds and butterflies of all shapes and sizes. Every animal known in the empire was fashioned out of gold or silver and placed in these zoomorphic gardens.

We can well imagine the impact all this wealth had on the Spaniards. It is estimated that over eleven billion dollars in gold and jewels was transported from the New World to Spain in years following, something that made the legendary wealth of the Oriental capitals of the Old World pale by comparison, and threw the financial market of Europe into near panic.

We are told by historians that the Inca priests hid the greater part of the gold, silver and royal treasures in lakes and secret caves after Pizarro assassinated Atahualpa. The Incas themselves told the Spaniards after the conquest that the portion which fell into the hands of their conquerors was but a very small amount of the gold and silver that actually existed. "A few grains of salt from the saltshakers . . ." ". . . a few kernels of corn from the storehouse . . ." ". . . a drop in the bucket . . ." some old writers tell us. In any event this lost treasure has never been found. Most believe the Incas spirited it away over the Andes to the jungles where the Spaniards could not follow. Legend has given the name of El Dorado to this region. It has escaped detection for over four centuries.

The tomb robber did not reveal the location of the desert city—we only knew it was located somewhere in the Sechura—10,000 square miles of desert! Mirko and I made a few sweeps over the vast sandy wastes in an attempt to spot the site, to no avail. A large number of desert ruins were observed; but we had no way of identifying the doomed city from which the treasure was being removed.

A short while later Rafael invited me to visit the hacienda at Uningambal. Douglas and Robert Sharon joined the field party and we spent several weeks combing the high sierra country by muleback and on foot. It was in this area that I discovered to my horror that some of the better ruins were being pillaged of their architectural ornaments and broken down for inexpensive building materials. Stone monoliths, obelisks and carvings cut in the shape of human heads, originally tenoned, Chavín-style, in the walls of ancient buildings, had been removed and sold to buyers at ridiculously cheap prices —250 to 500 soles, at that time $10 to $20—a fraction of their worth. Whole settlements were wantonly stripped of these stone decorations, destroying their architectural beauty and archaeological significance forever. Nothing remains but broken walls, gutted and falling. It was the same story throughout this whole region. Such is the present state of the best archaeological remains over much of the sierra north to Cajamarca, south to Santiago de Chuco.

One evening, when the last rays of the sun fell on a large white sandstone cliff dominating an Andean meadow, we came to a shepherd's hut and asked for food and shelter. The owner of the cabaña, an elderly fellow in his late sixties or early seventies, kindly invited us in. He closed a rickety door against the cold wind, offered footstools around a warm fire, coffee and bowls of hot, parched corn.

Dressed in sandals, wool poncho and a felt hat, he began to talk about the ruins of the area. One of his sons, wearing a funny straw hat purchased in Santiago de Chuco, asked him to show us his huacos. He attempted to hush him up, but then all the children insisted. He went into the back room and brought out four pottery vessels which were unmistakably Mochica. "Where did you find these?" I inquired, rather surprised to see coastal pieces in the highlands.

"Oh, in the ruins of Calamarca," he answered. "These are very common. We find them all the time. Some much better," he blurted.

"So the old man is plying the ancient trade," said Robert in English. No amount of argument from any of us, including his wife, could make him show us more pieces. He appeared to be most guarded in attitude. It was understandable since we were strangers.

However, he did allow his eldest son to bring in a very beautiful heavy stone carving with a finely chiseled serpentine design engraved on the surface, which had been used as a door stop. When I asked the old man if I could photograph it, he ordered his son to put it in the back room. He would have given us anything we needed, but the question of antiquities became a closed subject. I did not try to broach it. He had his reasons, I knew. Either he was robbing tombs for profit or for some religious reason, a custom in these remote regions whereby whole communities dig for ancient objects on certain nights of the year. I recalled having seen one of these strange ceremonies in Moche, in which several clans were working by lantern light in the dead of night at the Pyramid of the Sun. This colossal structure had yielded millions in gold and it is possible not all the treasure has been removed from its great hulk. Searching for relics to be used in divination by witch doctors, they must have used secret chambers because they disappeared into the depths of the pyramid and did not come out until early morning. I later examined a few bits of mother-of-pearl belonging to a confidant. He said he had seen a whole room inside the Pyramid of the Sun lined with the shiny substance. These people believed that objects removed from the pyramids had a religious significance and a power when used in sorcery. Some communities have brotherhoods of such mystics who carry on nightly.

I changed the topic of conversation and brought up the matter of enchantment. Our host agreed that all the ruins were enchanted, particularly those sites over the mountains to the east in the great forests beyond the Marañón. "You must never visit these places," he said, "because you will be turned into stone like the others."

"What others?" I asked, pulling up my saddle blanket against the cold wind that came in under the door.

"Our forefathers, a long time ago. They were turned to stone forever," he replied.

"How do you know this? Have you seen them?"

"Once I saw a stone head," he said. "I am sure it was once a real man."

"Do you believe in the enchantments?" I asked.

"Yes, I believe in them," he proclaimed in solemn tones. "It is said there are golden cities in the great forests."

I was determined to cross the Andes and explore the dense forest belt from the ground.

6 · The Vilcabamba Kings

THE STORY of Vilcabamba (Willkapampa, in the Quechua language) is a puzzle because so little is known about it. The name Willka was the old name for the sun. It also denotes lineage, descent, ancestry. There is a narcotic plant of the same name, used by the Inca priests to make contact with the spirits of the dead. The name has always held a special place among the Incas. Pampa means plain. Willkapampa was a name that meant the Plain of the Sun and had something to do with the ancestry of the Incas. Fernando Montesinos, secretary to the Spanish Viceroy and chronicler of Inca legend and myth, wrote that in the early days of Peru's history—many centuries before the Spanish takeover—the fifty-third king or *amauta* of prehistoric Peru had successfully defended the Inca empire against an invasion of barbarian tribes coming up from the plains of Argentina, Bolivia and the Titicaca region. Following the defeat of these aliens from the east, the Inca was given the name of Willkanota or Vilcanota. Later, during the reign of his son Pachacuti, a barbarian host again attacked the Incas killing the king in battle and forcing his armies to retreat back to the "place of their origin," Tamputocco, a territory that mythology says was in the Urubamba-Apurímac basins.

The vast Inca empire was known as Tahuantinsuyo, or the land of four parts. (Map II.) Much larger than modern Peru, the empire included parts of Ecuador, Bolivia, Argentina and Chile and its influence was probably felt into Brazil, Colombia and Venezuela. Cuntisuyo, the temperate region of the Cuzco area, was the land of the Quechua or Cuntis people. Kollasuyo included the high country of Bolivia, Chile and Argentina and was inhabited by the Kollas or Aymaras. Chinchaysuyo, the desert regions occupied by the Chinchas or Yungas, stretched clear up to Quito, Ecuador. The most interesting quarter, and the least known, was Antisuyo (for which the Andes Mountains are named). This was the world beyond the snowy mountains, that great jungle land of the Antis people, sometimes called Yungas, which was the

52

INCA TAHUANTINSUYO

N

CARACAS

TAIRONA   CAQUETI
QUIMBAYA   ORINOCO RIVER
BOGOTA   CARIB   ARAWAK
TIERRA DENTRO
SAN AGUSTIN
CHIBCHA   MAYAPI   EQUATOR   10°
QUITO   TOCANO   MANAO
                     SAIRIANA   BORA   MANAUS   MARAJO
ANTAS   CANARIS   JIVAROS   WITOTO   AMAZON   AMAZONAS   SANTARÉM   BELEM
TUMBES   MANARI   NAPO RIVER
             CHACHAPOYAS   RIVER   MIRAKANGUERA
CHIMU   HUAMACHUCOS   BASIN
             HUAROCHUCOS
YUNGAS

LIMA   CHINCAS   MATO GROSSO   CAYAPÓ
             CHANCAS   CUZCO   SHAVANTE   BOTOCUDO
             QUECHUA   LAKE TITICACA   TUPINAMBA
             ATACAMA   LA PAZ
TROPIC OF CAPRICORN   AYMARA   GRAN CHACO   CARIJO

             ARAUCANO   RIO DE JANEIRO
                                          PAMPAS   CHARRÚA
                                          QUERANDI
SANTIAGO

                                          PUELCHE   BUENOS AIRES

PATAGONIA
TEHUELCHE

SOUTH AMERICA

Showing the Ancient Inca Empire and Major Tribal Divisions
of South American Indians

SCALE

0   250   500

MILES

largest quarter geographically, and presumably densely populated. Legend tells (we are not certain just when this event was supposed to have taken place in Inca history) that Cuzco was overthrown by invading people from the eastern forests on the Bolivian side and the Incas were driven out. The story goes on to say that the empire was later solidified again. We do know that during the rule of Huayna Capac in the late fifteenth and early sixteenth centuries of our era, these forest tribes, who were rumored to be fierce fair-skinned warriors, continued to attack, posing a constant threat to the Inca capital.

During the course of my research I discovered that a fair-skinned people were actually known to have ruled an important jungle kingdom in the Chachapoyas region, conquered by the Incas in the fifteenth century, if we are to believe the Spanish chroniclers. Huayna Capac eventually brought these people under control, and had been impressed by the riches of this eastern region. He had moved his quarters north to Quito where he could better rule this large territory. Both he and his son, Atahualpa, went on to conquer other eastern provinces. They finally abandoned Cuzco, traditional Inca capital, which eventually led to the downfall of the empire. Huayna Capac had hoped to wed east with west, but died before his dream was realized.

More and more it appeared that the eastern *montaña* had been inhabited by high civilizations and even more important, that the Incas had been no strangers to tropical regions. If this were true, then it was quite possible that the last of the Incas, Manco II, had built his refuge down in the green jungles as the Augustinian monks had testified.

According to the oral traditions of the Incas, after the defeat of the early, unrecorded Inca dynasty (which I assume preceded the first known ruler of the Incas, Manco Capac, who established his capital at Cuzco sometime in the eleventh century A.D.), the whole empire collapsed and small kingdoms were formed out of the provinces. Folklore says the Incas were exiled for six centuries, a period of earthquakes and pestilence. When the exile ended, Manco Capac came up from his refuge at Tamputocco and returned to Cuzco and built a new dynasty of Inca kings who, according to the story, began to retake the old provinces, reuniting the people and establishing a sovereign rule up to the time of the Spanish Conquest. They were penetrating into the populous Amazon forests when the war between Huáscar and Atahualpa paralyzed the empire. With the triumph of Atahualpa, a conquering-type Inca with his eyes focused on greater expansion, the Incas were ready to begin again; but Pizarro put a stop to it. Perhaps the industrious Inca conqueror would have gone on to invade the eastern forests and the Chibcha, Maya and Aztec empires to the north. Spanish sailors reported having observed Inca sea vessels plying the coast as far as Panama and there is some evidence that they were aware of the existence

54

of the Atlantic Ocean. The Amazon River may have been the route taken, for the Spaniards also reported having seen settlements of the interior spread along the banks of the Amazon.

Had Manco II, descendant of the mighty Manco I (Manco Capac) who had originally led his people out of Tamputocco to found the city of Cuzco, imagined himself the leader of a new sacred cause? Was his cry, "back to the place of origin from whence we will rebuild and reconquer"? He may have believed history was being repeated. This is suggested by the religious fervor of his earlier movement. He took pains to remove the golden mummies of his ancestors and took along a large delegation of priests and Virgins of the Sun by which to preserve the solar arts and sciences of Inca civilization. He also retired with the *coya* and the royal harem to provide for his inheritance.

Was this land of Vilcabamba the Tamputocco of Inca legend, the cave of origin? Hiram Bingham, the Yale University professor, started looking for the "Lost City of the Incas" and chanced upon Machu Picchu north-west of Cuzco. He believed this mountain citadel to be Tamputocco as well as Manco's Vilcabamba—a hypothesis that has been criticized by scholars. As far as I could tell from my study of Inca mythology, there were three caves of origin, the most prominent being at Pacaricctampu in the province of Paruru, south of Cuzco. At least four great nomadic tribes were involved over different periods, the earliest of which seems to have originated in the Apurímac-Urubamba watershed.

While I felt that the region between the Apurímac and Urubamba, *i.e.*, the Vitcos-Vilcabamba territory, was more than likely one of the earliest homes of the Incas before their march on Cuzco, it was also probable that greater Antisuyo—that vast region east of the Andes—was the ancient home of many families that grew into the Inca people. If this were true, then the farther east I explored, the more primitive the constructions that would be found. Because Machu Picchu—and other ancient remains found in and around Cuzco—are the result of a classic period of Inca civilization, the stonework being most technical and the result of advanced skills, it had to be ruled out as both an early home and refuge of the Incas.

Spanish chronicles had placed the central city of Manco in that vigorous land between the Apurímac and Urubamba, deep down in the steaming jungles forty to sixty leagues (six to eight days' foot travel) northwest of Cuzco. (Map III.) On this assumption—and the records of reliable writers—I believed that I could expect to find the missing city in that vicinity. If I succeeded in finding it in the jungles it would lend strength to the idea that ancient peoples, Incas included, were no strangers to the jungle.

In early May 1532, Francisco Pizarro marched out of the port of Tumbes, in northern Peru, toward the inner regions of Inca land at the head

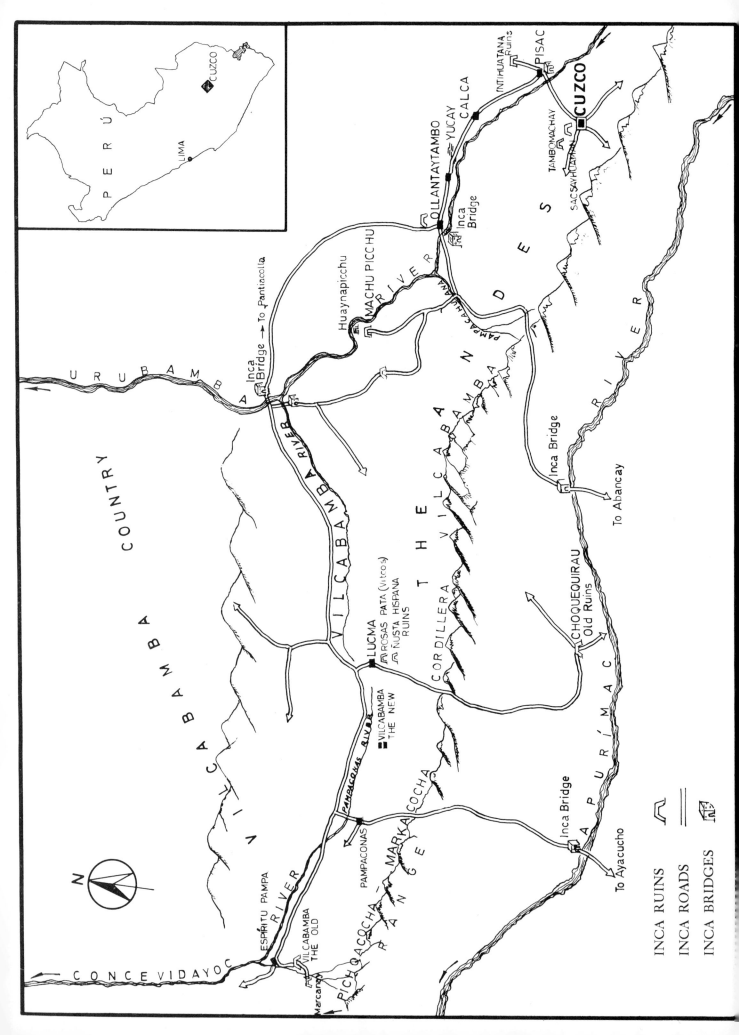

of a small force of 130 foot soldiers and 40 mounted troops. The small army soon entered Cajamarca and there met the Lord Inca Atahualpa, master of Tahuantinsuyo, recent victor over his half brother, Huáscar, rightful heir to the Inca throne. Atahualpa had observed with curiosity the entrance of these strangers bedecked in resplendent armor scintillating in the sun. His priests feared they were *Viracochas* (holy men), and thus restrained the ruler from ordering his 30,000 personal troops (and ten times this number should they be needed) upon the intruders. What followed is one of the most interesting episodes of history.

In a bold and daring move, the old conquistador Pizarro, thirsting for power and gold, struck headlong at the Inca's bodyguard and captured him before the army could act. Atahualpa agreed to pay a great ransom for his release and Pizarro shrewdly bided his time until it arrived. Upon hearing of the civil war, the old soldier told the Inca he would choose between him and his brother. This prompted Atahualpa to order the death of Huáscar and his family who were held prisoners. When Pizarro learned of this he executed Atahualpa—a foolish act which resulted in the withholding of the ransom, though some $15,000,000 in gold managed to find its way to Cajamarca—before he departed for the Inca capital. With the death of Atahualpa and Huáscar, Prince Manco II was recognized as next in line for the throne by the Cuzco clans. Acknowledging the technological advancement of the Spaniards, and suspecting them to be *Viracochas* who had harnessed the force of the sun, Manco II went forth offering his services. (Some of Atahualpa's troops harassed the Spaniards along the way, capturing several members of the expedition; but without the Inca as head these attacks were ineffectual.) Manco II met Pizarro at the Apurímac and the two forces entered Cuzco where Manco was crowned under the watchful eyes of the Spanish in 1534.

Manco co-existed with the foreigners until 1536, when he became disenchanted with their cruelty and greediness. With Francisco Pizarro away founding his new capital at Lima, Manco took command of a huge army and put Cuzco under siege. The great fortress of Sacsayhuaman was taken and lost. A battle was fought at Ollantaytambo with the Peruvians victorious; but it was soon lost in another battle under a lieutenant of Diego de Almagro (Pizarro's old sidekick and co-conqueror of Peru). Aware that his troops—though vast—were no match for cavalry, firearms and artillery, Manco II decided to retire. He might have succeeded in throwing the Spanish back into the sea by sheer weight of numbers (upwards of 50,000 men) had it not been for an unfortunate turn of events. Tahuantinsuyo was a confederation of a multitude of peoples representing different religions, languages and customs held together by the stern discipline, law and order of the Incas. Deprived of their power, the Incas were unable to maintain the government. Once the head of the dragon was cut, the body thrashed wildly about. Suddenly the Inca had lost his supreme power and tens of thousands of soldiers

(soldiers who could have won for Manco) returned to the place of their origin or went over to the Spaniards. Manco was forced to fight Spanish armor and the best troops of the once proud Imperial Inca Army—the fierce Cañaris and Chachapoyas who had been elevated to *alabarderos* (Royal Guards in charge of the garrison at Cuzco) by Huáscar. Naturally rebellious and sworn enemies of the Incas, these warriors jumped at the opportunity of striking back at their former conquerors. It was this fact that contributed to the quick victory of Pizarro, no other.

Manco, now desperate, withdrew to the province of Amaybamba in the year 1537, by way of the high mountain pass of Panticalla. He took with him the royal mummies and a great amount of treasure gathered from the temple of Cuzco and other parts of the empire, which included the great Golden Sun Disk and a magnificent golden chain made by Huayna Capac to celebrate the birth of Huáscar. King Manco called his nobles together saying, "In life we can't alter what is given us for well you know that we are compelled to do what we don't want to do. Therefore, I am forced to go to the Antis people who have for so long urged me to go to them." The king took an army of volunteers, which must have numbered into the thousands, and with a great retinue of nobles, the Chosen Women of the Sun, the *mamacunas*, common-folk and large herds of llamas, made a forced march into Antisuyo. Amaybamba had originally been conquered by the great Inca Pachacutec, who absorbed the provinces of Vitcos and Vilcabamba during the same campaign. In the reigns of Tupac Yupanqui and Huayna Capac, Amaybamba was settled by the defeated Chachapoyas from the north of the empire. Manco fought a battle with a Chachapoyas army, defeated them and depopulated the territory forcing them to accompany him into exile. Crossing over the Urubamba at the bridge of Chuquichaca, Manco had the Chachapoyas chief beheaded and his head cast into the waters as a warning to the Chachapoyas, an act that led to a revolt among his people. They left the refuge of Manco, and returned to Amaybamba offering their services to the Spaniards. Hernando Pizarro helped them build fortresses along the opposite bank of the Urubamba to guard it against attack from Manco. According to the son of Manco, Titu Cusi, the Inca moved on to the capital city of Vitcos across the Urubamba. While celebrating with the Antis people, he was caught in a surprise attack led by Captain Diego de Almagro and Gonzalo Pizarro. The Spaniards captured a large number of people and much treasure, including four gold-plated *malquis* (mummies) of former Incas and the Inca's son, Titu Cusi. Some historians believe this raid occurred at Ollantaytambo, but Titu Cusi records that it was at Vitcos, thirty leagues from Cuzco, too close to be the famous fortress. Titu Cusi knew the provinces of Vitcos and Vilcabamba like the back of his hand—he ruled the rump empire for some years—and had no reason to lie. He explains that his father was afraid to keep the mummies at Cuzco and Tambo (Ollantaytambo) for fear of Spanish troops. His account was prepared in the presence of an

Augustinian friar, Marcos García, and the Spaniard Martín Pando. Both men were familiar with the geography of the inner kingdom and neither contested the Inca's statement. Manco escaped to an impregnable mountain and the Spaniards could not dislodge him. During the night he, with his followers, escaped over a river, cut the suspension bridge and left the Spanish troops stranded on the other side. After this the conquistadores returned to Cuzco with their booty.

Manco fought several more battles against the Spaniards in other parts of the empire and then returned to the province of Vitcos and built a "long palace on top of a hill, calling the place Vitcos." From there he went on to the province of Vilcabamba and as it would appear from the writings of his son, occupied a city which he made his principal seat. History knows it as Vilcabamba. Operating from his new capital, he cut the bridges leading into his empire and closed all the key passes, heavily defending incoming routes available to the Spanish. Manco crossed the Apurímac River by balsa rafts, and struck at Huamanga (Ayacucho) and even as far away as the newly-established city of Lima on the coast. For two years he defeated the Spaniards. He "captured artillery, arquebuses, lances and horses," put Spanish prisoners to work on ordnance, manufacturing gunpowder, and forging horseshoes for his cavalry. Here was an Inca army in transition, equipped and trained in modern warfare as fought by Europeans.

Shortly after Manco returned to Vilcabamba with his loyal followers, Gonzalo Pizarro was unexpectedly defeated while leading a sizeable armed force against the rebellious Inca. It was clear to the Spanish that Manco posed a real threat. Francisco Pizarro, now Marshal of Peru, was greatly disturbed by the news. An army larger than the whole force that had conquered Peru a few years before was thrown into confusion by the rebel. That was enough to throw a real scare into the Marshal. The situation worsened when Diego Almagro, co-conqueror of Peru, vied with Pizarro for control. Manco's brother, Paullo, was crowned Inca and while some of the Cuzco faction accepted him, he did not dare contend with Manco, the legitimate ruler who offered hope to the people for the unification of Tahuantinsuyo. The Almagrists succeeded in assassinating Francisco Pizarro in 1541 and allied themselves with Manco. As the fates would have it, they were defeated on the field and Almagro was executed. Many of the survivors of this battle sought refuge with the Inca in Vilcabamba.

With Gonzalo Pizarro in power, Manco continued his war of attrition and appeared to be growing stronger. He controlled an army of around 10,000 well-armed troops with a nucleus of old Spanish soldiers who knew all the tricks of war. Manco was still in control of greater Antisuyo with many thousands of Antis Indians willing to fight, and each day more and more people from the rest of the empire under Spanish rule were going over to the Inca. A dark cloud had hung over Peru for many years. Now it seemed that the sky would clear and the Sun-god Inti would shine once more.

King Charles V of Spain, seeking peace with the Inca King, issued the "New Laws" recognizing the rights of the "Indians." A new Viceroy made contact and offered to negotiate with Manco. Seeing a possibility of coming to terms with Spain, Manco dispatched Gómez Perez, one of the many Spaniards residing as allies with the Inca, to Lima to come to terms. However, the Viceroy was overthrown by Gonzalo Pizarro and killed. The envoy returned to Manco reporting the sad news. Later, Perez and six other Spaniards attacked and killed Manco, according to one of his sons, Titu Cusi, who witnessed the assassination. Thus it was that 1545 became a tragic year for Tahuantinsuyo. One of the great Inca kings passed away and with him passed Peru's hopes of freedom and independence (which did not come for three more centuries). A remarkable king who fought the Spaniards on their own terms, Manco came extremely close to regaining the empire—or at least a large part of it—and returning Peru to its former glory. Had he succeeded, the course of history in the Americas might have been different.

Following Manco's untimely death, Sayri Tupac, a young son of the Inca, was dispatched to Cuzco by Titu Cusi and Inca chiefs at Vilcabamba, at the invitation of the Viceroy, where he received the Royal Fringe and was accepted by the Cuzco Clans. He took up residence in the beautiful Yucuy Valley where he lived in contentment until his death in 1560. Now the picture grows militant again. Titu Cusi, who held sway at Vilcabamba, was highly suspicious of the Spaniards. He had lived among them following his capture until he was secreted out of Cuzco by his father and taken to Vitcos and then to Vilcabamba. He had received excellent tutoring for leadership under Manco and the Vilcabamba regents. With the death of his brother, Titu Cusi accepted sovereignty in the confines of Vilcabamba where he refused to come out regardless of Spanish threats and appeals. Titu Cusi had seen his father killed by seven Spaniards at Vitcos, and seems never to have forgotten the words of the dying monarch, not to trust the Spaniards or to allow them in The Sacred Vilcabamba. He maintained patrols at all the entrances to the inner kingdom and managed the government of the neo-Inca state.

In the year 1565, Titu Cusi allowed a chief magistrate and ambassador of the Spanish Viceroy to visit him at the Inca capital. This was meant to pacify the Spanish throne which was insistent—even at the risk of open warfare—that the Indians of the interior be converted to Christianity. That he condescended to admit the representative, one Diego Rodriguez de Figueroa, shows his cunning. Titu Cusi was intent on continuing the rebuilding of Tahuantinsuyo. He was not ready to go to war and was stalling for time. Alexander von Humboldt, the famed explorer, had come across a manuscript obtained from M. Eugène Jacquet in Paris, sometime in 1833, that records the meeting of the friar and the Inca. The Ambassador of the Viceroy

writes that on the 5th of May, 1565, he reached the hanging bridge of Chuquichaca which was the key entrance to the Vilcabamba Kingdom, but seeing that it was torn down went farther down river and crossed over in an
oroya, a basket strung over the water by a rope, on May 6. Then he went on
to Lucuma (Lucma), which took him three days. From there he sent a note
to his Majesty, the King Titu Cusi, who was at Vilcabamba, farther along
in the *montaña*. On the 12th he went to Vitcos, the highland capital of the
Inca that defended access to the inner city of Vilcapampa. Between the 13th
and the 14th, the ambassador went to Bambacona (Pampaconas) hoping to
talk the Inca into coming out of his refuge. The Inca sent along two hampers
of peanuts, products of the jungle, and a message that the Spaniard need
journey no farther.

Next day, as the story goes, the Lord Inca arrived from the capital
amidst a crescendo of music produced by silver flutes and trumpets. He was
accompanied by an escort of 450 noblemen and attendants dressed in diadems
of plumes, gold belts, silver plates and armed with lances and wearing masks
to hide their faces. The Inca was robed in a mantle of vicuña and wore a
silver breastplate and a gilded dagger at his side. He carried a golden shield
and staff. Crowning his head was a feathered headdress of iridescent plumes
and the *maskaypacha*, the royal insignia. His countenance was hidden by a
colored mask. The company came to a halt on a wide plain and the king
strode to a place prepared for him. Twenty or thirty beautiful women stood
behind the royal figure. He looked at the sun, threw a *mucha* (a kiss) to it,
and sat down on a throne. The chief noble saluted first the Sun, then the
Inca with the words, "Child of the Sun, thou art the child of the day." Each
member of the throng did so, including the governor and two *orejones* (long-
eared nobles). Suddenly a large delegation of Antis Indians came up from
the jungle laying down their lances, bows and arrows. All this time the
ecclesiastic held up an image of the Virgin Mary.

Finally the sovereign, who was about forty years of age, sent for the
ambassador. Courtesies were exchanged. They ate a meal of "boiled and
roasted venison, fowls, macaws and monkey meat," brought up from the
montaña. The Inca said he had journeyed forty leagues to talk with him.
Light talk continued during the meal to the accompaniment of music and
dancing. During the meal, Don Diego told the Inca he must accept the
Christian faith. This disturbed the Inca and words became heated. The
ambassador told the Inca to come out of Vilcabamba and take up residence
in Ayacucho or Cuzco; otherwise, the Spaniards would make war on him.
"The entries into this land are no longer secret," boasted the friar. The Inca
cooled down and, diplomatically, said that he would first have a counsel with
his nobles before giving an answer. The envoy threatened the Inca saying
he must come out immediately. An argument ensued until Titu Cusi lost his
patience. Orders were issued. Some 600 or 700 Antis warriors appeared out
of the thickets. The Inca exclaimed that he had only to say the word and all

the Antis people and the whole Peruvian nation would rise to arms and put to death all the Spaniards in the kingdom. Like his father, he said he knew how to defend himself. Then more troops were sent for to impress the Spanish envoy. Some 200 more Indians appeared and a few days later 100 captains from the sacred sanctuary of Vilcabamba threatened to kill the cleric. Not wishing to start an open war with the Spanish, the Inca stepped in and saved the ambassador. He felt he had made his point. A military tactician, he knew that his strength lay in keeping his enemies on the other side of the Urubamba, until such time that he could lead a general revolution throughout the land. Again he was stalling for time. Thus it was that the Inca allowed Father Diego to remain in his land. This encouraged the priest and he sent word to Cuzco that a second ambassador be sent. It seems the Inca went down to the suspension bridge of Chuquichaca (perhaps rebuilt to receive the dignitary), but seeing that he was accompanied by twenty harquebusiers the Inca sent Father Diego back the way he had come, then cut the bridge and retired into the confines of his kingdom, keeping one Martín Pando, a mestizo(half-breed) who had a knowledge of Spanish and Quechua, as his personal secretary so that communications could be maintained between the two capitals.

Three years later, in order to pacify the Spaniards, the Inca condescended to accept Christianity and was baptized by Juan de Vivero, Prior of the Augustine Convent. Yet he stubbornly refused to venture beyond the borders of his sovereign state; but he did allow an Augustinian missionary, Marcos García, to build a church at Puquiura, where the Inca maintained his armies. It lay in the shadows of the highland capital, Vitcos.

In 1569 a new Spanish Viceroy, Don Francisco de Toledo, arrived in Peru with a large delegation of Augustinians with orders to missionize the Indians of Vilcabamba. Friar Diego Ruiz Ortiz was dispatched to the Inca with instructions to indoctrinate the people in the Christian faith. Here begins one of the most interesting chapters in Peruvian history because it gives us some firsthand information on the redoubt of Vilcabamba.

The friar made his way into the sanctuary and speaking with the Inca asked if he could remain. Somewhat alarmed to see another priest of the hated Catholic faith within his borders, Titu Cusi at first refused; but seeing that the priest was a gentle soul, he gave him permission to build a church, hospital and school at Guarancalla, some two or three *jornadas* (two or three days' journey) from the mission at Puquiura. Guarancalla was, according to the accounts, a populous community in the jungle near Vilcabamba—a city which the friars were not permitted to see under penalty of death. Antonio Calancha in his *Crónica Moralizada de San Agustín en el Perú*, details the lives of Fathers Ortiz and García who spent some time in the refuge state.

Father Calancha writes that the two friars went about their missionary work not without difficulty. The Inca kept them under constant surveillance and made it clear that he had no intention of giving up his own religion, and continued to participate in the rituals held at a great white rock known as Yurak-Rumi, upon which was situated the image of the Sun called *Punchao*. This rock was at a village known as Chuquipalpa near Vitcos. Father García irritated the Inca by calling him a pagan and criticizing him for keeping two wives (he probably had more than two, which was allowed him by Inca right). García threatened to take stern measures if the ceremonies did not stop. Friar Ortiz, on the other hand, seems to have pleased the Inca with his good works in the tropical forests, healing the Antis Indians who came up from the inner jungle to be cured of their fevers and other diseases.

The two priests continued to try to persuade the Inca to allow them to enter the capital city and there teach the people. Finally the Inca relented and told them he would accompany them to his principal seat. After a difficult three-day journey from Puquiura—which included a cold dunking in the waters of Ungacacha, an artificial lake caused by rain—the two Augustinians arrived at the outskirts of the sacred capital. They were allowed to preach only to those inhabitants living in the outer fringes of the city. Often the priests would walk in the great forests planting crosses along the roads. Determined to gain entrance to the principal parts of Vilcabamba, the priests kept after Titu Cusi. As a Priest of the Sun who belonged to the Inca Temple, which the friars called the University of Idolatry, he could not admit these uninitiated men for fear of offending his own priesthood, who were strict vegetarians and ascetics. Yet as a baptized Catholic (in name only) he did not wish to offend the Spanish Crown and thus bring war to his people. The Inca saw a stratagem. During the night he sent the Chosen Women, the most beautiful and pleasing—those from the hot jungles as well as the highlands—to seduce the two celibates. If they succeeded, this would lower the priests in the eyes of the people and would give him an excuse to send them back to Cuzco. After two or three weeks of this temptation the priests lost heart, each returning to his mission.

Once back at Puquiura, Father García decided to burn the pagan rock of Yurak-Rumi. He bravely (or foolishly) led a procession of people to the sacred rock and piling wood around it set it afire. Exorcism to drive out the "devil" that appeared in the temple! Upon hearing of the sacreligious act, Titu Cusi flew into a fit of rage and had the guilty friar cast out of his kingdom. Strangely enough, he allowed Ortiz to remain.

Some time after this event, Titu Cusi was taken with a bad case of pneumonia. Friar Ortiz and Martín Pando attempted to heal the Inca with medicine, which he is said to have taken with some reluctance, but he expired soon after. The two men were held responsible, particularly the friar. Inca law was specific: If the patient died from wrong treatment, the physician was killed. The priest, who probably did everything in his power to save the Inca, was set upon by a maddened throng who beat and tortured him unmercifully. It had been rumored that the Spanish had poisoned Sayri Tupac some years before while he was living with them, and now the Indians were fully convinced that the act had been repeated. The good friar was stripped, joints disjointed, bones broken and skin pierced. He spent the first night in the outdoors. Next day he was beaten again and dragged toward Vilcabamba to be judged by Titu Cusi's younger brother, next in line for Incahood. Barely twenty-five years of age, unschooled in military and diplomatic disciplines, the innocent youth had been allowed to live with his wife and daughters and the Chosen Women of the Sun at a place called Marcanay, two leagues from Vilcabamba.

The host of angry citizens took Ortiz over the Inca road that led down from Vitcos to Vilcabamba. On the third day they arrived at Guarancalla where the priest was subjected to ridicule, abuse and more torture. Then they entered the outskirts of Marcanay. The impressionable Inca, under the influence of his chiefs (sworn enemies of all Spaniards), ordered his captains to execute the man who had dared kill his brother. The unfortunate Catholic was bullied down an incline to a site called La Horca del Inca (hanging place of the Inca) situated on a pampa between two rivers. Slivers of *chonta* (palm) were slipped under his fingernails, arrows driven into his flesh and his body was impaled on a shaft. Miraculously alive, he was clubbed and beaten again. Finally he was hit a terrible blow over the head. There under the pale shadows of the great forests, eight years after having set foot in Peru, shortly before his thirty-ninth birthday, the life was taken out of Diego Ortiz by those whom he sought to befriend. This was sometime between May and July, 1571. The site later became known as Mananhuanunca meaning, "he would not die." It became a shrine to the Spanish and a curse to the Incas.

Don Francisco de Toledo, Viceroy of Peru, had been in the conquered territories two years, long enough to know that the neo-Inca state of Vilcabamba was a thorn in his side. He had been sent to put the empire in order, though he overstepped his powers in doing so. Son of a notorious Spanish family, he delighted in his office. It is common knowledge that he intended exterminating the Royal Inca line. Driven by a personal hatred for the Indians and driving ambition, he set out to provoke the Vilcabamba Incas, threatening war unless Tupac Amaru came out to Cuzco.

He had sent ambassadors to make contact with the Vilcabamba chiefs. Atilano de Anaya, head of an armed force that tried to force entrance across the Chuquichaca bridge, was captured and put to death by the Inca's captains. When word of the defeat reached Cuzco (coupled with news of the martyrdom of Father Ortiz), the Viceroy decided to strike a blow.

The Spanish Viceroy called his men to arms ordering a general invasion of Vilcabamba. The heathen infidels had mocked God and King for the last time! In a burst of charged energy he shouted vengeance, called the expedition a crusade, a holy war, a fight to the finish. Under the guise that it was being sent to Chile (Inca spies at Cuzco kept careful watch on all Spanish activities), an expedition was hurriedly outfitted.

Messages were dispatched to Huamanga (Ayacucho) calling for an armed force to guard the entrances to Vilcabamba along the Apurímac gorge. Another was sent to Abancay. The Viceroy was determined to keep the Inca bottled up inside the refuge state, cutting off all possible escape routes. He had no intention of letting Tupac Amaru slip through his fingers.

The main army, under the command of General Martín Hurtado de Arbieto, an able soldier and old veteran of the civil wars, left Cuzco during the month of May, 1572. The large force of Spanish knights, Cañaris and Chachapoyas Indians, armed with harquebuses and field pieces, made haste for the Chuquichaca bridge so as to force entrance from the Urubamba side. Reaching the suspension bridge that hung low over the water, the army rushed across in single file. The harquebusiers sent a volley of shots resounding up the valley which scared off the defenders before the cables could be cut. The vanguard caught Tupac Amaru by surprise near the hanging bridge but he managed to escape into the thickets (he confessed later that he had been visiting the House of the Sun). The Spanish army gave hot pursuit. A battle was fought at the Coyacchaca River (river unknown) where they routed the Incas. Following their victory the force moved through the inter-Andean mountain pass of Ccolpa Casa and camped at Pampaconas. Ten days later, on June 16, the main force moved in the direction of Huayna Pucara (Young Fortress) over a difficult trail. A small force was stationed to guard key passes, particularly Ccolpa Casa. Baltazar de Ocampo, who recorded the official report given by Captain Martín García de Loyola (married to a daughter of Sayri Tupac), writes that the captain, in company of fifty harquebusiers, twenty-five shield-bearers—to protect the harquebusiers from slingshot, arrow and bolas—and one hundred Cañaris, led the attack. The Spaniard records the fortress was "situated on a high eminence surrounded by rugged crags and jungles, very dangerous to ascend and almost impregnable. Nevertheless, with my aforesaid company of soldiers, I went up and gained the young fortress, but only with the greatest possible labor and danger." Following this, General Hurtado, who had been observing from below, advanced with his artillery. Inca general Callqtopa abandoned the fortress and fled with the remnants of the army.

The road to the sacred city of Vilcabamba was now open and undefended, except for possible ambush. Making their way cautiously, the victorious Spanish force went through Guarancalla and on June 24, 1572, occupied the city of Vilcabamba. The standard-bearer, Pedro Sarmiento de Gamboa, claimed the city for Don Felipe, King of Spain. Even then the victory was empty, for the Inca, taking his treasures and valuables, had fled into the jungle. He left a burning city behind, having ordered the best buildings set to the torch.

Tupac Amaru had escaped to the Valley of the Simaponte, a name not shown on modern maps but undoubtedly the Cosireni, into the territory of the Antis Indians (the Mañaries), and thence by balsa raft into the interior. The Spanish force, under the command of Captain García de Loyola, pushed through the difficult jungle trails until they came to a large river called La Plata (probably the Urubamba). Five rafts were hurriedly built and the pursuit continued, as it would appear from the account, through the Pongo de Mainique to Momori (a settlement near the Picna, a tributary of the Urubamba). From that point fifty Spaniards, ragged and tired, but determined to bring the Inca to heel, continued the hunt some three leagues' distance into the interior.

Then the unexpected occurred. The Inca sent a message that he would agree to parley. The surprised Spaniards quickly agreed, but kept a tight grip on their firearms. The Inca said to continue the fight, in which many people, both Inca and Spanish, were being killed, was senseless; and since he was innocent of any wrongdoing, he would accept the terms of the Viceroy to live in peace in Cuzco, if no harm would come to his royal person, his family and principal chiefs. If his terms were not acceptable he would continue into the interior and there seek refuge with the Antis people over which he was Lord. If this transpired he could not guarantee the safety of either the captain or his men. The Spanish captain gave his word that no harm would come to his royal personage. Dressed in his imperial robes, adorned with the golden image of the Sun and wearing a headdress of brilliant plumes and jewels, Tupac Amaru, accompanied by his queen, three children, body-guard and royal treasure, which included the great Golden Disk of the Sun, the mummies of Manco II, Titu Cusi and the *coya*, were escorted over the road they had come. They passed through the smoldering city of Vilcabamba. The remains of Father Ortiz were exhumed from Mananhuanunca and taken up past Pampaconas and through Ccolpa Casa. A new city was founded (the New Vilcabamba), named San Francisco de la Victoria de Vilcabamba, in Antisuyo, twenty leagues from Cuzco in the east, on September 4, 1572, settled by the remnants of the Inca army. It was later peopled by the monks of Our Lady of Mercy and a convent was established to house the blessed remains of Ortiz, until they were officially removed to Cuzco in the year 1595. Old Vilcabamba was abandoned for good.

The procession continued on to Cuzco. General Hurtado triumphantly presented the Inca before the Viceroy. A mock trial was held and Tupac Amaru, together with his chieftains, was judicially sentenced to death. The Bishop of Cuzco begged for the Inca's life to no avail. Even after Tupac Amaru consented to be baptized and made an appeal to be presented to the King of Spain, the Viceroy carried out the sentence. The Inca chiefs were tortured and killed, and a Cañari Indian cut the throat of the Inca in the great square of Cuzco before a riotous crowd of 300,000 onlookers.

The death of Tupac Amaru brought the reign of the Vilcabamba kings to a climatic close. Yet the Vilcabamba tragedy was to continue.

With the Inca out of the way and his army demobilized, the Spanish poured into the Sacred Land, ravaging and despoiling the countryside. Captain General Martín Hurtado de Arbieto was made the first Governor of Vilcabamba under the Spanish Crown. He seems to have encouraged the total destruction of the territory. Pedro Sarmiento de Gamboa, cosmographer, and Captain Baltazar de Ocampo, soldier and miner, tell us that the Incas had selected "the best land in Peru," and that it was rich in gold, silver and treasure, especially at the legendary ravine of Purumata, which contained a fabulous huaca. The Spaniards spread panic among the populace, slaughtering and burning as they went. Many villages were razed and many others set to the torch by the inhabitants to keep them from falling into Spanish hands. In this way many important townships disappeared.

Viceroy Toledo continued to persecute the survivors of Royal Inca blood —including half-breeds. Those not killed outright were deprived of rights and property and banished to Chile or the swamps of Darien where they soon died. The purge continued under Toledo until his term of office ended in 1581. By the time he was replaced it was too late. The killing of the Emperor and the Inca aristocracy was an administrative blunder that resulted in disorder, famine and pestilence. A great empire fell into collapse, from which it never recovered.

7 · The Vilcabamba Expedition Is Born   1963

HISTORIANS GENERALLY AGREE that Manco II took a large force of volunteers into exile in the *montaña*. Spanish troops who were eyewitnesses to the fall of the neo-Inca government told of having marched into the tropical forests while tracking down Tupac Amaru, Manco's youngest son and the last of the Incas. The young Inca was not wandering aimlessly about the jungle, but was marching to reach an Inca settlement deep in the interior. Agricultural terraces have been observed on the banks of the Yavero, a tributary of the Urubamba near the Pongo de Mainique, and at other jungle sites, which suggest that the Incas maintained several jungle cities in addition to the capital, Vilcabamba. We know that the Spaniards, as well as Tupac Amaru, partially destroyed the old city of Vilcabamba. With its re-location in the sierra a curtain seems to have fallen across the legendary city.

Our aerial flight two years before over the eastern limits of the Department of La Libertad and the western limits of San Martín had shown that roads did drop down from the highlands into the *ceja de la montaña*, the eyebrow of the mountain, as the Spaniards used to call the thick forest regions that swept up from the great expanse of jungles eastward. We knew from our coastal work that the big desert arterials led to urban centers; so had the highland roads. Jungle roads would undoubtedly follow the same pattern— the Pajatén road seemed to indicate this. The problem was to find others. A task not without difficulty, considering there were absolutely no written records of Inca or pre-Inca road systems of the jungle. So the Pajatén road was the first real clue. (It later proved to be more important than any of us realized at the time).

We had attempted to lead an expedition into Pajatén country, an expanse of undulating terrain over which we had flown while scouting for

68

ancient roads; however, we could not find men who would take part in an exploration of the area. Several others had made attempts to penetrate this terra incognita and had failed. In 1919 Dr. Augusto Weberbauer, a German botanist, struck out for The Pajatén, and though he succeeded in locating ancient remains on the edges of the forest, he did not penetrate into the lower *montaña* because his guides from Bildibuyo, a pueblo of the sierra, were afraid to go. He had planned to visit the legendary Franciscan mission of Pajatén, several days' march into the *montaña*, but had to give it up. He did locate some hilltop ruins on the edge of the jungle at a place called Puerta del Monte. From his drawings of this scattered remain, published by the Geographical Society of Lima in 1920, the ruins looked exciting. They showed rustic buildings with zigzag design. He also mentioned a road running off into the *montaña*. I can well understand his reasons for wanting to explore deeper in, and his disappointment at not being able to go on.

Other explorers had disappeared into The Pajatén—never to come out again. The simple hill-folk said they had been enchanted. Had they been killed by wild animals? Had they lost their way in the trackless regions and starved to death? Or had they been killed, put out of the way by bandits or rustlers or poppy planters? The one man who could have helped guide us through this wild country, Teodoro Ganoza, had died the year before. He was only forty-eight years of age. Some said that the trip he had made through this region in 1953 and 1954 had resulted in his premature death—a curse. This had been the greatest single blow to our early expedition plans. Something was doing its best to keep the secrets of this mysterious region hidden. Then in early 1963, Carlos Lopez, a miner, cattleman and hunter from Huamachuco, chanced upon some scattered ruins in this area while opening up a trail. He later signed on as my trailman.

They appeared to be the lower parts of the great cliff we had spotted from the air a year earlier. It confirmed what we had suspected for some time. Large ruins *did* exist in the jungles.

By this time membership in the Andean Explorers Club was growing. Our explorations had attracted the interest of a large number of persons scattered about the world. I decided to send out an appeal to all members asking for support of our first jungle exploration. Within two weeks checks poured into our headquarters at the Savoy Hotel, Lima, from over twenty-two different countries. With these funds—and with what each resident member could throw in from his own pocket—we prepared to launch our first Vilcabamba Expedition.

I began studying old church documents and historical works compiled by the Augustinian, Jesuit and Franciscan orders in hopes of finding clues to jungle roads. These orders had maintained missions in the jungles—and still do. Old libraries are filled with voluminous reports of their activities, many of which make reference to the Indians and their settlements. The Franciscans had worked in Pajatén country; traversed the jungles by means of older roadways built up by the Indians in times past. The Augustinians actually managed to get into the legendary redoubt of Vilcabamba, the last refuge of the Incas under the illustrious Manco II, which fell to the Spanish Crown. According to the friars who worked with the last of the Vilcabamba kings, the sanctuary was down in the jungles. Juan Cancio Saavedra, Manuel Ugarte and Manuel Lopez Torres, rubber planters who lived in Espíritu Pampa, reported scattered remains in a place called Eromboni Pampa. This report, in which they speculated that these ruins represented a small military outpost which defended other ruins "deeper in," occurred around 1895. Hearing that ruins existed at Espíritu Pampa, Hiram Bingham went to investigate. But he could not locate what he was looking for. He wrote: "Calancha says that 'Vilcabamba the Old' was the largest city in the province, a term hardly applicable to anything here, far more applicable to Machu Picchu or even Choquequirau—the ruins Antonio Raimondi believed to be Vilcabamba —than to Espíritu Pampa."

Bingham concluded it was Machu Picchu and went to great pains to prove it. Yet, being a historian and knowing the geography of Vilcabamba, he was forced to conclude: "There appears to be every reason to believe that the ruins of Espíritu Pampa are those of one of the favorite residences of this Inca (Titu Cusi). It may have been the place from which he journeyed to meet Rodriguez in 1565." He reasoned that the valley met the requirements of the place called Vilcabamba, but he could not find sufficient ruins to justify calling it a city. Neither had Saavedra, Ugarte or Lopez Torres. When Bingham's guides chanced upon an Inca group of two houses, he described the event in the following words: "Nothing gives a better idea of the density of the jungle than the fact that the savages themselves had often been within five feet of these fine walls (those of Eromboni) without being aware of their existence." Had the jungles hidden much more? It seemed that they had, for Bingham acknowledged that it was the valley, or so it would appear, to which "Tupac Amaru, the last Inca, escaped after his forces lost the 'young fortress'. . ."

He was forced to write it off as a possible site of the legendary Vilcabamba because of the small number of ruins Saavedra's son and the "savages" showed him at Eromboni Pampa; also because: "It did not seem reasonable to suppose that the priests and Virgins of the Sun (the personnel of the 'University of Idolatry') who fled from Cuzco with Manco and were established by him somewhere in the vastness of Vilcabamba would have cared to live in this hot valley. The difference in climate is as great as that between Scotland and Egypt. They would not have found in Espíritu Pampa the food which they liked. Furthermore, they could have found seclusion and safety which they craved just as well in several other parts of the province, together with a cool, bracing climate and foodstuffs more nearly resembling those to which they were accustomed."

While acknowledging that Espíritu Pampa met the geographical requirements of Vilcabamba, Bingham dismissed it entirely as the possible site of the old refuge because he was not shown by his guides, nor could he find for himself, sufficient archaeological remains. Thus, he turned back to retrace his footsteps and claimed Machu Picchu as the lost city of the Incas. (Machu Picchu was seven days' foot travel from Espíritu Pampa, due to poor trails at the time; that much closer to Cuzco and removed from the location where history placed Vilcabamba.) His reasons seemed to be justified considering he was looking for the "largest city in the province" and did not find it at Espíritu Pampa. He appears to have suffered from the fatal error of thinking the Incas did not inhabit the jungles, and thereby left after only two or three days' exploration of the place, caused in part by his men from Pampaconas wanting to leave due to their fear of the savages.

My thinking was somewhat different on this point. I considered that the records of the Augustinian Order and the early Spanish chroniclers were most reliable. If the friars and soldiers placed the city of Vilcabamba in this valley, then it had to be here. There was no sense in trying to decide whether the Incas inhabited the jungles or not. Fathers Marcos and Diego had confirmed that Vilcabamba was in the tropical forests; so had the Spaniards who tracked down Tupac Amaru and later occupied the sanctuary for a brief spell until they founded another city of the same name higher up in the mountains.

Here was an account by a reliable reporter that Inca remains existed in the tropical rain forest. When Bingham left Espíritu Pampa he said, "we still have not identified Vilcapampa—the principal city of Manco and his sons." While he did not find a large number of ruins there, nor did he believe that the Incas would have selected a hot, tropical valley for their last refuge, I decided to take the word of the Spaniards and follow this trail in search of the lost city.

The Vilcabamba plan was simple enough: Pick up the roads and follow them using historical references, including those of Bingham and other explorers who had visited the area off and on over the past seventy years or so. According to the findings, the arrow pointed to a place called Espíritu Pampa, Plain of the Ghosts. I stuck a red flag on the Club map to a remote region less than a hundred nautical air miles northwest of Cuzco; a week's traveling by mule deep into the Peruvian montaña, whose physiography makes it one of the roughest and most dangerous places in the world for explorers. Thousands of square miles of undulating, jungled peaks shoot up into the high, Andean air like a giant washboard of green pyramids stretching for as far as the eye can see—and farther. The virgin rain forests cover everything. A green, impenetrable forest that grows in the Brazilian plains and fights its way west, up over the cloud forests that grow to 10,000 feet above sea level, where it is finally defeated by the towering Andes whose rugged peaks soar 20,000 feet or more. The Vilcabamba! A remote region, uninhabited except for tribes of nomadic savages whose heritage goes back to the Stone

Age. Save for a few settlements of pioneer farmers who have been colonizing the territory for some years, there is no sign of civilization. One of the most isolated spots on earth, it is a hot, humid jungle teeming with poisonous snakes, plants and insects, jaguars, pumas, bear and wild pig that resent man's presence. To gain access to this country one must traverse mountains which were thrust up when the world was born; negotiate deep canyons and valleys gouged out by violent streams that rush down from the Andes to debouch into the Amazon River a thousand miles away. It was enough just to explore these forest lands of the Southern Andes, much less to set out looking for the Inca redoubt of Vilcabamba, which had escaped a good number of explorers ever since the remnants of the last Incas fought their way through the Spanish ranks to settle into this overpowering wilderness.

While others had depended upon Machiguenga Indian guides (notorious for their unreliability), and spurious maps, I planned to follow the roads . . . those mentioned by the Augustinians and followed by Bingham.

It is known that the Inca armies under the militant Manco II, tramped over the backbone of the high Andes into the greater Vilcabamba country. They would have to travel over roads unknown to the Spaniards. The Incas had probably retired into the Antisuyo quarter (composed of the huge areas east of the Andes) and settled into the section nearest the traditional capital of Cuzco, the gateway to a jungle world. Undoubtedly the fourth quarter was crisscrossed by roads which linked the new capital city of Vilcabamba with the rest of the territory. I hoped to find these roads. No simple task, since the Spaniards unwittingly closed the door on the jungles of Antisuyo centuries ago.

PART II

THE VILCABAMBA EXPEDITIONS

1964-65

8 · The Legendary Lost City of the Incas

ON THE MORNING of July 1, 1964, Doug and I caught an airplane for Cuzco. The trip had been saddened by the news of Mirko's death a few days before in an airplane accident. He was to have flown us.

Sucking oxygen from small rubber tubes placed between chattering teeth, we looked down on the snow-crowned heights of the Andes sharing the loss of a friend.

We made the descent and touched down at Cuzco, ancient capital of the Incas, settled on an alpine plateau 10,800 feet above sea level and surrounded by grassy hills and sparse groves of eucalyptus trees. Today the city is vastly different from what it must have been five hundred years ago. The pink-tiled roofs and whitewashed houses of the Spaniards have long since replaced the primitive stone structures of the ancient Incas, but the spell of the Incas has never been broken.

We scrambled out of the plane carrying our cameras and warm clothing. A bright sun shone and the brisk, dry mountain air was exhilarating after the warm, humid coastal climate. We were met by Antonio Santander, amateur archaeologist of Cuzco, who had accepted an invitation to join the expedition as our guest. A tall, thin man in his early sixties, Santander had lost an eye due to an infection two years before while exploring the high Madre de Dios territory in search of Paititi. It has never been determined whether Paititi is a city, an empire or simply the name of an emperor, but most explorers consider it to be a city in the eastern forests beyond Cuzco. The search always seemed fruitless to me because there is so much confusion about its whereabouts—and identity. But who could be sure?

The following day we caught a train headed for Huadquiña, six hours from Cuzco. Rambling along through the brown hills, we reached the valley of the Vilcanota, and began a serpentine descent through one of Peru's most beautiful river gorges. We passed the imperial terraces of the Inca ruins of Ollantaytambo laid out on the hillsides and farther down river caught glimpses of the hanging city of Machu Picchu, on a peak high up over the river. As we dropped down into the valley the weather grew uncomfortably hot and by the time we arrived at the small village of Huadquiña we were down to our cotton shirts.

The gear was loaded on a broken-down six-wheel truck, which took us on a bumpy drive over a washboard dirt road into the tiny pueblo of Chaullay. We were met by Victor Ardilles, Governor of Vilcabamba, who had agreed to supply the expedition with mules and porters. A short, stocky man in his early forties, he shook hands and welcomed us to his territory. He was optimistic about the expedition and felt pride in his mission with us. Of all the hired members of the expedition he was the most valuable because of his knowledge of mountain trails and the fact that he was the governor of the district with official status and control over the porters, who were known to be unreliable and rebellious.

A police corporal commanding the Guardia Civil post ceremoniously inspected our papers and then said with candor, "Do you truly expect to find Vilcabamba la Grande, Señor?" The afternoon radio had mentioned our expedition.

"That is my intention, corporal."

"You do not believe Machu Picchu is the last refuge of Manco Inca?"

"No."

He pulled his ear and pushed his cap to the back of his head, "I have heard reports of an Inca city in the *montaña* from several *campesinos*. The Machiguengas have told them. But they are all afraid to see for themselves."

"Because of the *antimonia*?" I asked, referring to the dreaded malady of spitting blood and coughing spells caused by breathing the dust while excavating old tombs.

His brow furrowed. "They are more afraid of the *relámpago*. It is said that when anyone ventures close to the ruins it begins to rain . . . the thunder comes . . . and the lightning strikes." Then he smiled and laughed softly, "That is what superstitious people say."

"Do you believe it?" I asked. He shrugged his shoulders and said nothing. I knew enough about the folklore of the southern Andes to know that the old beliefs were deeply ingrained in most of the natives and that while the policeman spoke lightly about superstitions, he was not a confirmed disbeliever. I was familiar with the legends of Illapa, an agent of the Sun-god Inti, who struck down those who offended sacred grounds with thunderbolts and lightning, and the legend of Ccoa, who enslaved the spirits of its victims forever to its service. Time has not diminished the people's superstition of enchantment.

My plan was to follow Bingham's old trail in hopes of locating the "illusive city" guarded by the "forest spirits." There was no question about it: there had to be something at the base of all these rumors and fears of enchantment.

We returned to the truck and took a dirt road that circled down from Chaullay to a steel bridge that spans the Urubamba River. The driver pulled over to the side of the road and I jumped down to survey the scene. The foaming waters of the green current came tumbling down with a roar. On the other side, the Vilcabamba River rushed down from the sierra to debouch with a great crash into the larger Urubamba. A marvelous spectacle! Victor Ardilles had joined me with the other men. "An old Inca suspension bridge used to span the river somewhere around here," I said, pointing to the modern bridge. I knew from the chronicles that the old Inca "Bridge of the Lance" or the "Bridge of Fine Gold" as it was known, led into Vilcabamba country near this spot.

"No, Señor," Ardilles said, pointing to the other side. "The bridge of Chuquichaca is around that bend over the Vilcabamba River. The base is still to be seen."

At that moment two men who had been standing on the opposite bank to the left of the Vilcabamba climbed into a small metal cable car and pulled themselves hand-over-hand toward us, swaying back and forth over the treacherous waters. I could imagine that the original Inca suspension bridge, made of vegetable fiber, must have offered an equally hair-raising trip.

When the men reached our side of the river I asked them about the bridge Ardilles had described and they knew of it too. I decided to investigate.

We drove across the modern bridge to the other side of the Urubamba and got off the truck. We walked to the top of a knoll above the confluence of the two rivers, then pushed our way through the forest above the banks of the Vilcabamba until we came to the remains of an Inca bridge. A narrow, deep gorge stood between us and the far side of the river. It would have been a serious problem for armored cavalry to cross had the bridge been cut (much more difficult, I believe, than it would have been over the Urubamba where the river widens out some distance down from the conjunction of the two rivers.) Which bridge then, was the original Chuquichaca?

In ancient times the route from Cuzco did not come down the Urubamba River, known then as the Vilcanota in its higher reaches and the Vilcamayu farther down, but up over the pass of Panticalla and down the Lucumayo River. So it seemed to me that the present village of Chaullay was the key pass to Vilcabamba. Victor Maurtua, a Spanish chronicler who recorded the Spanish campaign that stormed Vilcabamba and took the Inca prisoner, spoke of the suspension bridge spanning the *río grande* which enters Quillabamba. Undoubtedly he meant the Urubamba. Yet another chronicler of the Vilcabamba episode, Barrantes, wrote that it crossed the smaller Vilcabamba River. Wherever it crossed, the bridge was somewhere near the conjunction of these two rivers and more than likely over a large rock a short distance up river from the present steel bridge over the Urubamba.

The question was partially cleared up some time later by another member of the Andean Explorers Club, Richard H. Hawkins, a Yale undergraduate, who traced the road up from this bridge and discovered that it led to Yurak Rumiyoc and a cluster of ruins in the neighborhood of Llactapata and Machu Picchu. This seemed to be positive proof that Machu Picchu was linked to the refuge state of Vilcabamba by means of this very same bridge and road system and was quite a distance from the Vilcabamba territory. (Tupac Amaru had been surprised by the Spanish force near the Chuquichaca bridge. After his capture he confessed that he had been visiting the "House of the Sun." This would suggest that he had been up to see Machu Picchu and had come over this very same bridge that spanned the Vilcabamba River.)

The Spanish ambassador to Vilcabamba, Diego Rodriguez de Figueroa, after crossing the bridge at Chuquichaca in 1565, took three days to reach Lucma; then he went to Vitcos and Pampaconas, which required several more days of travel. The Spanish force under General Martín Hurtado Arbieto took the same route, keeping the Vilcabamba River on the left for some days. There was no questioning the fact that Machu Picchu did not fit into the picture. It lay in the wrong direction. Had one wished to reach this site from Cuzco one would have gone via Ollantaytambo, crossed over the Urubamba by a suspension bridge, and then by an Inca road in the Pampaccahuana Valley and thence to Winay Wayna and direct to Machu Picchu. It could also have been reached overland direct from Cuzco where the road intersects below Pumamarca. This would have been no problem to mounted Spanish troops, had the site been occupied as a refuge by the Incas.

We hiked back up the hill and returned to the truck.

A twenty-five minute drive around gradient, hairpin turns brought us to Cuquipata and the end of the road, still under construction. It would link Chaullay with Lucma when completed.

I can remember the next day vividly because it was my first day in Vilcabamba country. Extracts from my expedition log read as follows:

Sunday, July 5. Cuquipata

At six o'clock we are up. The men engage in loading the equipment on five mules. Cases are placed in rawhide nets and tied down to wooden pack-mounts with ropes. The men manage to scrounge up two old saddle blankets from somewhere and carefully wrap them around the cameras until they are firmly secured in the racks.

We have breakfast at a small thatched roadside hut which serves as a grocery store and bar. The proprietress, a nondescript, rather hefty lady with black, furtive eyes, gives us a stern lecture on the merits of Hugo Blanco, a local figure thought to be a communist leader who was arrested not too long before our arrival and later sentenced to twenty-five years' imprisonment. Discreetly, I explain that my aim is to explore archaeological remains; I have

78

no interest in politics. She looks at me with a hollow smile. There is a distinct tension in the air, a feeling I can't quite define. (We had no way of knowing at the time that a band of rebels was operating in the area. It haunted our second and third expeditions, eventually coming to a head just prior to the fourth trip, which brought my explorations of Vilcabamba to an abrupt end. While the countryfolk were aware of what was going on, they would not say a word about it. They were scared.)

Thanking our hostess, we step out into the bright morning sunlight. The cargo mules have been sent ahead a half hour before and we hurry to our saddle mounts to catch up. I check my altimeter. We are 4,500 feet above sea level and it is already 80°. It will soar much higher before the day ends. Warmed by the hot air currents that rise up from the jungle floor, these altitudes are semi-tropical. The *montañas* to the east of the Andes, which lie under a sea of warm air, are hotter still and far more dense.

We ride quietly along through thick woods, hanging vines and red and yellow air plants. Flocks of parrots chatter back and forth, and, at the sound of our mules clattering on the rocky trail, swoop down the hillside toward the green, rushing Vilcabamba River.

At midmorning we stop at a tiny farmhouse constructed of poles plastered with mud and thatched with grass, surrounded by banana trees. A smiling, middle-aged couple offer us fresh melons and papayas; they are old friends of Governor Ardilles. I purchase a stalk of sweet-smelling, ripe bananas, divide them among the men and stuff the rest in my saddlebag.

We continue along up the mountain trail, passing through a series of tunnels cut out of the rock and over makeshift bridges that span small tributaries of the Vilcabamba River. Though overgrown by thick brush, pieces of old Inca roads crop up from time to time suggesting that we are on the right path into Vilcabamba country—and hopefully to the "Lost City of the Incas."

Climbing steadily higher into the sierra, the forest thins. Lush foliage gives way to waving grasslands. Late in the afternoon we arrive at a small pampa called Qucllomayo where there is a small thatched hut. The owner comes out and invites us to coffee. Once inside he extends the hospitality of his home, which we cordially accept since rain threatens. But we are six and there is barely enough floor space for three or four guests, and then with some discomfort. So Doug and I give up the room to Victor and Antonio and the two muleteers to go outside to pitch one of the tents. Everyone is watching us. It is the first time they have seen tents or sleeping bags and we put on quite a show what with our crimson duffel bags and green tent. It causes a sensation. Even the stock animals look at us suspiciously.

It is almost dark when we finish preparing for the night. A fine mist starts to fall. We are invited into the house for a modest meal of boiled yucca, eggs and potatoes, served with a hot sauce made of green pepper called *ají*. We eat amid the confusion of chickens, turkeys, pigs, dogs, and *cuy*, little long-haired guinea pigs, scampering about on the dirt floor looking for scraps of food, and everyone huddles around the fire for warmth.

When gourds of coffee are served, the owner of the house, a small, middle-aged man, stands and waves his arms up and down, shooing all the animals but the *cuy* out into the yard with a great fanfare. His wife fetches a plate of parched corn, places it on the table and sits down on a tiny little stool next to the fire. She is probably in her early forties, but looks much older. Her hands are gnarled from field work, her eyes dark and curious. Her tiny bare feet, cracked from the cold and hard stony earth, are partially hidden by thick layers of skirts that hang limply on the dirt floor. She pulls a shawl about her neck against the cold. A typical example of the Indian of the impoverished sierra who is accustomed to heavy labor and few comforts, she speaks no Spanish, only the Quechua language of her ancestors. The passing centuries have brought few changes in this part of the Peruvian highlands.

At eleven o'clock, blankets are spread out on the floor for the governor, Santander, and the mule skinners; Douglas and I bid everyone good night and walk out to our tent. It is terribly cold. What a difference two thousand feet in altitude can make! We fall asleep with the sound of rain drumming on the canvas roof. So ends the first day of the expedition.

Early the following morning we were on the trail moving through the thinning woodlands. At one point the trail became a narrow, crumbling shelf cut into the sides of a hanging precipice several hundred feet above the river. Farther along, a donkey train laden with bags of coffee beans on its way to the lowlands came down the trail. We stuck close to the inside to prevent being pushed down the mountain slope by a bolting animal.

We forded a small tributary of the Vilcabamba chartered as the Palmayoc on my map, a drawing of the region by the naturalist, Christian Bues, who mapped the area from 1916 to 1928. Then we took a high bridge made of logs that spanned the Vilcabamba River. Finally we arrived at Victor Ardilles' home in Lucma, the capital of the district, which would serve as our base of operations for exploring the eastern *montaña*. (Map IV.) A small high-land community of mud cottages with thatched roofs situated 8,300 feet above sea level, it is like so many towns of the sierra, without electricity, running water, hospital, or physician. Mass has not been said in the church for some time; a priest calls only occasionally. However, a large school is maintained for children of the whole district.

The pack animals were unloaded and the expedition goods taken to our quarters. We would spend the rest of the day at Lucma hiring porters for the *montaña* and gather what information we could from the local citizenry. We didn't meet with much success in either department. No one at Lucma would have anything to do with the *montaña* beyond Espíritu Pampa. We hoped to have better luck farther ahead. Ardilles said we would have little difficulty in hiring men once we penetrated the forest region since pioneer settlements were scattered along the trail. I explained to him that I wanted to explore the Espíritu Pampa area thoroughly and Santander wanted to press on to a place called Aconcharcas and the lower Urubamba country, home of the ancient Mañaries Indians (the Antis who were allied with the Incas). Almost everyone offered some idea of where to find an Inca city but nobody had actually seen ruins and no one offered to guide us. They simply told us to investigate a nameless hill or valley on our own. Bingham told of these fruitless searches. Other explorers had wasted time on wild-goose chases. I wasn't for blindly entering unchartered regions without something tangible to go on. No, we would search for roads—roads were the whole key.

Next morning at daylight we set off across the grasslands. Our mule train consisted of five pack and four saddle animals. We had managed to hire three muleteers and one machete man. A modest beginning, but I hoped to employ others. I only hoped I could shake them out of their fears and superstitions and get them working in concert.

Skirting along the upper banks of the Vilcabamba River, we moved over an old Inca road that took an erratic course up a mountainside, crossed over the Vilcabamba and eventually led into the small community of Pucyura situated on a flat strip of wooded land around 8,900 feet. We ran into our first difficulty at the police control, a ramshackle house held down by a nattily dressed sergeant and four *guardias*. Santander had left his identity papers in Cuzco and the sergeant refused to allow him to pass. A policeman had been killed at the post less than a year ago by Hugo Blanco and his rebels. The sergeant didn't want to accept the responsibility of letting any unauthorized person pass his post—the last one in this part of the country—for fear they might be part of a guerrilla band suspected of operating somewhere in the jungles.

Only after two hours of arguing and a thorough inspection of our equipment did the sergeant appear content enough to allow Antonio's passage. Just as we were about to leave Pucyura, a peasant woman invited the four of us into her home for a cup of hot cocoa. Accepting her kindness, we followed her inside to a table. Halfway through my second cup of the bittersweet liquid, I happened to catch sight of a pottery figure resting atop a dusty shelf. A smaller and less imposing object stood next to it. They were partially covered by a dirty piece of material. "May I look at your huacos?" I inquired of our hostess. She tried to ignore the question but as a I grew more insistent she reluctantly placed them on the table explaining they were mementos from her late husband. I examined them with great interest, asking Doug in English to see if he could find out their origin and history. The larger piece, an incised effigy vase with spout, stood about seven inches high.* The second ceramic

---

* Alan Sawyer of the Textile Museum of Washington, D.C., later identified this piece from photographs as Middle Horizon dating back to the eleventh century of our era—which showed that the Tiahuanaco or Huari culture appears to have settled in the region centuries ago, before the Incas rose to power under Manco Capac.

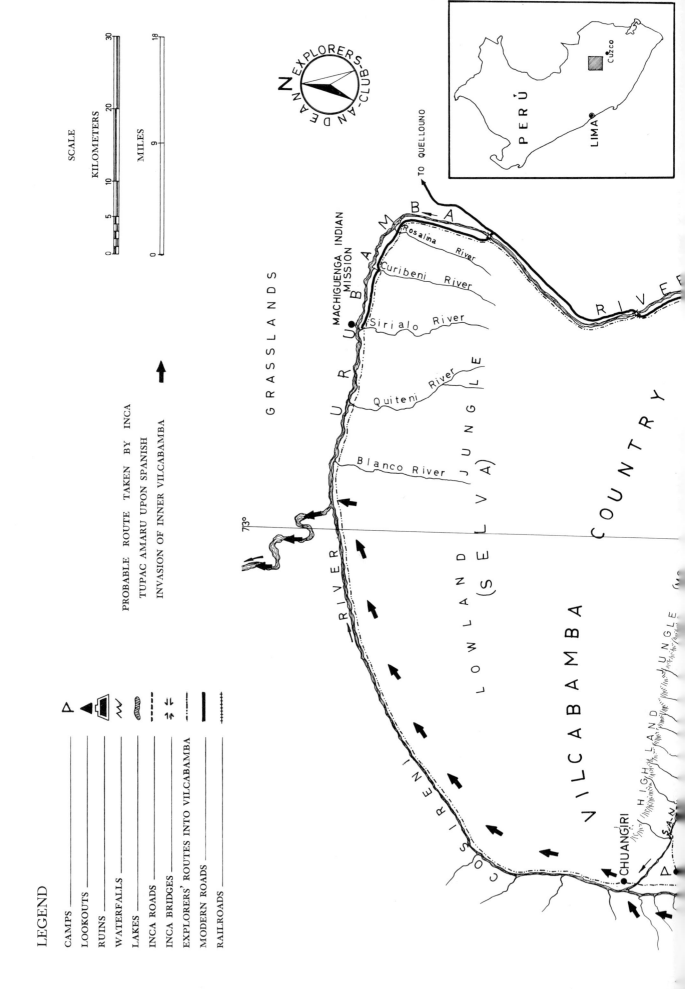

LEGEND

CAMPS
LOOKOUTS
RUINS
WATERFALLS
LAKES
INCA ROADS
INCA BRIDGES
EXPLORERS' ROUTES INTO VILCABAMBA
MODERN ROADS
RAILROADS

PROBABLE ROUTE TAKEN BY INCA
TUPAC AMARU UPON SPANISH
INVASION OF INNER VILCABAMBA

SCALE

KILOMETERS
0   5   10   20   30

MILES
0   9   18

EXPLORERS AND ANDEAN CLUB

PERÙ

LIMA
CUZCO

TO QUELLOUNO

U R U B A M B A   B ← A

Rosalina River

Curibeni River

MACHIGUENGA INDIAN
MISSION

Sirialo River

GRASSLANDS

Quiteni River

Blanco River

73°

U R U B A M B A   R I V E R

L O W L A N D   (S E L V A)   J U N G L E

C O S I R E N I   R I V E R

V I L C A B A M B A

C O U N T R Y

H I G H L A N D   J U N G L E

CHUANGIRI

S A N.

PICH

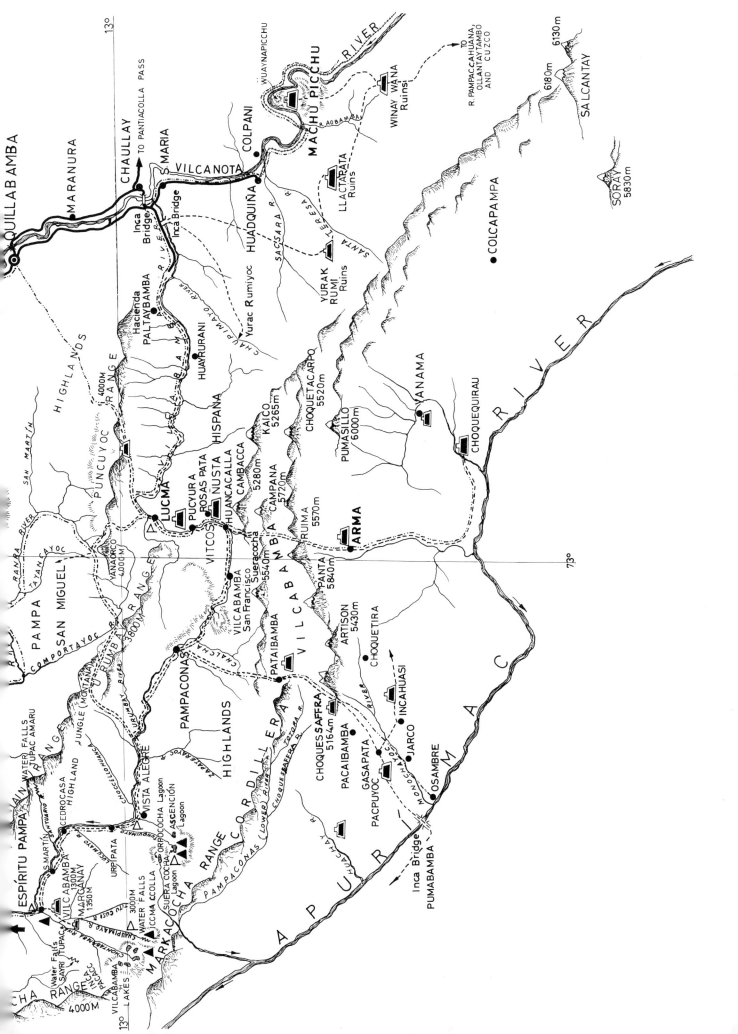

vessel, a goblet with polychrome painted designs in orange-red, red, white and black geometric patterns with dots, was also very interesting.

"They came from Espíritu Pampa," said Douglas in a low voice. "Seems her husband had a small collection before he died three years ago."

The woman disappeared through a door into the kitchen and Doug leaned across the table and whispered, "Ardilles says he died of antimonia." The governor nodded confirmation. The people of the area believed he was involved in tomb robbing and met his end through the curse of the Incas.

Our mules jogged along the trail grunting their protest of tightened cinches, drawn around fat bellies bloated with lush grass eaten during our sojourn at Pucyura. We urged them on by cracking our long rawhide quirts. My mind unraveled the events of the past hour. I couldn't help thinking there was much more to Espíritu Pampa than anyone imagined. Had Bingham, who had searched for the "Lost City of the Incas," missed something down in the jungled Plain of the Ghosts? I couldn't help thinking he had.

Bronze-faced Indian shepherds and their flocks of sheep scattered up the sides of the grassy ridges as our mule train trotted by. They chattered in Quechua and stared wide-eyed at the Viracochas (fair-skinned people) who had invaded the sacred privacy of the inner Andes. In a half hour we entered the small pueblo of Huancacalla, where we planned to spend the night.

Early in the afternoon we set out with one mule loaded with camera equipment to make a reconnaissance of two old Inca sites located atop a dominating mountain peak named Usnuyoc. We crossed over a wooden bridge spanning the Vilcabamba River, climbed a forested slope and reached a grassy verge. A short hike brought us to an elevated spit of land called Rosas Pata (Hill of Roses), a sequestered place cloaked in an aura of Spartan-like austerity at some 9,300 feet altitude.

There before us, broken and bleached, lay the remains of what had once been a beautiful Inca temple. Three or four large doorways made of white granite blocks stood in mute testimony that kings and lords of royal lineage had passed through these portals. (Plate 6.) They were built on the order of the famous Inca sun temple at Vilcas Huaman.

I had the cameras unpacked and the mule tethered on a grassy courtyard. Drifting around the far side of the buildings, which stretched nearly a city block in length, I reached a level terrace which commanded a sweeping view of the countryside. I stood there gazing at the incredibly beautiful world of The Vilcabamba with its majestic maze of valleys, ridges, gorges, precipices and forested groves. Rising over the landscape stood the towering peaks of the Vilcabamba massif, "El Señorio de Vilcabamba," as Inca and Spaniard knew it, with resplendent, snow-crowned Pumasillo dominating the scene.

Looking out from this "eagle's nest," I could see the Vilcabamba River far below shimmering in the sun and to the north a range of granite peaks that soared up 13,000 feet or more. According to my map a cluster of ruins

crown its heights. Christian Bues explored a main group known as Puncuyoc consisting of white limestone buildings located on the route known as Abra Puncuyoc emanating from Quillabamba. This route was taken by Bingham and other explorers. I scanned it carefully with my field glasses. Ardilles had told me he had seen the ruins. Henrik Blohm, Richmond Lawrence and Pepe Pancorvo explored these same ruins during the Victor von Hagen Inca Road Expedition in 1953 when tracing Inca roads of the District. Since the ruins had been reported by previous expeditions, I decided against taking time out to re-explore them. I was interested in opening up new ground in Vilcabamba, something that no one had done up to the present time. I studied another map which revealed an alternate route leading to Puncuyoc from the lower Pampaconas via the Sacsarayoc or the Salt Pass, as it is known. How did these ruins figure into the Vilcabamba story? The thought struck me they might be the Huayna Pucara fortress attacked by Captain Martín García de

85

Loyola. Nearly impregnable, the site fits the description given by the Spanish captain. The ruins consist of a long two-story building built atop a platform with niches and roof pegs. Spanish artifacts have been found on the premises, but from all appearances it was built as a bastion guarding the route from Quillabamba. Ocampo, the Spanish chronicler, actually visited a place called Pitcos. He wrote of Pitcos as follows, "There is an extensive level space with a very sumptuous and majestic building erected with great skill and art, all the lintels of the doors, the principal as well as the ordinary ones, being marble elaborately carved." Was this a description of Rosas Pata or Puncuyoc? Or Machu Picchu? We may never know after all these centuries and all the conflicting reports that have been written. When King Manco occupied the Vitcos Province he must have constructed many buildings, including a mountain fortress, abandoning many of the older structures as he withdrew deeper into the Vilcabamba Province. The name Huayna Pucara (young fortress) would describe his fortress. Bingham believed Rosas Pata to be the Vitcos of Manco, the one visited by the Spaniards. But it was more likely that the old Vitcos was abandoned once the Spaniards learned its whereabouts and a new Vitcos erected to fit the special needs of the fighting Inca. In my opinion, Rosas Pata would not have offered any great obstacle to Spanish troops; whereas Puncuyoc and Machu Picchu would have been almost inaccessible. It is curious that the Spanish do not write of having taken Vitcos, but Huayna Pucara. Does this suggest that it had been given a new name? Whatever the speculations on the whereabouts of Vitcos, one fact stands out: Vilcapampa La Vieja (Vilcabamba the Old), constructed by Manco as his principal city, was beyond the Province of Vitcos to the east, some several days' journey into the steaming, tropical *montaña* of the Antis Indians. All the chroniclers are clear on this point.

After conquering Amaybamba, Inca Pachacutec moved his armies across the Urubamba to the provinces of Vitcos and Vilcabamba. He tells of having been met by emissaries of Vitcos who submitted peacefully. This was in the fifteenth century. The Inca withdrew his army and inaugurated a building program which implies that Vitcos experienced a hundred years of building before the Spanish takeover. The finer construction methods found at Machu Picchu (which stands in the Vitcos Province) suggests that it was the older capital of this province. Rosas Pata could have been one of the later townships, which, too, received some attention from Manco. Puncuyoc, on the other hand, appears to have been occupied during the colonial epoch.

The Vilcabamba Province, the land of the Antis Indians that includes the jungle regions to the east, was brought into the Inca Empire so as to absorb the great wealth of the *montaña*. Unquestionably, the Incas would have erected many cities in the jungle in order to collect tribute from the nations of Antisuyo, to show the strength of the Inca and to store many rich products such as cocoa, feathers, hides, timber, bamboo, medicinal herbs and roots, gums, resins, fruits, gold washings, emeralds and all the other tropical goods necessary to the economy of an imperial power. Manco, aware of these outposts, no doubt selected a convenient city as a springboard to Cuzco, and there built his capital city which became known as Vilcabamba.

Standing on the high terrace at Rosas Pata, I shifted my vision to the east and followed an old trail that wound its way up from Huancacalla toward the source of the Vilcabamba River. With the aid of my binoculars I could distinguish broken bits of an Inca road in the rolling countryside. On the other side of the great hills and mountains lay the forest regions of Vilcabamba. Surely Espíritu Pampa could be reached over this road in three days.

On the expedition map I traced the line of Inca monuments, the fortified citadels on the eastern frontier—Pisac, Ollantaytambo, Machu Picchu, Rosas Pata and a number of others. The Incas had protected all incoming routes to Cuzco from the *montaña*. Because it is commonly believed that the high and low jungles were not densely populated, some historians question the need for these bastions. These writers forget—or choose to forget—that Inca legend tells of confederated nations who fought their way up from the rain forests on the eastern watersheds of the Andes into the sierra, conquering Cuzco and driving out the Incas. During the fifteenth and sixteenth centuries Incas Pachacutec and Tupac Yupanqui fought back subsequent invasions and Huayna Capac used fifty thousand troops to keep down these bothersome tribes. All along the central Andes a string of fortifications was erected to prevent further invasions. Had the Incas been content to fortify their highland regions by building a ring of fortress citadels around their capital? I thought not. The Incas were known to have moved deep into the jungles where they subjugated many tribes and nations and settled them in newly built cities and tambos. These conquering Incas absorbed the Mañaries, Pilcosones, Chunchos, Yana-simis, Opataris, even the fierce Chirihuanes of the Gran Chacu. Later they conquered the Chachapoyas to the north, the Cañaris and the Cofanes. With the conquest of the Kingdom of Quito in what is now Ecuador, Huayna Capac established a new city from which to rule the greatly extended empire. From this new capital city of the northern provinces the Inca ordered the building of a network of jungle roads to bring the wealth of the eastern *montaña* to the highlands.

Dropping down an overgrown trail past stone terraces, canals and fountains, we arrived at a place known as Ñusta Hispana. Making our way through the Inca ruins, we came to a huge, white boulder perched in the center of a marshy plain. Smaller stones were cast about, including a large Intihuatani, a hitching-post-like column used by ancient Inca Sun Priests to ceremoniously tie the Sun during the winter solstice. There were other sculptured blocks, apparent religious symbols of reverence to the Sun-god Inti, the visible representation of light. Kon Tiki Viracocha (or Illa Kon Tiki Viracocha) was the name of the Inca Supreme Being, the Creator, the first cause and fountainhead of generated being and form.

One side of the large rock was built over a spring of water. A carved fountain stood nearby. This rock appeared to answer the description of the historical Temple of the Sun at Chuquipalpa, which contained a great white rock called Yuracrumi (Yurak-Rumi). According to the chronicles of Antonio Calancha, this rock was close to Vitcos. Undoubtedly the rock was a sacred huaca and had a religious significance to the Incas. Each important Inca town contained one of these *huancauri*, usually in the center of the community. The Supreme Creator of the Incas, Kon Tiki Viracocha, was believed to have made the first man from stone; thus men were sons of stone, animated by God. Stone contained the divine spark of fire which would come alive when struck by flint or metal; thus stone was related to the Sun, the progenitor of man. While huacas were not worshipped, they served as the *apu*, the focal point for priests, for it was generally held that the spirit of their ancestors were bound up inside these special stones. In a way that is comparable to the oracle of Delphi, they were important in divination rites. Like the eternal flame that burned in ancient temples, these huacas were a link between the past and the world of the living.

Stone was a building block of the universe, magically united with fire and water. The life-giving rivers were born from the stone of the high mountains. Stone drew its energy from the Sun. The earth was made from the dust of stone, from which the sacred *choclo* (maize) was nourished by rainwater and sunlight. Corn was prepared for human consumption by being ground between stone mortar and pestle. So it is that the Incas chose to build their cities from the sacred matrix of life.

Calancha tells us that atop this great rock stood "the idol of Punchau" which symbolized the Sun as the giver of daylight, and we can assume this was the great Golden Sun Disk taken from the temple at Cuzco and brought to Vilcabamba by Manco. Here oracles were sought by the High Priest of the Sun.

I noticed that the spring of water originated from a cave-like opening. Niches were cut into the rock, and gave the impression of once having been a burial vault. Could this have served as the tomb of Manco following his death? Beyond question, the place was a sacred shrine of some kind, possibly before Manco came here to establish his refuge.

The following morning we climbed a trail up a tight rocky valley toward the source of the Vilcabamba River, arriving at a ghost town of fifty or sixty unoccupied thatched huts. Most of the inhabitants were away in the fields tending their flocks and potato patches. The local caretaker of the tumble-down church, a short little man the other side of sixty years, with a dark wool poncho thrown over one shoulder and his hat in his hand, explained that the town was deserted, save for a few huts. The townfolk lived in their *chacras*, returning to the village at fiestas only. The community was the New Vilcabamba settled by the Spaniards. They called it Vilcabamba Chico (Little Vilcabamba). Vilcabamba Grande (big Vilcabamba) was farther along.

88

A long thatched church building made of stone cemented with mud stood near the main plaza. I estimated it to be less than half a century old. The remains of an older and undoubtedly more substantial stone church with three bells still hanging in the tower and slightly inclined like the leaning tower of Pisa, stood off to one side. It may have been the original church that housed the relics of Father Ortiz after they were removed from Mananhuanunca. We came across the foundation of still an older structure in the center of the plaza. This raised some doubts as to which had been the original church. Rectangular in shape, the foundation measured 90 feet long by 70 feet wide. There were two smaller structures inside the main building, one circular, the other square-shaped.

We found a stone carved with an inscription that included the word "Vilcabamba" and several Inca artifacts in the modern church. A young boy from the village led us up the side of a hill to an old colonial cemetery where we examined a large rock, probably a crypt, with a rough cross cut out on the surface. The natives of the area claim that fire shoots out of this rock during certain nights of the year.

My maps indicated this was the legendary San Francisco de la Victoria de Vilcabamba, founded by the Spaniards 392 years before. Modern historians refer to it as the New Vilcabamba. What existed here in Inca times? Some artifacts in the church and the remains of building foundations suggest it had been an Inca community at one time.

Pukiu means spring of water in Quechua (springs abound in the vicinity). Because it is so close to the ruins of Rosas Pata (Vitcos), it appeared to me that it was possibly the original village of Puquiura where Manco II maintained his armies and where Father García had his mission. Strategically located at an altitude of 10,000 feet, looking down on key passes of the region, it must have been important to the Vilcabamba kings, a fitting site for the New Vilcabamba.

Dropping down to a large pampa watered by springs and streams that feed the Vilcabamba River, we drove our mules carefully over the *fango*, the soggy tundra country, then continued higher up into the cold sierra, with a bone-chilling wind at our backs. At 12,000 feet we came to the pass of Ccolpa Casa (Kollpa Kasa, strong pass), and went through it as determined to make the grand assault on the Inca city of Vilcabamba as any Spaniard that may have passed this way four centuries ago.

The brown hills rose up on either side to 13,000 feet or more. To the south, the magnificent Cordillera Vilcabamba with the snowy, serrated crests of Artison and other peaks averaging 18–20,000 feet, cut a saw-toothed outline against the sky. Calancha says that the Province of Vilcabamba ". . . is a hot country of the Andes and is mountainous and includes parts that are very cold . . . intemperate bleak uplands." The only signs of life were hawks swooping across the sky or occasionally a fox darting into the underbrush.

We continued on past cascading waterfalls and the echoing reverberation of the newly born Pampaconas River (soon to become the Concevidayoc) churning away in a steep gorge on our right. The trail dropped down. We left the cold wind that had plagued us since leaving Lucma behind on the other side of the mountains. We came out in a sheltered green valley to find ourselves on an old Inca stone road that staircases a quarter of a mile down the slope. Another hour's ride and we swept into Pampaconas where we stayed the night.

We were up at the crack of dawn. Our little hut faced east and the sun came up in a blaze of white fire. I went out to catch the first shafts of light as they shot up from behind the rocky heights of Yanaorco (black peak). The highlanders are early risers, and each day the village begins to stir around four o'clock. By sunrise, smoke was billowing up through thatched roofs and the aroma of fresh coffee scented the dry, winter air.

At 11,000 feet above sea level, Pampaconas is a community of fifty families situated on a lofty plateau on the edge of the cloud forest. Measured by the standard of living in the sierra highlands, it is a prosperous village, and while it lacks all the modern conveniences, its inhabitants possess a dignity and pride that is rare in isolated hamlets. Life is simple and goes on in much the same way as it has for centuries. Perhaps it seems like an excessively hard life to outsiders, but if one looks beyond the windowless homes, and the patched and worn clothing, there is a well-being and security about the people. By modern standards, these people are abysmally poor; but they manage to provide themselves with the basic necessities of life. I saw well-fed, happy children with rosy cheeks and delightful laughs. Their parents are independent, community-minded property owners. A school building for 160 children was under construction. Transistor radios keep them informed of the outside world. Families make regular trips by mule to markets in Quillabamba and Cuzco. Nevertheless, they are isolated and live according to past traditions. They speak Quechua, but with changes in government literacy programs, everyone is under obligation to learn Spanish. The highest respect is maintained for elders of the village who are called *papa*. Fair-skinned, narrow-faced gentlemen, who are taller and thinner than the coastal people, expressed astonishment when learning we intended exploring the pampas lower down the valley. They had heard that ruins existed at Espíritu Pampa.

We moved painstakingly across swampy plains, forded a stream, our mounts plodding across the soggy ground until we came out on a dry trail leading to the *montaña*. Was this the Ungacacha (actually Yunkakasa, gateway to a temperate or hot land in Quechua) mentioned by Father Calancha, the place where Friars Marcos and Diego entered the water up to their waists, when making the long, difficult journey with Inca Titu Cusi from Puquiura to Vilcabamba? Perhaps the Inca had damned up or diverted a stream over these *pajonales* as described in the chronicles of Calancha. He described the sierra as a "cold place," which seemed to indicate that Ungacacha was the damp plains below Bambacona, presently known as Pampaconas.

The *teniente gobernador* of Pampaconas had promised to send three carriers to our base camp at Espíritu Pampa the next day, and we hoped to hire other men farther down the trail. We had been told that a man named Ascensión Luque, who lived at a place called Vista Alegre, was friendly with the chief of a small tribe of Machiguenga Indians near Espíritu Pampa. Luque had been a young man when Bingham passed through Pampaconas in 1912 and later served as a guide for the naturalist Christian Bues. He told the men from Pampaconas that he knew the whereabouts of ruins near his *chacra*, both in the upper heights and in the jungle. From my point of view, he was indispensable to the upland trek since he was the only living man who knew the access trails.

We plunged headlong into the cloud forest. My altimeter registered 8,300 feet. A warm draft wafted up from the dark jungle valley which was alive with wild sounds. Crickets and song birds—their forms lost in a hundred shades of green moss, shrubs, vines, bright flowers and huge trees spreading their upper branches in a closed canopy high above our heads—chimed in with the roaring resonance of the Concevidayoc River to produce a pleasant symphony of nature. Occasionally a *chicotillo* would slither across the trail. This long emerald-green snake, called *látigo* in the *montaña*, is harmless, but can cause quite a fright. When provoked it whips and throws itself at a man, dropping bodily out of a tree to wrap itself around the neck.

At 3 P.M. my altimeter showed we had dropped 5,000 feet. We were now deep in the Concevidayoc Valley—a sunny land where pumpkins and bananas, coffee, tea, pineapples, oranges, yucca and sugarcane are grown in the fertile alluvial soil on small *chacras*, cut out of the thick jungle by a few hardy pioneer farmers who have fled the crowded highlands for a new life in the *montaña*. Men like Ascensión Luque, master of Vista Alegre, have been here for many decades. Many newcomers had arrived from the sierra only a few months before our own visit, and land had been recently cleared at intervals along the trail.

From my diary, our entrance into Vista Alegre is so recorded:

Thursday, July 9. Vista Alegre

The expedition reaches Vista Alegre with a great fanfare. We ride up in a clatter of pounding hoofs, whiplashes, braying mules, squeaking pack mounts and banging kettles, sending chickens, ducks and pigs scampering across the yard. The elderly Ascensión stands in a doorway of one of the huts, watching us dismount. He walks over to the Governor, giving him a dignified *abrazo*, then cooly shakes hands with other members of the expedition. We are invited into the larger of the two cabañas for coffee.

Ascensión speaks Quechua and only a smattering of Spanish. Tall and lean, he gives the appearance of great austerity. An aquiline nose and thin lips grace his long, chiseled face. In a soft, flowing voice he tells us we are welcome. He says nothing else until the *gobernador* asks him about the possible location of ancient ruins. He fusses over the clay pot of boiling water before answering. He has seen small ruins in the Markacocha Mountains, an extension of the Cordillera Vilcabamba. He also admits to knowledge of an Inca road nearby and agrees to guide us there.

Cutting our way by machete down the bank of the Concevidayoc River we come to a fragment of Inca road. It appears to be a continuation of the same road which we had followed down from the heights above Pampaconas. We set up our tents and stay here overnight.

When the forest is stilled and bright fireflies blink about in the darkness, Ardilles suggests we all have a drink. I instruct one of the boys to fetch a bottle of aguardiente. Before long, everyone is feeling the effects of drink. The old man, while being most cordial, had given evasive answers to my questions about ruins in the lower pampas. Now that his tongue is loosened, he talks freely about the pampa spirits and how Apu Manco guards his secrets. He explains in great detail how a man can be turned to stone even by touching the sacred territory, by coming too near it. His face takes on a ghostly look in the candlelight. The others listen spellbound, catching every word in quiet fascination. He agrees to accompany us in two days hence and promises to talk with the Machiguenga chief. But he will not enter the pampas. We shake hands on it, then retire for the night.

With Ascensión, who agreed to join the expedition until it reached the pampas, we set out at dawn pushing farther into the *montaña*. The weather grew much warmer. Fording a number of rushing streams we found ourselves on a muddy trail, the mules up to their bellies in the sticky ooze, slipping and fighting for balance. We finally dismounted and walked them up treacherous inclines. Farther along we saw a man on muleback coming toward us. Ardilles said it was Julio Cobos, the man responsible for putting in the trail between Espíritu Pampa and Vista Alegre. Wiry, in his early fifties, he is a typical frontiersman from the highlands of Armas who makes a living by growing coffee beans. In 1957 he had replaced the Machiguengas as the lord of the lower pampa. He listened attentively while the *gobernador* told him our business, then scratched a note with pencil to his eldest son. He bade us good-bye then trotted his mule up the trail disappearing into the foliage.

In a stifling heat, we moved deeper down into the valley through a tangle of undergrowth, great ferns and giant elephant-ear-like plants. Parrots squawked back and forth above the leafy canopy. A pair of large, black monkeys crashed through the tree branches high overhead. Machetes sang a metallic note, twanging the air, and the acrid smell of fresh-cut vines filled the nostrils. It was late afternoon when we finally arrived at a place called San Martín, altitude 4,500 feet. Espíritu Pampa was another league ahead.

We did not know the trail and since darkness threatened we decided to stay the night in a little hut near the trail, rather than risk getting lost or injuring an animal.

Next morning I scouted around with two machete men and uncovered an ancient building made from irregular stones cemented with mud; also scattered potsherds, unmistakably of Inca origin. Bingham had found similar artifacts up the valley at Concevidayoc when it was owned by Juan Cancio Saavedra. But when Cobos took over the valley he made his home here at San Martín before moving down to Epríritu Pampa. It was Saavedra along with Manuel Ugarte and Manuel Lopez Torres, rubber gatherers, who had first heard of ancient remains at a place called Eromboni from the Machiguengas who were living at Espíritu Pampa before the turn of the century.

In addition to the Inca remains found at San Martín, I came upon some old structures, which were either Spanish colonial or re-worked Inca constructions. I picked up several square pieces of floor tiling and Spanish *ladrillo*, possibly old fragments from the mission of Father Diego Ortiz at Guarancalla. It is told that his church, hospital and school had been very close to Vilcabamba, in the jungles near the Mañaries Indians whom he frequently healed. These finds suggested we were on the right road.

Sunday, July 12. On the Trail to Espíritu Pampa

Our little caravan sets out again, moving slowly over the fern-covered trail. The lead men have a hard time cutting a swath wide enough for the pack animals. Winding our way along the path—which looks as if it may have been an old Inca road centuries ago—we come to a promontory that overlooks the lower Concevidayoc Valley spread out directly below, a forested pampa guarded by a 6,600-foot peak and graced by cascading waterfalls. A tiny toy-like farmhouse and a dozen acres of land stand on the edge of the dense virgin rain forest. A series of forested pampas are fed by several rivers that have their origin in the high, rocky Markacocha-Pichqacocha range, a 12,500-foot series of granite peaks some fifty to twenty miles to the west. (*Marka* is the Quechua word for high region; *cocha*, lake; *pichqa*, five.) Ardilles tells me there are a number of lagoons situated on these heights. He adds that one of these lakes is called Yanacocha. Ascensión is the only person who knows the upper range. The uppermost peak is called the Ñusta, the sacred virgin mountain which no man has ever touched. He points his finger to the purple peak and explains that local folklore says it is Manco turned to stone because he angered the lake goddess when he left his people to the Spaniards and retired to Vilcabamba.

Surveying the locale, I can't help analyzing the practical advantages of the Vilcabamba Valley. Because it was defended by a series of old *miradores* or lookouts called Tikuy Rikuqs (to see all, in Quechua), which were perched on hilltops and other strategic points in the valley, a surprise attack would have been impossible. It will be remembered Captain García had to storm several fortifications before he could enter this valley. When attacked, Tupac Amaru retreated into the forests. Had he known military strategy, he could have defeated Captain García and his small band. No Spanish army had ever dared venture into the sacred valley when Manco and Titu Cusi sat on the throne.

A fertile valley irrigated naturally by rivers, the pampas of Espíritu Pampa could have supported a large population. History does not tell us how many people Manco took with him but we can estimate that there were thousands; sources place the figure at anywhere from 30,000 to 100,000. Just how many he maintained at the principal city we do not know. Titu Cusi must have kept his army in the capital city and since it was the metropolis of the province, it can be assumed that constant water supply would have been a chief requirement for the livelihood of a large population. Small mountain citadels like Machu Picchu could neither accommodate nor sustain the agricultural needs of large numbers of people.

Located at the crossroads, Espíritu Pampa affords access to the sierra by means of the road over which we had come. No doubt there were other roads that led up over the Markacocha-Pichqacocha range and down to the Apurímac where an old Inca bridge spans the river. Manco crossed this stream on numerous occasions to attack the Spanish supply lines operating between Huamanga or Ayacucho and Lima, with surprising success. Navigable waters were only two days down river; thus making the highways of the inner jungles accessible to the Incas.

Our mules negotiate a wide stone Inca road that staircases down the slope into the valley. Overgrown by thick vegetation, it is only partially cleared. A second road drops down from the upper regions (it is later traced and found to run off in the direction of the Markacocha-Pichqacocha Mountains). A quarter of an hour later we pull up in front of the Cobos house. It is made of fieldstones cemented with mud and thatched with sugarcane, there being no *paja* grown in the valley. Two men, later introduced as Benjamin and Flavio, eldest sons of Julio Cobos, step out into the hot midmorning sun to greet us. I can tell from their faces they have been following us hawkeyed from the moment we first appeared on the promontory. We are invited into the hut, and treated to coffee locally grown on the *chacra* and freshly ground on large stones. I inquire about the Inca road we have been following. Benjamin Cobos informs me that it disappears into the great forest, beyond the coffee fields. I ask if he knows the location of the Eromboni ruins. He explains he and his father were shown these ruins in 1958 by the Machiguengas who abandoned Espíritu Pampa several years ago for a new camp farther down river. My next question animates his black, piercing eyes. "Will you guide me to these ruins?" He mulls over the matter, tosses a glance at his younger, thinner brother. "*Bueno*," he replies.

After sharpening our steel machetes on the large mortar used for grind-

94

ing toasted coffee beans, Douglas, Ardilles, two of our highland men and I fall in behind Benjamin. Shortly, we are in the fields, making our way in and out of coffee plants that soar over our heads, their branches bending under the weight of ripe red coffee beans. We come to several circular structures which would have gone unnoticed had our guide not pointed them out in the dense foliage. He explains that for several years his family has undertaken the Herculean task of cutting down timber trees, some of which towered 150 feet high according to his account, in order to clear the land for planting. During this process they encountered a large number of these constructions which they left intact, mostly because it would have been too much trouble to cart off the stones.

I was struck by the curious fact that these old buildings were circular in design. Considering the Incas employed straight lines in their architecture, this was an odd thing to see. Other than the sun temple in Cuzco, the semi-circular Temple of the Sun at Machu Picchu and scattered circular structures in the vicinity of Choqetacarpo, I knew of no other round constructions of Inca origin. Conical huts were known throughout Amazonia. Did this bit of information suggest a possible link between the Incas and tropical peoples? Were these round houses used by the Antis Indians during their stay with the Vilcabamba Incas? I remember Bingham commenting on these round houses when he was here half a century ago.

We amble along through the coffee fields until we come to the edge of the great forest. Benjamin and the two highland men plunge headlong into the green maze cutting a swath as they go. Less than half an hour later we find ourselves deep in the woods. The spreading crowns of Cedrela, which push up 70 to 120 feet high or more, blot out the light from the sun. Creeping vines wrap around our feet and ankles; delicate nettles sting through our light cotton trousers bringing red, itching welts to the surface. The underbrush seems to be a solid wall of thorns. It is difficult going, more difficult trying to keep up with natives who are able to hunch over and make their way through on all fours. All well and good for men built close to the ground, but no mean trick for taller men. This is virgin *montaña* and the only trails besides those tunnel-like paths used by Machiguenga hunters, are those made by machete and a good right arm. It is unbearably warm. Our shirts stick to our backs, sweat trickles down our spines. Clouds of mosquitoes descend upon us. Curious little black bees, quite harmless but irritating as the devil, alight upon our exposed skin by the hundreds. No amount of agitation can dislodge them; they must be brushed off, only to return like flies to sticky flypaper. I can quite agree with whoever it was that first called the jungle a "green hell."

Rounding a tropical headland, we come out on a flat piece of ground. Benjamin informs me that the ruins of Eromboni are just ahead. We take a short rest. Ardilles passes out black cigarettes and everyone lights up.

We scramble up a wooded incline and find ourselves on an elevated platform. Benjamin motions for me to follow. He chops his way along a stone wall and drops down into a depression. I wiggle my way through an opening and nearly bump my head on the upper half of a large Inca aryballoid water jar, perched atop a fallen tree. I straighten up and, looking around, see that we are standing inside an ancient Inca room. We set to work clearing the ruins, pulling vines off the walls exposing niches and a doorway at one side. (Plate 7.) I had crawled through without knowing what it was. My attention is drawn to the large number of ceramic fragments scattered about the floor. Benjamin tells me there are many such pieces. Minutes later we press into a second, adjacent room. Atop the platform are a series of galleries so overgrown with vegetation I cannot estimate their size or importance. (When I had the buildings cleared, a task that took three precious days out of our schedule, the two-story platform group was found to consist of twelve rooms graced with niches and doorways, including a semicircular room, inner and outer courtyards, a fountain, hallway and stairways, the whole surrounded by high walls decorated with roof pegs. The terraced complex measured 165

[PLATE 7] *Inca group of houses showing room with niches and a door. A dozen men worked three days to clear forest growth.*

by 105 feet.) I notice an unusual piece of orange-red ceramic protruding from the ground. I pick it up and discover that it is roofing tile, the kind used by the Spaniards during colonial times. Kicking up a pile of dead leaves with the heel of my boot, I find there are several layers of tile strewn about the floor. Many pieces are well preserved, colors still vivid. One piece is incised with serpentine lines, an Inca characteristic. The men scratch around the soft floor of the jungle with their machetes and expose piles of similar *teja* mixed with pottery fragments. (Plate 8.) Who had used these tiles? Unknown in old Peru, roofing tile was introduced by the Spaniards shortly following the conquest. The Incas preferred ichu straw. Then I remembered that Manco had taken Spanish prisoners of war. These and the Augustinian friars under Titu Cusi may have passed on the use of this permanent roofing material. The Incas would have been adept at making such tiles; they had worked clay for centuries. The Viceroy had ordered the city of Cuzco tiled in the year 1560, a preventative against fire (Manco had put the old capital to the torch in 1536). From our findings it would appear that the Incas of

Vilcabamba learned the art of manufacturing roofing tile and were utilizing it in their modern buildings; proof that they were experiencing a kind of transition, absorbing Spanish refinements while retaining their own. I marked this group "Bingham's Group" or simply the "Spanish Palace" because of the large number of tiles found within its walls, possibly due to the influence of Father Diego Ortiz's mission at nearby Guarancalla. For the moment I had no way of telling what place these ruins had in history. Did they form part of a larger city? The object would be to try to locate additional remains.

I inquire of Cobos whether there are more ruins. He nods, wipes his brow and moves out into the jungle, hacking away at hanging vines and fern trees, lobbing off huge palm fronds with his curved machete. Everyone is afraid of being separated, so we stick close together behind him. A half hour's march brings us to a swampy spot choked with palms, reeds and vines. The sound of running water comes to our ears. Looking down through the darkened shadows we discover that our expert trail guide had guided us to an Inca stone bridge. Not far away he shows us a fountain with three spouts. Turning back over our trail we find a long Inca building, its walls fallen, covered by a carpet of dense vegetation. I cannot estimate its dimensions. It is built of rough-hewn stones cemented with mud. Our guide explains this was the extent of the ruins of Eromboni as shown him by the Machiguengas. This compared to what Bingham had described in his book on Machu Picchu. Upon my return to Lima I reviewed his volume *Along the Unchartered Pampaconas*, also his plan of Eromboni Pampa, our Spanish Palace, and found he had observed the roofing tile, ". . . half a dozen crude Spanish roofing tiles, baked red. All the pieces and fragments we could find would not have covered four square feet. They were of widely different sizes, as though someone had been experimenting. Perhaps an Inca who had seen the new tile roofs of Cuzco had tried to reproduce them here in the jungle, but without success." While he dismissed this find as vague and unimportant, I seized upon it at once. To me it was a key find. Bingham had also been shown the long structure. He gave its measurements as 192 feet long by 24 feet wide and guessed it originally contained twenty-four doors. It seemed odd to me that this was the extent of the ruins of Espíritu Pampa or Eromboni Pampa. Why hadn't the Machiguengas encountered more? Later I learned that their old hunting trail to the higher ground intersects the two major groups of ruins encountered by Bingham—and our own expedition. A practical people, not being curious about anything outside their primitive world of reality, any ruins which they might encounter are cast off as natural stones. Having no concept of numbers or size, they are not able to recognize the significance of antiquities. These reasons, plus their superstition regarding the pampa, explain why they confessed ignorance of other ruins upon Bingham's careful questioning through Saavedra. This prompted Bingham to bring his explorations of the area to a close.

It is with a sigh of relief that we come out into the open air and sunlight some minutes later, away from the steaming forest. A refreshing breeze blows over the valley. We saunter over to Benjamin's cabaña, a quarter of an hour's walk from the main house. Learning of our interest in antiquities—I had mentioned the pottery I had seen at Pucyura—Benjamin informs us that he and the other men of the family have come upon similar objects during their farming. He produces three Inca ceramic pieces and a fourth which appears to be of Tiahuanaco style. Other assorted pieces are displayed, including a blue stone carved in the shape of a tooth, a copper rod, and an old-fashioned Spanish-type horseshoe—a large, flat type used in colonial days. The object had been uncovered while erecting the main house. This isolated valley must have been the site of the refuge cities of Manco and his sons. How else could the presence of Spanish horseshoes be explained? The roofing tile we had found earlier strengthens this hypothesis.

Back at the main house we check our gear and find that one of the large wooden crates has broken and a medicine box is missing. It contained penicillin, sulfa, antibiotics, antidotes and snake-bite serum packed in a special watertight container. Everything else is in order, including all other medical supplies. I am greatly concerned about the lost case. We are in tropical country where without medical treatment the slightest infection can spread like wildfire. We will soon be in snake country where the deadly bushmaster, the largest venomous snake in the Americas growing up to twelve feet in length, abounds. The *chimuco*, as it is known, attacks anything on sight. This deadly pit viper is the most feared of all baneful creatures in the jungle. Then there is the fer-de-lance, the jergon, and many others whose bites spell death. The dangers of tarantulas, scorpions, vampire bats, biting ants and poisonous plants are exaggerated without proper medicines. Fortunately, we have many other medical supplies with us. (However, there is nothing in our medicine chest that will handle yellow fever, malaria, leprosy, beriberi and many other tropical diseases. Nor is there medicine for the bite of a special fly that is believed to cause uta, a malady that eats away the soft tissue of the mouth, nose and ears.) The water and food is infested with parasites that invade the delicate intestines, liver, and blood. Nevertheless, these are dangers we are prepared to contend with. But the missing medicines and snake-bite serum is an unnecessary risk.

In a land where every discarded item of the expedition—scraps of paper, tin cans, cartons and the like—is avidly scooped up and put to use, a bright-colored package like our medicine case would attract the eye. Nothing large or valuable ever disappears. A misplaced gold watch, valuable camera or expensive light meter would be cheerfully returned to the owner. Not so with a small item. To take it is not considered stealing. The Governor lectures the men sternly. They are told that with the next thing that disappears—no matter how insignificant—there will be the devil to pay! In this way a modus vivendi is established. (We never found the medicine, but nothing was ever lost again.)

Afterward we hold a council. I explain to the men that it wouldn't make sense for the Incas to build a few isolated ruins here on the pampas. There would have to be many more. I propose we start out by looking for roads and trying to trace them. I suggest we re-visit the Inca bridge—particularly the Spanish Palace—and start exploring the vicinity. The Governor agrees to send to Pampaconas for machete men who are familiar with the *montaña*. A price is settled. Benjamin condescends to be hired for a few days and to provide four or five men at the same rate of pay. With the problem of manpower solved, the expedition stands a chance of succeeding. Without it we would have had little hope.

So my pencil had recorded the events of the day.

Bright and early the next morning twelve of us set out up the Concevidayoc. The Cobos boys had told us about a stone bridge over the river and I wanted to see it. The men were in a surly mood. It had rained the night before and they blamed the expedition. Anything foreign in the valley upsets the balance of nature and brings cloudy, unruly weather—and rain at this time of the year is bad luck. Human skulls are set out along the river banks and in other appropriate places to ward off the rain. The dry season has a special significance for an agricultural people in the rain forest. It is their spring after a long, wet winter. I can't really blame them for resenting intruders who upset the balance.

The day turned out to be exhausting and pointless. The "bridge" proved to be an overhanging section of cliff that had slipped into the river at some time. Our only compensation for the grueling trip was the great quantity of wild bees' honey found in the trunk of an old tree.

Rain caught us on the trail back to the house. We returned to our base by the old Inca road we had come over the day before and found Ascensión waiting with three new men from Pampaconas. Santander said the men were grumbling about the change of weather. They were convinced that "The City of the Incas" was trying to hide itself. They complained about having to explore the pampas. They were afraid of the *relámpago* and the *espíritus*. Ascensión boldly proclaimed that even the Machi, poor ignorant savages that they were, knew better than to go into the pampas. One of the men, a barefoot, volatile fellow with a curvo machete draped around his neck, said in Quechua that the pampas were inhabited by Purun Machu, an old devil that enchants abandoned ruins. This was the same spirit believed to have enchanted Machu Picchu. The natives believed that men could live on the edge of the jungle, as they did when Bingham arrived, but that no one should dare venture into the ruins. This is why the ruins have remained unknown for so long, though their whereabouts were known to the local populace. Ascensión told us that by failing to perform the "proper ceremonies" we would never succeed in penetrating the pampas without arousing the wrath of Apu Manco (Lord Manco).

I allayed the men's fears somewhat by suggesting to the Governor that we limit each man's contract to two or three days only, and double the pay. Over the next three weeks we hired a total of seventy men from the surrounding area, shuttling them back and forth over the mountain trails at a rate never seen in these quiet valleys, at least not for centuries. It was a successful game of psychology. Governor Ardilles would dispatch written orders with his official seal requesting that the lieutenant governors send men to Espíritu Pampa. When this failed, we would coax, plead, bribe, flatter and hound the men, appealing to their emotions until they agreed to hire out for a few days. We were not able to overcome all their fears of the enchanted pampas, but at least we got men.

Monday, July 13, Espíritu Pampa. New Discoveries

At dawn we send Ascensión down river with a can of salt, a machete and a small axe from our stores (money has absolutely no value to these isolated tribes) to barter with the Machiguengas. He is instructed to speak with the chief (tribal custom forbids them from giving out their names for fear of losing their souls, so he is to address the chief as Mariano) and to try to obtain information about ruins. Ascensión is told to give the items to the chief if he agrees to tell us of the whereabouts of ancient remains. This will be our only chance to make contact, we are told. Once our man enters the "Machi" camp they will fade away in the jungle and not come out.

I set out with a dozen men to explore the pampas. Packs of wild pigs, forty or fifty head each, are said to frequent the jungle plains. Vicious when disturbed, they will charge a man. If he attempts to escape by climbing a tree, they uproot it and try to tear the man apart. I have the rifle and ammunition broken out. We head for the bridge we had seen two days before, where we start cutting trails into the dense vegetation. I fan the men out and shortly one of them reports he has come to a wall, below the fountain with three spouts. It turns out to be another stone fountain with a single waterspout; but better worked than the first. (Plate 9.) Incredible! Not more than twenty feet from the other fountain and no one was aware of its existence, so thick was the tangle of jungle growth.

We find another stone wall directly behind the fountain. It proves to be a walled avenue of some kind. It is under a thorn forest so thick we would have been hours cutting through it. We give up trying to breach it and turn our attention to the other side of the bridge where one of the men has found a retaining wall of an elevated group of Inca houses. Across from this group we fall into a depression and discover we have accidentally stumbled into a sunken group of Inca buildings under a mass of twisting vines and growth. It is below street level, completely walled. An hour of exploring the colossal group reveals inner streets, stairways and eighteen independent rooms. The group measures a stupendous 297 feet long! A canal with flowing water runs

on one side. Tons of dead vegetation top the old ruins. One Inca house measuring 40 feet long by 18 feet wide is graced with thirteen niches and a broken doorway. The stones are cemented with adobe, as with the Spanish Palace. The architecture is Inca, but strangely different. Clearing the site, we discover some twenty odd circular buildings 15 to 20 feet in diameter. My men show surprise at finding these ruins.

We scramble back up to the upper wall over which we had come and find it is a walled passage 15 feet wide. We cut our way over this street for 300 feet until we reach the upper walls of the long structure observed the day before. Making our way blindly along the inner walls we come to a slab of white stone, which appears to have been some kind of altar. Outside we find an elevated platform some 150 feet long by 115 feet wide. Atop the walled structure sit two Inca buildings with three rooms, each topped by jungle. We find evidence that the wall of irregular stones had been covered with a red ceramic-like stucco or terra-cotta. Between this unusual find and the long building we had chanced on, we found a huge boulder weighing hundreds of tons. It is topped by a great *matapalo* tree whose bole is 12 feet in diameter and covered with layers of moss and tropical vegetation. The buttress roots of the great tree enclose the boulder in a tenacious grip like arms of an octopus. The forest is so dark and dense it takes a long time and much effort to uncover a stone platform which supports the large stone. A stone stairway and walled avenue lead to two rectangular Inca buildings below the big boulder. The building materials used in construction are rough, white limestone blocks, but the corners of the buildings are hand-hewn and well-cut. But so much of the construction is covered with vegetation and displaced by the numerous vines that have dislodged the stonework, it is difficult to determine exact dimensions (field sketches were made at a later date when the buildings were cleared and the huge tree covering the elevated boulder cut away. The latter was found to measure nearly 65 feet long and 20 feet wide and oriented north to south). The big rock is an important discovery and we would have passed by this curious stone had I not been on the lookout for one of these large white stones or Yurak-Rumis, as Father Calancha calls them at Ñusta Hispana. The boulder suggests we are inside an important ancient Inca community; for such stones were used for oracles and called huacas by the Sun Priests. These stones also served as a kind of war idol, a mother Huancauri that inspired the Incas to victory in battle. The use of this stone as a war idol would have been most fitting for the last refuge of the Incas. Resting atop its dark platform, it has the appearance of a giant egg. Inca folk myth tells of the Sun having sent down three eggs that generated the three Inca estates.

I am greatly excited by the find of the giant boulder and cannot move ahead fast enough. The natives feel differently. If it weren't for the money, none of them would be here on the enchanted pampas. We forge ahead on the road we have been following. An excitement has taken over, an excitement that only discovery produces, an intoxicating feeling.

A hundred feet later, we come to three terraces. The outer wall is nearly 300 feet long. Together they staircase up 25 feet high. The top is gained with difficulty. We approach a wall, clear some growth away with our curvos, then take a stairway that leads to a spacious courtyard, now a wild garden of exotic tropical flowers, lianas, fern and palm trees. Seven houses, their walls in ruins, rise up in the center of the terraced citadel in an atmosphere of deathly silence (in keeping with the mood of the machetemen).

We drop back down to the road and soon come to another group of rectangular buildings built atop a terraced platform 306 by 178 feet. The men chop away some of the growth that clings to the walls of large stones and then we jump back to the floor of the jungle and resume our search for other ruins.

The road we have been following comes to a halt. Rather than retrace our steps, we decide to keep going in the same direction hoping to pick it up again. I have the men spread out. It is a half hour before we find two small Inca houses perched on a promontory overlooking a river, and another group of buildings. The stonework is of better quality than what we have seen before. It is evident that the cut white limestone blocks had once fit snugly together, although many had now been broken by feeder vines that had wormed their way between the stones and pried them apart. One of the buildings, a rectangular construction with two doorways, guards a green-lit temple; a high elevated bulwark of stone consisting of rooms with niches and fallen door lintels, inner courtyards and enclosures. It must have been very impressive when the Incas lived here. A large huaca boulder rests beside one of the walls. It looks as if it may have fallen from the top of the platform wall. A magnificent *matapalo* tree with a spreading crown some one hundred feet above our heads locks one of the walls in a grip of gnarled roots. Some of the rocks are squeezed out of place by its vice-like grip. Rattan vines hang down from its upper branches, forming a screen through which we must cut our way.

Tramping on blindly through the jumbled growth, cutting a path with our blades, we intersect a trail of dead leaves. Our circuitous route has brought us to yesterday's trail. Benjamin shouts, "The Spanish Palace is ahead!" Strange how the shallow little footpath of the day before gives the men a sense of assurance. Even I feel it. It is our mark upon the jungle, a meandering ribbon we had claimed from the unknown. It is our link with the outside world. A trail is everything in the jungle. Without it a man is unsure of himself, on unfamiliar ground.

The virgin jungle can truly be beautiful in the daytime; when one has time to enjoy it, when it isn't raining and there is space enough to see. We are on higher ground now, above the boggy swamplands caused by dammed and overspilling canals. Cedrela trees, tree ferns, cane, bamboo and palm thickets of various species: Iriartea, Euterpe, Bactris, hem us in on all sides. Lianas creep and twist over the jungle floor winding up feeder vines toward the light. The trunks of the trees are covered with mossy bryophytes, lichens and bromeliads. Even without strong sunlight, vegetation thrives in the rich alluvial soil and the heavy rains. Nowhere have I seen such vivid colors as the deep red, orange and yellow of the tropical flowers overhead. With a single blow from a machete, they cascade about our heads and shoulders by the dozens, so delicately balanced and fragile is their hold on upper vines. Flowering parasite plants and bromelia add a touch of red and yellow to the hanging garden. A cardinal finch blares its song from above, no doubt saluting the sun from its lofty perch. Other than this sound the jungle is deathly still, as if we were the only living creatures. The monkeys have moved to higher ground and won't be back until the rainy season. It would have been pleasant to hear their chattering. Of all marvels of nature, the jungle has the power to evoke both fear and wonder in man.

We return down to the lower group of white stone ruins and I put the men to work clearing so plans and a photographic record can be made. Watching the first sunlight fall upon these ancient walls after a lapse of several centuries is a memorable experience. The white granite blocks, covered by thin layers of delicate lichen, take on a ghostly appearance. An ominous quiet falls over the jungle as the axemen bite into green wood. The forest seems to shudder. The men chop at the base of a tall tree until it hangs suspended from a spiderweb of vines, like a tottering mast of a ship. Machetes glint in the sun. Vines snap. The tree falls. Leaves flutter earthward, caught in shafts of light. Thin, diamond-marked snakes coil like corkscrews and slither for cover.

For the first time I realize what we have found. We are in the heart of an ancient Inca city. Is this Manco's Vilcabamba—the lost city of the Incas? I am certain we are in parts of it. I experience an overwhelming sense of the history the ruins represent. For four hundred years they have remained in the realm of legend. Some even doubted they existed. But I always knew they were there, somewhere, awaiting discovery. To me they were the most important historical remains in Peru. Important because Manco was a glorious hero who gave dignity to Peru when all was lost. Important because so many great names had looked for them. Some would expect to find cyclopean walls covered with sheets of gold, or finely cut stone of the classic Cuzco style. Old Vilcabamba wasn't this at all. She was old and worn. The walls of her buildings were toppled, covered with thick, decaying vegetable matter; their foundations under tons of slide and ooze. She had been put to the torch by the Incas who had built her and ransacked by the Spaniards who were looking for gold. Four centuries of wild jungle had twisted that part which remained. But she had not lost her dignity. One could easily see she had been a great metropolis, a colossus of the jungle. A wave of melancholy swept over me. It would require an army to clear these ruins properly; cost a fortune to restore the buildings to their original form, and they were so far from civilization that it might never be accomplished. The city represented everything for which the Incas stood. It was a monument to their industry, their struggle with nature, their fight for freedom against overpowering odds. This was immortal Vilcabamba—that legendary city of a thousand history books. If I never succeeded in finding another city it would not matter. Legend had been turned into history.

Darkness comes early in the *montaña*, so we want to get out of the woods before the trails become shadowed. By five o'clock we are home, just as the first chorus of sounds of the nocturnal creatures takes over the jungle.

We have been out all day and the Cobos family and Antonio are eager to know if we have found anything. Everyone is surprised to hear of our discoveries. Don Julio, who had returned in our absence, is jubilant for he sees possibilities of a road coming to his farm. He said he had always suspected there were more ruins in the pampas. We were the first to confirm it. A paradox. While perfectly able to explore the jungle—he is far more familiar with it than we—ancient superstition weighs heavily on the minds of these backland Peruvians. They are content to let someone else show the way to discovery.

Old Ascensión comes padding into camp. We wait expectantly for news. He wipes his hands on his cotton chaparajos, takes the presents we had intended for the Machiguengas from an alforja and places them carefully on the bench outside our quarters. He shakes his head. Chief Mariano refuses to collaborate with the expedition; knows nothing of ruins. Ascensión wants to go home. He keeps muttering about Apu Manco and the enchantments.

Right after dinner we tumble into bed. I write my daily entries by flashlight. While I feel the Gordian knot has been cut, there is still an imbroglio. Bingham had reached the outskirts of this old Inca city. There is no doubt about that. By failing to press on to discover additional ruins he dismissed its importance. This explains why he wrongly assumed Machu Picchu to be the Lost City of Vilcabamba. All he could find on the Eromboni Pampa was the one Inca group, the Spanish Palace, consisting of the road leading into the city, a small watchtower, the fifteen to twenty round houses on the edge of the forest, the bridge, fountain and traces of terraces near the twenty-four-door structure. Our findings show the site to be far more extensive. Weighing the new information on hand against that previously known, I reach some sensational yet logical conclusions.

Because of the big rock, the twenty-four-door building seems to fit Father Calancha's description of the "Long House of the Sun." Yet I cannot bring myself to accept this site as Chuquipalpa. I am convinced, as was Bingham, that Chuquipalpa is at present-day Ñusta Hispana. However, we find many fountains and a canal nearby. Surely the great stone is a kind of Yurak-Rumi and the building is very long (when cleared it measured 229 feet long by 28 feet wide). Perhaps it was this building which was burned by Father Marcos García, and not that of Chuquipalpa (Calancha could have been wrong). It is quite evident from the condition of the building that at some time in the past it had been destroyed, probably by fire. When the Spaniards invaded Vilcabamba the Old and took it on the feast day of St. John the Evangelist, June 24, 1572, in the name of King Philip, they found the city abandoned and smoldering. The veteran Victor Maurtua recounts in his original manuscript entitled "Vilcabamba"—now filed in the General Archives of the Indies at Seville, Spain—that the sworn statements of the Spanish soldiers who took possession of the old city found it burning. Inca Tupac Amaru later testified in Cuzco that he had given orders that the "principal residences of the Inca" be put to the torch before his flight into the interior. The eyewitness accounts at the Vilcabamba scene make it clear that Vilcabamba the Old was known to the Spaniards, that the best buildings were burned by the Incas themselves—which forced the conquerors to abandon it—and that they chased the Incas into the jungle.

The "Lost City of the Incas" was said to be the largest in the province, a metropolis of the lower jungles. Two other pueblos were close to it. Father Ortiz had his mission at Guarancalla and, two or three days' traveling distance away, García had his mission at Puquiura. When Father Ortiz was captured, he was taken to his own mission at Guarancalla and thence to Marcanay on the third day. Marcanay was only two hours' distance from the refuge city. This information is confirmed by the accounts of General Martín

Hurtado Arbieto, who pursued the last Inca down through Guarancalla when the Spaniards occupied the old city of Vilcabamba.

Father Ortiz had requested permission to build his mission as close to the sanctuary as possible, "in the lands of the Antis Indians." He was barred from entering the sacred precincts of Vilcabamba, where the Priests and Virgins of the Sun performed their rites and ceremonies in the temples— much to the chagrin of the Catholic priest. He finally beseeched Father García to help him gain entrance. When the Inca did give his permission, they were both confined to the outskirts of the city where they could do little else but teach the Antis and post crosses in the great forest.

The Antis Indians used to "come up from the jungles" to be healed by Father Ortiz at Guarancalla, a populous village. I know that we are in a valley which was occupied by these Indians. Their descendents are still here. But where is the Guarancalla of Father Ortiz? And Marcanay where Tupac Amaru resided? What of Mananhuanunca, the place where Father Ortiz was martyred? Each of these sites had to be identified within the greater Vilcabamba complex.

Three pueblos of great historical importance were situated within a short distance of one another—two or three leagues at most. Vilcabamba is believed to have been the principal city of the province, the site of the "University of Idolatry," according to Calancha, where the idol of Punchao (the Golden Sun Disk) was worshiped. Guarancalla was a pueblo of the popular classes, including the Antis Indians. The Incas seemed to have isolated themselves in the upper section, away from the masses. Marcanay, also a pueblo, was the residence of the last Inca, Tupac Amaru, two leagues from the city of Vilcabamba. Then there was the matter of Father Ortiz' mission.

It seems most likely that the ruins at San Martín, or Concevidayoc, were the mission of Father Ortiz. (But I did not eliminate outer Espíritu Pampa as a possibility.) They probably formed part of Guarancalla (the friar was undoubtedly isolated from the main village). We know that Guarancalla was "populous." The greater part of the Espíritu Pampa ruins consist of circular structures and are close to the conjunction of the two rivers, the Concevidayoc and the incoming Chontabamba. The ruins in fact were found to run all along the Concevidayoc River. These appear to have been residences of the popular people. Located at the edge of the great forest, the Espíritu Pampa ruins are outside the more complex ruins. I am sure that the inner pampas contain many additional ruins and that they represent the greater extent of the Vilcabamba complex. Tomorrow should tell me what I want to know. I close my journal, turn out the light, and roll up inside my sleeping bag.

Tuesday, July 14. Farther into the City

In the gray light of dawn we start out again. A cool mist hangs over the valley. I send one party over the higher Inca road that runs up the western pampa and lead a party of eight men over the bridge near the walled fountains. We come to a quagmire of soggy earth buzzing with gnats and mosquitoes, and decide to cross an immense growth of thorny vines instead. We cut our way through to the other side. Immediately we come upon the first ruins.

Before the day is over we discover three big groups. One measures 100 feet by 84 feet, consisting of two very spacious rooms with about twenty windows and three large doors. A platformed plaza or courtyard extends down the slope. Higher up the hill, we encounter a second group of houses. It has three separate terraces. The upper level is over 150 feet long, and overlooks a canal. The third group is the most interesting—more of the peculiar circular buildings, and probably originally fitted with a center pole that supported a conical roof. The largest measure 15 to 20 feet in diameter with eight interior niches and a central doorway. Many are staircased on the sides of the hills and enclosed by stone walls. Round structures do not conform to Inca architecture. An Amazon characteristic, they raise the possibility of the neo-Incas having built upon an older site. Or did the last Incas integrate Amazon people into their refuge? Of still greater consequence, was the jungle the cradle of the Incas, and the ruins we were now seeing representative of their jungle architecture?

Most of the day is spent surveying an extensive urban settlement scattered about the slopes. Amazing, I say to myself, that Bingham was just the other side of the canal without knowing of the existence of these fine buildings.

Slashing through the jungle with machetes, we follow a stone stairway that leads to the top of a high prominence. At the summit, overlooking the valley, we find two curious stone structures that may have been lookouts. Returning the way we had come, we cross an Inca bridge (found earlier in the day) that spans a dry canal.

We find two major groups of ruins, each accessible by separate roads which join the upper plateau with the lower like links of a chain. It is a notable feature that the Inca buildings were situated on stone terraces. Streets and passageways joined buildings of wide and varied architectural designs. Most curious to me are the numerous circular buildings interspersed with rectangular houses. Sometimes we come across a series of two or three rectangular-shaped terraces, fifty yards or more in length, supporting several of these round buildings. Others lay scattered over the pampas. Were these storage bins or granaries? I could not be sure. The fact that there are so many suggests that they might have been used for depositing coca leaves (had the Incas actually moved into a large coca plantation and modified it as a refuge city for the Vilcabamba line?). On the other hand many were residential units with doors and niches.

It was unfortunate that so much of the Vilcabamba ruins were topped by jungle. It would have been interesting to know what lay underneath. It reminded me of Pompeii, so much of the old city was covered and hidden from view. The city was not a Machu Picchu, a small village-temple of well-worked stone on a mountain summit on the edge of the *montaña*. Here was a rambling metropolis in the jungle, spread over what seemed to be an extremely large area. The Incas had built a city utilizing materials at hand. (Plate 10.) Although we found well-cut stone, the larger number of buildings were constructed from rough stones cemented with mud. Exterior walls had been plastered with thick, red stucco. Timber appears to have been used for roofs and upper framing. Long ago Vilcabamba must have been a primitive

[PLATE 10] *Eye-bonders, roof pegs and assorted building accessories found in the ruins of Vilcabamba.*

109

but beautiful city which filled the Mañaries and Pilcosones of the deep interior with awe.

One day, soon after we had actually found Vilcabamba, we made what I thought was a significant discovery of another group of ruins. We had been following a road that serpentined over narrow V-shaped valleys. We came to a little knoll above a river and stopped to rest. The men engaged in their morning ritual of chewing coca. They select the tender leaves from little pouches they carry on their belts, pluck the stems and place them reverently on their laps. Cupping the green tea-like leaves in their hands they blow upon them uttering the words, *"Pachamama, Pachamama, Pachamama, Pachamama, Pachamama"* (the Blessed Virgin and Goddess of Earth), making obeisances to the cardinal points and to the Sun and invoking the protection of Pachamama against the forest spirits. Only then do they stuff the leaves into their cheeks and dab wet ashes (in the absence of lime) into the tight, little balls of coca leaf so as to extract the alkali. When passing around the bottle of aguardiente, each man pours out a little as an offering to this ancient deity of the Incas, who, while dead in the thriving industrialized coastal areas of Peru, is very much alive out here in the *montaña*. Strengthened by the mild narcotic—they believe no one can live out here unless he chews the sacred leaf—their stomachs warmed by alcohol, they seemed quite cheerful, considering we were deeper into the pampas than we had ever been before.

After honing our machetes, we continued along the road through the jungle growth until we broke out of the woods to a slightly forested pampa. We came to several stone buildings topped by a dense blanket of vegetation, and I dropped down inside one and started cutting away some thick vines from a series of niches. Once we had cleared off the surface growth and compiled crude sketch plans, there seemed to be no doubt that we had uncovered another extensive sector of ruins about a league's distance from Espíritu Pampa. Curiously, there were large numbers of boulders scattered about the dead city. Perched at the corners of walls and strewn carelessly about, they didn't seem to have any function or purpose. We found a line of these stones along one side of the plaza and a circular house on the other side of it.

Our initial explorations of the pampas had shown this ancient metropolis to be composed of large, terraced groups of Inca buildings, separated like islands in a green sea. Now we were finding whole communities of these groups, each separated by an hour's walking distance. Bingham had neither discovered these groups nor the roads leading to them. He had found the circular buildings down by the old Machiguenga camp and the isolated "Eromboni" (our Spanish Palace). Separated by such distances of wild jungle growth, the other groups would have been difficult to locate without time and enough men willing to explore the area. Dependence upon Machiguenga guides also contributed to his unsuccessful exploration of the area. The Indians would have stuck to their hunting trails which, though passing through some of the ruins, bypass the major groups. It would have been difficult getting them off these trails into the "spirit-infested" woods. Fortunately, we had the availability of good men (the best available in these parts), and had followed the roads which led to other groups. The explorations would have been impossible without the help of the Cobos boys who kept the men in line and did their best to assist the expedition.

We explored the Vilcabamba for several days. Vines, rattan trees and saplings covered everything, methodically the machetemen cut and chopped through the thick growth uncovering the countless stone structures which staircased up the mountain slopes. Although the city was buried and in ruins, there seemed to be evidence of careful planning and it occurred to me that Vilcabamba must have been built in divisions, with the upper sections probably having been occupied by the ruling class of Incas. I felt an overpowering urge to start exploring in all directions but fought it off. Each group had to be measured and mapped as found, otherwise the expedition would have no scientific value. I did not want to be criticized later for playing the part of the excavating archaeologist. I restricted the men to clearing the upper surfaces of the buildings so that their dimensions could be measured with tape, a compass reading taken and a plan made. Photography offered a genuine challenge. The jungle sucks up light like a sponge. I could do little more than fit the corner of a building into the lens of my camera, the rest was lost in a thick mantle of growth and shadows. In any event, my preliminary work would serve until scientific instruments and engineers could come in to do a proper job. Potsherds were collected from the surface of each group, placed in watertight plastic bags, dated and properly labeled. The archaeological evaluation of potsherds is one of the most accurate means of determining the age of a site. Our potsherds would be boxed and transported to Lima, where they would be washed and classified by a specialist and turned in bulk over to the Peruvian Government Department of Archaeology.

The days flashed by. With each new day the impact of what I had found intensified. At first my notes consisted of individual groups. We reclaimed one building at a time until it became a group of buildings. Then we would fan out, find another, and add it to my plan of the ruins. Slowly I mapped out the dimensions of a city—a city with streets, temples, houses, public fountains, canals, bridges. (Map V.)

One vital question kept gnawing at my mind: If Espíritu Pampa was the Guarancalla of Calancha, why had Titu Cusi allowed Father Ortiz to get so close to Vilcabamba the Old? Then I began to reason. Espíritu Pampa and San Martín are on the road leading from the jungles up to the highlands. To enter Vilcabamba one passed through Guarancalla—not more than a short distance away, two or three leagues at most. But Calancha writes of the long journey of Ortiz and García in their attempt to gain access to the sacred city. Of course their journey started from Puquiura, but even at that Ortiz would

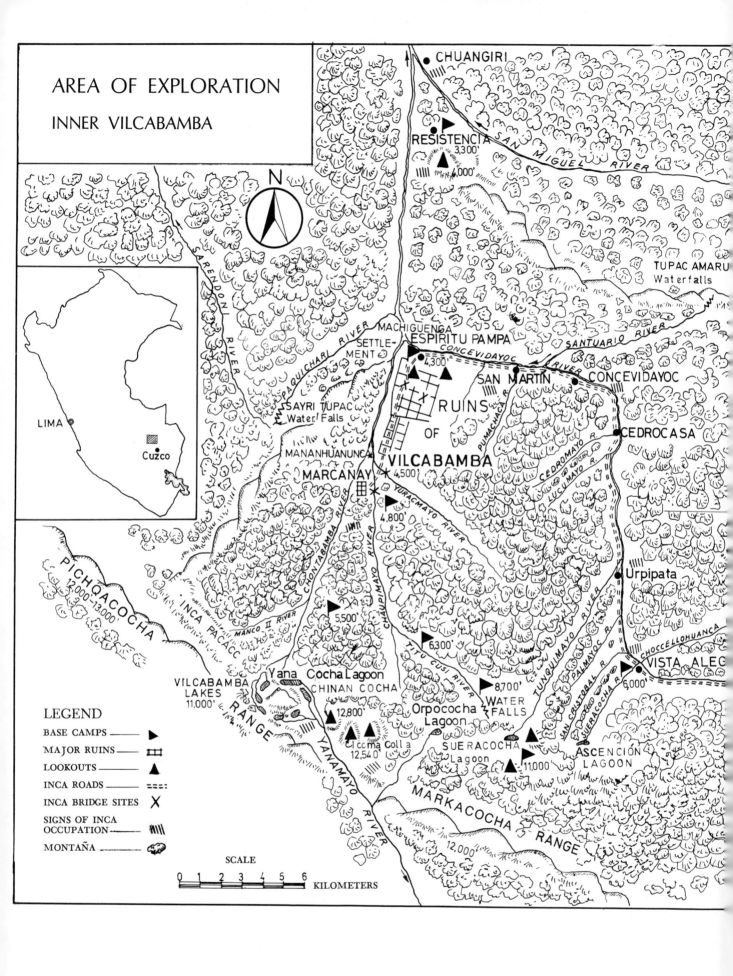

AREA OF EXPLORATION

INNER VILCABAMBA

N

LIMA

Cuzco

SARENDONI RIVER

SAN MIGUEL RIVER

CHUANGIRI

RESISTENCIA
3,300'
6,000'

TUPAC AMARU
Waterfalls

PAQUICHARI RIVER

MACHIGUENGA
SETTLE-
MENT

ESPIRITU PAMPA
4,300'

CONCEVIDAYOC R.

SAN MARTIN

SANTUARIO RIVER

CONCEVIDAYOC

SAYRI TUPAC
Water Falls

RUINS
OF
VILCABAMBA
4,500'

PUMACHACA R.

CEDROMAYO R.

LUCUMAYO R.

CEDROCASA

MANANHUANUNCA

MARCANAY

YURACMAYO RIVER

4,800'

CHONTABAMBA RIVER

CHAUPIMAYO RIVER

MANCO II RIVER

5,500'

6,300'

TITU CUSI RIVER

Urpipata

TUNQUIMAYO RIVER

CHOCCELLOHUANCA

VISTA ALEG
6,000'

PICHQACOCHA
12,000-13,000'

INCA PACACC

Yana Cocha Lagoon
CHINAN COCHA

Orpococha
Lagoon

8,700'

WATER
FALLS

SAN CRISTOBAL R.

PALMAYOC R.

SUERACOCHA R.

ASCENCIÓN
LAGOON

VILCABAMBA
LAKES
11,000'

RANGE

12,800'

Ucma Colla
12,540'

SUERACOCHA
Lagoon

11,000'

YANAMAYO RIVER

MARKACOCHA RANGE
12,000'

LEGEND

BASE CAMPS ——— ▶

MAJOR RUINS ——— ⊞

LOOKOUTS ——— ▲

INCA ROADS ——— ====

INCA BRIDGE SITES X

SIGNS OF INCA
OCCUPATION ——— |||

MONTAÑA ——— 🜁

SCALE

0 1 2 3 4 5 6
KILOMETERS

have been familiar with this part of the jungle. Calancha was not familiar with Vilcabamba and wrote from secondhand information and with religious fervor. It seemed to me that Titu Cusi purposely led the two priests over a circuitous route to confuse them. He did not want them in the populous center of the old city and, trying to keep its whereabouts hidden, only permitted them entrance to the outskirts of the city. We did in fact locate two roads leading to Vilcabamba—a higher and lower road, the latter entering the Espíritu Pampa area. Inca guards posted at the roads could have kept the priests from entering the main part of the metropolis. It seemed obvious that Titu Cusi had no intention of giving the friars access to his inner kingdom. So he put García near Vitcos, Ortiz near Vilcabamba. What cunning! Father Ortiz had no way of knowing how close he was to the secret city until he was led up to Marcanay. Then it was too late to matter.

The boulders strewn about the confines of the city still remained a puzzle. I could understand the function and practical use of oracle stones such as that in Ñusta Hispana and even the one in the lower parts of this city. But surely all of these stones could not be huacas. Natural and uncut, they simply stood within a group as if they had fallen from the sky like meteors. Then it dawned on me that the city was actually a city of huaca or vilca stones as the dominating feature. That fact probably explained why the place had been called Vilca Pampa—a pampa of vilca stones. If this were true, the city must have been very sacred to the Incas.

I decided to probe higher up the pampas toward the source of the Chontabamba River, a tributary of the Concevidayoc that waters the lower pampas, to see how far the Vilcabamba ruins reached. We hired several half-breed Indians that had come up the valley. Reluctantly they agreed to hire on as cargo-bearers for the upland trek.

July 19, Rinconada Pampa

At one o'clock the rains came. Torrents of rain unlike anything I have ever seen, by three o'clock it was impossible to keep going. We put up the two tents for shelter. With no firewood, no hot meal, no herb tea, only cold tinned sardines, crackers and slabs of chocolate, we ate lunch and waited inside for the rain to stop. Trees loomed up like ghosts out of the pale light and dark shadows. The men were furious, blaming me for their misery. Their thoughts chimed in with the rumbling thunder to say the enchantment had befallen us.

Soaked to the skin, teeth chattering, depressed, we had managed to reach an altitude of 5,500 feet where the weather grows chilly after nightfall. We had crossed three rivers—the Yuracmayo, the larger Chaupimayo and the still larger Chontapampa. Our camp was situated above a smaller tributary of the latter river, which I had marked Manco II since it had no name of its own. I was worried we might not be able to cross back over if the rain continued.

Ita, tiny wormlike parasites, had drilled into our waistlines by the hundreds. They are like tiny pinpoints of fire that burn and itch. Pasting wet tobacco leaves over the bite brings them to the surface. No part of our bodies seemed missed by the *monta blanca* mosquito which finds its way inside our clothes, even into our boots and stockings.

Daybreak brought a flicker of light through the swirling mists and wet foliage. It had stopped raining. On our way again, we slashed a trail through the wet vegetation. Benjamin Cobos told me we were in the old hunting grounds of the Machiguengas, a large alluvial fan called Rinconada Pampa.

We moved steadily along, anxious to get to the river before it started raining again. We found the Chontapampa River to be a raging torrent, swollen by the night's rain. We searched along the river to find a narrow part where we could cross. We cut a long length of vine the thickness of a man's arm and took hold of it to form a human chain in the water. We waded up to our chests until we reached the opposite bank, another large pampa called Chonta Pampa.

I wanted to explore the pampas, but there was no way to convince the men that this was a good idea. Nervous and irritable, they complained that the spirits were against us; that we had been very fortunate to have escaped from the *relámpago*, the deadly light that strikes from the sky without warning. Again the jungle was flooded in a tropical downpour and we splashed our way through the almost impassable growth. Sometimes we took an animal path. Occasionally we found an old Machiguenga branch trail; but most of the time we were forced to blaze our own trails. It was slow, miserable going and with the men set on turning back, I had no choice but to give up the idea.

Three hours of travel brought us to the Chaupimayo River. It took us a full hour to find a place narrow enough to cross. Up to our waists in freezing water, we moved across the rushing stream holding our gear above our heads. Late in the afternoon we arrived back at the small clearing of Espíritu Pampa.

Victor Ardilles returned to Lucma promising to send men to help with exploring. The whole population of the Concevidayoc Valley consisted of less than a hundred people, about fifteen of whom were Machiguengas. Without help from the highlands the work would have been impossible since the local citizens refused to work. Fortunately, Julio Cobos returned and lent a hand.

As it turned out we were successful in our attempts to map several important groups. We had also managed to maintain a system of main and secondary trails interconnecting the first major groups. These paths saved time and energy.

One day while photographing some of these ruins, the men were cutting down a tall tree to allow more light upon the obscure scene and suddenly without warning, the tree crashed down upon me, sending camera, tripod and equipment flying. I dove for cover, and my leg struck hard against a white limestone rock. Something stung my left kneecap and a spasm of pain shot up my leg like a hot iron. The men rushed to help me out of the branches and in a flash one of them raised his machete and lunged toward me. A yellow and black serpent, about a foot long, its triangular head puffed up, lay squirming on the ground cut in two. The bearer lifted it off the ground with his machete, showing it proudly. A *candonga!* The Machiguengas treat the bite of this poisonous rock snake with *itininga* or *sacha-jergon*—jungle herbs known only to them—or they find a cool stream, immerse themselves and stay there two or three days without moving a muscle, hoping that this will keep them alive. Had it stung me? My snake pants came up to my knees. There was a tiny hole just above the leather, but whether this was from thorn or serpent I could not tell.

That evening my leg began to swell. The next day the men left for good. They said the pampas were definitely enchanted. Apu Manco was angry. That was it. No more men would come down. But I wasn't concerned about that now, I was worried about my leg. I sent a runner up to Lucma requesting that mules be sent immediately for the return journey. I grieved the earlier loss of our snake-bite serum and drugs.

Five days later the mules arrived. By this time my leg had swollen to twice its normal size. I promised the Cobos men that I would return to complete the exploration and then we began the long trek back to Cuzco. With luck we could make it in five days. It was a long, muddy trail to Urpipata, a small plot of land on a high hill close to Vista Alegre. We could see it was raining in the highlands. I shuddered at the thought of the cold, wet sierra. A thunderclap reverberated down the narrow valley. Our pack animals strained at their ropes, rearing and kicking; a mule started to bolt and one of the men ran up to restrain him. *"Carajo! Hombre! Mula!"* he yelled, putting a switch across its hindquarters.

A frail, thin woman in her late seventies came out of a house to offer us shelter from the rain. She greeted me with the respectful title: *"Viracocha."* But when she saw me being helped off my horse, she came nearer and said, *"Imaykin nanan? Wayna wakcha."* (What hurts thee? Poor young man.) I pointed to my leg. *"Wakchacha"* (poor little one), she said, helping me through the door, sitting me next to the fire. "Thou needest hot soup. Thy body wilt be warmed by it," she said in Quechua.

She watched me adjust the poultice of herbs plucked from the jungle by one of the men, worn over my swollen knee to ease the pain. She sighed, "This life is a river of tears," and sent a boy to fetch a new batch of herbs. She turned a kindly, wrinkled face to me and said, "Thank the Creator we are not left alone."

She began to ask me questions about myself and the journey and was amazed that I had come so far to explore for Inca ruins. She stared into the fire and said wistfully, "In the olden times this land was great and powerful. Now all we have is memories. *Tukuy imapas manam winaypaqchu kause, tuquyniyoq."* (All things do not live for eternity, everything has its end.) She spent the next hour comforting me as best she could and applied some thin leaves to my swollen leg, promising they would heal me.

Like many others, she had migrated down to the *montaña* to eke out an existence by reclaiming land from the jungle. The old agricultural terraces that have been exposed are proof that the eastern slopes of the Andes were once the breadbasket of old Peru. With the agricultural limitations of the coast and the expanding population of the sierras, the recent migrations seem to give hope that Peru is expanding eastward where rich soil, abundant water and timberlands offer new prosperity.

The rain stopped and we moved on again. At Vista Alegre my temperature rose to 103°. A deep red line ran up the side of my leg to my groin. My lymph gland was the size of an egg. It would be ironic if the snakebite healed and I perished from blood poisoning. The infection was rapidly spreading. I had a splitting headache and palpitations of the heart. My skin was cold and clammy.

The men uttered mournful tones when they saw my leg—a swollen mass of black and purple. Antonio suggested I allow him to pound it with his fists, but I chose hot packs instead.

At daybreak, August 2, we flagged on through the muck and rain. My leg was even worse, the swelling immense. We spent twelve hours in the saddle that day and climbed over 6,000 feet. Dropping down from the cordillera, we stopped at Vilcabamba "Chico" for hot tea. Antonio had finally persuaded me to let him beat my leg with his fists. I set my jaws and told him to go ahead, only to recoil at the last minute. Back went the herb poultices and hot packs. I promised myself if the swelling didn't go down I would cut and drain the leg myself the next morning. I remember experiencing the sensation that I would never reach Cuzco alive.

Upon reaching Lucma the miracle happened. A message had gone ahead to Governor Ardilles that I was seriously wounded and suffering from a bad leg. He had sent a *chasqui* runner to Chaullay for medicine, who had returned shortly before our arrival. I was helped into the house and Ardilles proudly displayed two bottles of penicillin crystals. I quickly opened one of the bottles and dumped the raw powder directly into the gaping hole in my knee—a black, ugly, open wound. I then put steaming hot packs on my leg and herbs sent over by the *curandero,* the local medicine man. At 5 A.M. I administered the second bottle of penicillin and more herbs.

On August 4, we reached Paltaybamba. The sore began to drain and the swelling went down. When we reached Chaullay a sergeant of the Guardia Civil post dressed my leg. My fever was gone and the wound healing. Twenty-four hours later we were in Cuzco.

9 · Quest for Marcanay and the Sacred Lakes

August 1964

UPON RETURNING to Lima, we discovered that several articles covering the explorations had appeared in national and international newspapers. On the twelfth of August the Peruvian President Fernando Belaúnde Terry, requesting an explanation of the discoveries and their significance, received me at the palace. In describing the findings to him I explained that Vilcabamba, in the heart of the *montaña,* was no doubt the Lost City of the Incas. A metropolis of independent groups built atop terraces, the average altitude of the city is about 4,500 feet, but the ruins spread up the rivers to a higher altitude. I explained that we hadn't found stonework on the order of Cuzco; the city was buried under vegetation with only the upper portions of the buildings showing. The importance of the site would be measured by its archaeological value and what it could reveal of Inca history. Broken and twisted by four centuries of tropical growth, it was a miracle that Vilcabamba existed at all.

For the next few weeks I prepared a preliminary report of my field activities at Espíritu Pampa for Dr. Valcarcel, then President of the Government Department of Archaeology. I took my collection of potsherds and assorted artifacts to Gary S. Vescelius, chief archaeologist at the Vitcos Peru-Cornell Project, who washed, sorted and classified specimens from the ruins. The scientific analysis included a report of 320 fragments of pottery, 32 Spanish-type tiles, a Spanish horseshoe, a copper or bronze knife, a throwing stick for arrows, a lance point, a turquoise-colored artifact in the shape of a human tooth and a piece of obsidian. The report showed Imperial Inca ceramics, rough pottery of the late epoch and Tiahuanaco pottery types. Emilio Harth-Terré, professor of Peruvian Archaeology and Art at the National University of Engineering, examined my field sketches. We spent weeks together going over these sketches, preparing plans of the ruins. When I returned after the third expedition to Vilcabamba the following January, Harth-Terré prepared plans of study for President Belaúnde.

According to the experts, the artifacts and building remains verified my discovery as the Lost City of the Incas. But I felt that it was an isolated discovery and I could not be satisfied until certain other sites, including Marcanay and Mananhuanunca, which were inherently related to Vilcabamba's history, were located. Only then would our findings be conclusive.

A short time later I met an Augustinian monk, Father Avencio Villarejo, a well-known scholar in Peru who later became the Director of the Augustinian Order in Peru, and who had written numerous books on the geology, biology and ethnology of the jungle. He was as interested in my work as I was in his, and at our first meeting he brought along part of a manuscript he was writing on the history of the Augustinians in Peru (later published under the title: *Los Agustinos en el Perú y Bolivia, 1548–1965*). "I believe you have found Old Vilcabamba," he said in buoyant tones, "and I want to include it in my book. The location of your city verifies the writings of Father Calancha. If we could only find Mananhuanunca there could be no question about it." I explained my plans to return for the specific purpose of locating this sacred shrine and he offered to help me research the project, enthusiastically suggesting we go over every available volume on the subject to be found in the old library in the Monastery of San Agustín.

For days we leafed through three centuries of worm-eaten volumes and letters. It was marvelous to study a first edition of Antonio Calancha; to read his version of the Augustinians in Vilcabamba. Father Avencio had typewritten copies made of the more important transcripts and assisted me with the translations from archaic to modern Spanish. Painstakingly we formed a picture of what I must look for. We knew that after Inca Titu Cusi died, Father Ortiz was taken to the new Inca—a three days' journey from Vitcos. He went from Guarancalla and on to Marcanay on the third day. Marcanay was two leagues from Vilcabamba the Old. The "saint," though never canonized, was judged by Tupac Amaru's captains. And as was mentioned previously, was then dragged down a hill to a place called Horca del Inca, later known as Mananhuanunca, nestled among the hills between two rivers. I should look for a road leading out of the lower ruins, follow it for two or three hours until it comes to a river. No more than half an hour's distance across the river, I should come to hill ruins. Once these ruins are located, I should search for a second river. These findings would prove conclusively that I had correctly identified Old Vilcabamba.

September 15, 1964

Some weeks later, members of the Vilcabamba II Expedition gathered in my room at the Savoy Hotel in Cuzco. We were to leave for the interior the following morning. Standing in front of a large map, I explained that our

118

objective was to find Marcanay and Mananhuanunca. Douglas listened attentively, taking notes. Restless, hard-working, inflamed with a desire to meet every challenge of the jungle, he was indispensable to the team and the most likely choice to take charge of the expedition's equipment.

Geza de Rosner, a giant of a man who towered head and shoulders above everyone else, would be our cameraman. He stood next to Governor Ardilles who once again would supply us with pack animals and act as foreman of the men. Wilfredo Cabrera Escajadillo, Sergeant Second-class of the Guardia Civil, had been assigned as our escort. He spoke perfect Quechua, which would be a great help. Augusto Pastor Díaz, another new member of the expedition, had signed up only the day before. A small-framed man in his late twenties, he was from the *montaña* and wanted to work. He said he knew the Urubamba and was familiar with much of the country we planned to explore. He offered to be my personal bearer, to work for his food and whatever we could pay him. I detected sincerity and advanced 500 soles for a heavy coat, boots and a pair of pants.

That completed our expedition crew. None of us were scientists, but I had no doubts about the ability of the men as a team of explorers.

The next morning we made an aerial flight over greater Vilcabamba in a DC-3, which helped my map-making efforts and gave us a glimpse of the highlands of Markacocha and Pichqacocha. That afternoon I radio-telephoned Dolly in Lima that we were leaving the next morning.

September 20th saw us once again in Lucma where, after much bargaining, I hired the local *curandero* to join the expedition. It seemed a good idea, considering the natives were even more superstitious about the higher pampas than they were of the immediate area of Espíritu Pampa—and we had had enough problems there on our first expedition. A few days later we traveled to Pampaconas, where we hired twelve bearers. At Vista Alegre, Ascensión, seeing that we had a witch doctor, also hired on.

The heavy rains of the wet season bogged us down and slowly we struggled into Espíritu Pampa, terminus of the mule trail. We stayed with the Cobos family who all agreed to join the new expedition. That night the *curandero*, who by this time we had christened the "Wizard," conducted his first *pago*. It lasted from 8 p.m. until two o'clock the next morning. Everyone attended. About twenty of us crowded into the large room in the Cobos' hut, watching spellbound as the Wizard laid out the paraphernalia necessary to perform his sorcery. He used a shaky wooden box covered by a soiled linen as a makeshift altar. On it, he reverently arranged several items: four bottles of liquor, gold and silver tin foil (to represent gold and silver), candy beads (to represent jewels), leaden images (representing idols), conch shells, coca seeds (each grain representing 25 pounds of coca), bits of colored wool, colored string, a dried starfish and the dried placentas of a llama and a vicuña (food for the spirits). In the pale candlelight, pouring libations as offerings and chewing a huge wad of coca leaves, he delivered his incantations to the spirits of the dead. He then turned his attention to the altar and using his fingers, molded a lump of llama fat into a human form and sprinkled it with shavings from a sea conch (called *llampu*) and the delicate seeds of the *sacsacuti* tree. These images, when properly sacrificed, appeased the forest spirits and kept away the rain, fog and the deadly *relámpago*. (He would later plant several of these little figures in odd places about the ruins—one of which was later dug up by a police official who reported that I had been practicing witchcraft in the ruins.)

The natives chewed coca leaves and drank alcohol with the Wizard, their skins a chalkish green in the pale light. About midnight we made a strange procession through the fields, walking by torchlight to one of the large Vilca stones—or Ñustas as they are popularly called—in an old cemetery on the edge of the ruins. The Wizard placed several packets near the huge rock, mumbling his abracadabra, fondling a talisman about his neck and stirring up a witch's brew while making incantations to propitiate the spirits. Then bundles of wood were stacked about the Ñusta and set on fire. We stood around the rock watching the Wizard toss his little fetishes that looked like tamales into the glowing embers. (Bingham noticed burned rocks at Machu Picchu but could not account for them. Undoubtedly it was the work of a *curandero* who got there before him.)

With the first light of dawn the next morning Ardilles, Sergeant Cabrera and Augusto set out to enlist the Machiguengas down river. They returned that afternoon to say that the Machis had agreed to guide us to the upper pampas.

Early the next morning the Machis arrived at our camp. They stood nervously in the center of the clearing, their chief distinguished by red designs painted on his face. Dwarflike, they looked sickly and undernourished. The chief's arms and legs were covered with abrasions, which we treated with Vaseline and penicillin ointment. All were suffering from bloated stomachs, signs of beriberi and a long diet of yucca. I could do nothing about this except offer them each a handful of vitamins. We led them over to the goods we had laid out—pants, shirts, axeheads, string, needles, mirrors, machetes, bright-colored handkerchiefs and other items. The Machi threw down a quiver of long arrows and a bow made from hardwood and picked up a handkerchief, revealing his coca-stained teeth in a whimsical smile. A beautiful plumed *huacamayo* (macaw), placed earlier near the edge of the trail, and a small monkey fetched their companion named Pancho a pair of trousers and a box of matches. I said they could have the rest if they took us to "Erombori," their name for the ruins. They agreed, much to my surprise. News of my miraculous recovery and return to Espíritu Pampa had reached their camp and they saw me as somewhat of a wizard.

The weather had been threatening and the next day it poured. I remained in camp with a sudden fever while the others went out with the

Machis only to return in the late afternoon drenched to the skin, shivering from the cold, to say their guides had taken them straight to the Spanish Palace and then run off leaving the gifts behind.

The Machiguengas are notoriously unreliable. A forest people who claim to be related to the Incas, they now constitute a shifting society of tribal camps inhabiting this part of the Peruvian jungle. They do not trust strangers and, as they demonstrated today, never reveal their hunting trails. Most Machis are nomads (they are linguistically related to the Campas) who hunt and fish in the jungle. Some settle in one place to grow yucca and live in chozas, circular huts of bamboo, cane and palm leaves. They keep numerous wives and will raid other camps for their women. They live in a closed society, practicing customs that go back thousands of years. It was presumptuous of me to have hoped they would cooperate with the expedition.

We did learn from an old Machiguenga woman that there were circular ruins farther up the Chontabamba River at the foot of the Iccma Ccolla—a big mountain in the Markacocha. Legends say the Incas buried their treasure there when fleeing from the Spanish. The woman spoke of sacred enchanted lakes which were a long way off. I felt certain I had seen these lakes from the air and from the description it seemed very possible that the ruins were Marcanay. After hiring porters, we started on the upland trek.

October 1. Alagón, 4,800 feet

My journal reads: We are taking half a ton of equipment, mostly food, tents and assorted gear into the highlands, planning to establish a series of intermediate camps en route, using Espíritu Pampa as a base. Hopefully, with a string of overnight stops all the way up to the Markacocha, we would be able to make a thorough exploration of the craggy, jungled heights—a hundred square miles of unexplored country which we suspect to be dotted with ruins. I send the porters up to a place called Alagón, an hour and a half from our base camp, while Benjamin, Douglas and myself strenuously cut our way with machetes over an old stone road overgrown with vegetation. We follow it across the Yuracmayo River, over the dense pampa to the larger Chaupimayo River where we find what we believe to be the remains of a bridge foundation. The men cut down a tall tree a hundred yards upstream, and by sunset we have built a bridge. We make camp at Alagón.

Dawn breaks. We cross the bridge and the men fan out looking for the road which I believe continues on up into the pampas. The first ruins, found close to the river, turn out to be two elongated oval structures. We pick up the road and follow it up a steep incline. An hour's search brings us to a cluster of ruins situated atop a series of terraces. The main building is circular, about 25 feet in diameter. Its stone walls, constructed from flagstone and roughly dressed riverstones cemented with mud, are graced with sixteen niches. The group is topped by layers of earth and rotting vegetation.

What we have found answers the description of La Horca del Inca, that legendary site known as Mananhuanunca where Father Ortiz was martyred, supposedly located in the hills between two rivers below Marcanay. I immediately dispatch three men to search for the Chontabamba River which should be off somewhere on the other side of the pampa, while the rest of us slash our way uphill through the undergrowth along a walled road some 27 feet wide. We follow it a hundred yards or so to a spacious courtyard, and on to an elevated platform or plaza some 15 feet in length. We find two Vilca-type stones at one end of it, and at the other end, under the spreading trees and hanging vines, a group of three stone buildings; rectangular structures some 100 feet long. A half dozen circular chuclla-style structures are on the floor of the jungle at the base of the raised platform. Three hundred yards to the west we find another elevated platform overlooking the Chaupimayo River far below. A crude wall of Vilca stones form a kind of wall at the western side.

The men spread out looking for other ruins. Soon the three men return with the exciting news that they have found the Chontabamba River. We are on a hilly pampa locked between the Chaupimayo and Chontabamba rivers some two to three leagues above the lower pampa ruins. Exactly where the Spaniards placed Mananhuanunca and Marcanay! There can be no question about it. We have recovered two legendary sites. The key to Vilcabamba. Except for a few Machiguengas, who may have passed this way over their old hunting trail, we are the first men to visit these ruins since 1572.

Hours later the rains came. Sitting in our tent we watched the Wizard predict that the rains would force the expedition back from the Markacocha so that we would not be able to attain our goal.

The men were slow to move the next morning. Reluctantly they packed up and continued on past the 7,000-foot mark where we encountered a swift uncharted tributary of the Chaupimayo. I marked it Titu Cusi. The men complained about the difficulty in cutting the trail. They were tired from the loads and wanted to return. At noon they all sat down in a tight little circle and refused to go another step. Ardilles was powerless to help. They would not listen to Sergeant Cabrera's pleas. I offered them an extra day's pay if they would work until three o'clock. They agreed. Three hours later we reached a fairly level spot and the men put down their loads again. I gave myself up to anger and despair. How was I supposed to explore the pampas without men; I had the men paid off and scribbled a note to Geza, who had returned to Espíritu Pampa:

Upper Chaupimayo. October 5, 3:30 P.M. 8,100 feet

Dear Geza,

The men refuse to go any farther. We are in the upper heights of the Chaupimayo, five days' hard trail above the first bridge near the ruins of Mananhuanunca. The jungle is terribly thick and the going rough. The lakes above us must be fairly large because we are crossing numerous streams. It is impossible to follow the road. We are climbing west.

I am pitching a large camp at this point. It is virgin country and the trail will be easy to follow because twenty-four men have just come over it. Try to send men up in three or four days to check our progress. We can use another small tent. Also fresh yucca, lemons and sugar.

Tomorrow I will set out with the others in hopes of reaching the lakes. The men will be able to find our trail. If they are afraid to go higher, just have them leave the food at the big tent. We will have someone there on the 8th at noon. No need to come up until I advise. As yet no ruins. Wish us luck. We are depending on you to get the men up to us again.

Sincerely,
Gene

I stuffed the note into a plastic envelope and gave it to Flavio Cobos. Our plan to set up a string of camps had failed. With this the men, all nineteen of them, picked up and disappeared down the trail leaving the six of us—Victor, Ascensión, Augusto, Wilfredo, Doug and myself—alone under the falling mist.

That night the spiders began to come out. We had set up our tents over an old rotted timber stand which was infested with huge, black spiders. The black spider, according to Ardilles, inflicts a bite that results in a terrible sickness. It deposits its eggs in the skin, which begins to swell in four to eight days. He described how the flesh rots away, the disease eventually spreading to the rest of the body through the bloodstream. There is no known cure for the lingering malady, which can last for several years and eventually results in death. The description was enough to send us out of the tents like men shot from a cannon. We burned the ground with gasoline and dug a big trench around the tents, hoping to seal the tents so that nothing could get in. We kept the lanterns burning all night and sat upright, afraid to fall asleep for fear of being bitten. We knew the noxious creatures were atop our tents like ants, drawn to our body heat and the light from the lamps. About two in the morning we found several spiders inside with us. We killed two, but the third got away. We searched for nearly half an hour until we found it in the cuff of my pants. I pulled mosquito netting over my head, slid my hands inside my sleeves and dozed fitfully, Akhenaton's "Hymn to the Sun" burning in my mind:

> *When you sink beyond the western heavens*
> *The earth is darkened as though by death;*
> *Then men sleep in their bedchambers,*
> *Their heads wrapped up . . .*
> *Every lion comes out from his lair,*
> *Serpents emerge to sting,*
> *Darkness is supreme, the earth silent;*
> *Their creator rests within his horizon.*

The following day we explored the surrounding area and decided to follow the river we had crossed earlier, traverse a granite cliff and then ascend the backbone of a mountain spur to the 11,000-foot mark; from there to the upper grasslands.

The river is the only place where sunlight penetrates the deep jungle. The air was filled with strange birds, dragonflies, flying ants, wasps and hornets, their curious hanging mud-nests perched up in the branches of flowering trees. Sometimes a hummingbird would flit by, or hover near a fragrant blossom. Most people know the jungle only from the movies; imagine it to be alive with wildlife. Actually one sees few large animals in the daytime. The great majority of predatory beasts are nocturnal and come out only after sunset. During the day they hide in the safety of thick undergrowth. In the daylight hours, the jungle is taken over by myriads of insects and creeping things that are found under every leaf and log, on every branch and tree. Their bite or sting can be fatal, and for man they are much more deadly than the larger jungle creatures we are taught to fear.

Boots slung around our necks, we walked in single file over sharp rocks and slippery boulders. The cool water was refreshing. We came to a waterfall tumbling down over a precipice. We pulled on our boots and slashed our way once more into the forest of hardwoods and palms. The sun beat down; it was warm and we were sweating profusely under our heavy packs. With good weather, we were optimistic about making the upper lakes. If it continued, we would beat the jinx of the Wizard.

The hours dragged on. The heaviest part of the virgin timber stands were behind us and the evaporation rate was increasing. We were getting close to the puna country. But it was still tough going. Stunted trees and the thick underbrush of the cloud forest combined to make a thick wall. Often we scaled a high peak, pulling up our packs behind us with the aid of a long rope, hoping to reach a spur that would lead us above the *montaña* to the open sierra. But it was hopeless. We would attain a crest only to observe a continuous sea of summits rising before us. We traversed a cliff and roped down to the riverbed, hoping to follow it up to the highlands. An hour's rough going brought us face to face with the first cataract, a thundering waterfall looming above our heads for hundreds of yards. There was nothing to do but work our way up through the jungle-clad forest and try to reach the crest. We moved through a shower of fine mist, belaying near the halfway point. Then the clouds opened and it began to rain. For hours we stubbornly persisted and only halted when the rain and the risk outweighed the practicality of continuing. We bivouacked on an outcropping of the cliff and spent a miserable night trying to keep our tent from being blown away. Next morning at sunup (though we never saw it) I stuck my head out the tent door. Taking out my altimeter, I took a reading—10,000 feet—and marked our approximate position on my map: latitude 13° 3′ S., longitude 73° 24′ W. The rains were beating us back, just as the *curandero* had predicted. Realizing that we could not manage this trail, we drew up another plan to reach the Markacocha range and the Iccma Ccolla peak. There was a trail that led from Vista Alegre to the uplands and to these lakes. We headed back to base camp.

Three days later the mules came down from the highlands and the next evening we were in Vista Alegre. Hiring six porters, we set out the following morning climbing up through the jungles. In the afternoon we managed to reach 11,500 feet, where we came out on the flat grasslands. It was exhilarating to be up out of the humid jungles in the cooling breezes of the Peruvian altiplano. It had been incredibly easy over this route, and we regretted not having come this way from the start. We tramped along in full view of Choquessaffra (18,141 feet), Totora, Huaswacocha and a dozen other great snow-peaks. Soon we entered marshy ground and felt our way over cold puddles of brackish water and numerous streams that fed a series of tiny lakes. That evening we pitched our tents at the edge of a small mountain lagoon named Suera Cocha. Not far away stood an Inca platform.

At daybreak, with feather-light packs strapped to our backs, six of us set out to explore the highlands in quest of the lakes we had heard so much about. Geza elected to hold down the camp and do some filming of the spectacular view. Our chests aching from oxygen shortage, we reached 12,400 feet above sea level, just in time to meet the sun peeping up through the clouds. What a transition the sun makes in the highlands. A million points of reflected light dance off the frosty earth and shimmering stretches of water, and the fog burns off the ground in billowing, vaporous sheets. The icy heights of the Vilcabamba sparkle in the royal-blue Andean air and parrots wheel above us, squawking and crying.

Plodding along over the soggy grasslands, picking our way like mountain goats, we passed a series of small lagoons veiled in a cloudy mist. Not far away stands the purple-peaked Iccma Ccolla, looking like a human face carved by time and nature. An hour later and 13,000 feet above sea level, we reached a stone Inca platform, 45 feet in length, 25 feet in width. We burned off the grass and I picked up samples of potsherds from the ashen ground. Glancing off to my left through the swirling mists, I caught sight of a large, dark body of water shimmering like an obsidian mirror. "Yana Cocha" (black lake in Quechua), said Ascención, who stopped cutting grass and came beside me. Evidently the lake was known to him. We strained our eyes through the vapor. A great tableland of lush swampy ground and another long, narrow lake came into view. Several small streams poured out from the lake, cascaded over cliffs and dropped down toward the Apurímac River. "Chinan Cocha," said Ascención. "There are others to the far side of those *patas*." He pointed toward two white granite peaks that rose up some 13,000 feet. "We will climb those mountains," I said, taking out my field glasses for a closer look.

Three hours of hard work brought us to the summit of the north peak and we looked down on one of the most beautiful views any of us had ever expected to see in Peru. Two thousand feet below, a string of seven lakes encircled the peaks—Yana Cocha, Chinan Cocha and five others called Pichqacocha. The Sacred Lakes of Vilcabamba! We could see the majestic heights of the snow-crowned Cordillera Vilcabamba perforating the cloudy mists, icy glaciers dipping down their sides like chains of sparkling jewels in the sunlight. The purple and brown sierra sloped down to meet the vast jungle that spread around us from the Apurímac to the Urubamba rivers, tributaries of the distant Amazon. From this altitude, we could imagine how the conquering Manco and his army were able to drop down over roads known only to themselves and lay siege to Ayacucho, Cuzco and a dozen other points. We were in the heart of the Markacocha-Pichqacocha range—the crown to the Vilcabamba kings!

Our explorations continued for several days. We found pieces of roads, Inca watchtowers and bits of broken ruins, but heavy rains and hail hampered our efforts. Cold mists brought visibility down to zero and we had to return to the tents. Next day the porters left and we were abandoned again.

The expedition broke up on October 16. Eight days later we arrived in Lima for a badly needed rest, supplies and additional funds. I was determined to continue the explorations and appealed to the government for support.

Not long after we returned to continue the exploration. From the log:

November 27 through January 12, 1964–65

During the fifty days of the third Vilcabamba expedition we had difficulty hiring porters and were on our own much of the time. There was something in the air: the pueblos, usually friendly, were less cooperative; the men staying close to their farms, unwilling to journey with us. I thought at first it was due to certain radio reports that we were robbing tombs. We were accused of transporting forty muleloads of gold over the back trails, attempting to break out across the Apurímac and thence to Lima. Governor Ardilles and Sergeant Cabrera complained about these false tales when they returned to Cuzco. But this wasn't the real problem. It didn't explain why the natives refused to work with us. They knew that our expedition was not a treasure hunt. We couldn't have taken a thing out without their knowing it. The cause was determined some months later when guerrilla warfare broke out in the Vilcabamba (later put down by the Peruvian armed forces).

December 21

Exploring the highlands north of Lucma we came upon another Inca stone road. It passed up over marshy grasslands leading to numerous ruins, some of which were known, and snaked over the precipices. One fork led over the Salinas Pass and entered the Concevidayoc Valley to Espíritu Pampa.

126

This could have been the route taken by Fathers García and Ortiz when they waded through the Ungacacha of history. We found a swampy morass along the route and a place called Padre Huarcuna where, according to legend, they hung the Father. We followed the second fork up over the 12,000-foot pass of Huarina into the beautiful San Miguel Valley, a tropical locale that produces corn, tea, coca, coffee, tobacco, yucca, oranges, lemons and bananas. With the dangers of malaria and huge bushmasters, we found exploring difficult. Near the junction of the Concevidayoc and San Miguel, where the Concevidayoc becomes the Cosireni, we found that the Incas had absorbed this valley into the Vilcabamba complex. We scoured the heights and valleys for potsherds, carrying long sticks to kill the bushmasters. The area between Espíritu Pampa and Chuangiri produced little more than scattered remains and pottery fragments; but we explored numerous watchtowers on the grassy summits and sighted others with our field glasses.

Returning over the high cordilleras we dropped down to Espíritu Pampa where we spent the better part of thirty days completing sketch plans of the lower ruins. One afternoon we walked down to the small Machi community to speak with an old woman who had first told us of the existence of ruins higher up the pampas, only to learn that she had been thrown out to fend for herself because she was too old to be of further use. We found her in a small hut on a partially used farm where she was able to pick up scraps of food thrown out to the animals. Weighing no more than seventy pounds, skin pulled tight over her frail bones, she was at least ninety years old, alone and waiting to die. We gave her some food which she grabbed from our hands and stuffed in the folds of her long cotton *cushma* that hung to her ankles like a robe. She refused to speak a word about ruins. Ardilles supposed she had been beaten recently for having previously spoken with us. In the meantime three Machis appeared as if by magic to ask for cigarettes. One was the chief. He refused to even look at the old woman, who was his mother. According to Machiguenga custom she was dead to him. When she began to scold him, he left with his two companions. Then she huddled up in the corner of the hut and cried. We stood silent and one by one emptied our packs giving her what food we carried, promising to send more the next day. When I turned to leave, she lifted up two hollow eyes and looked into my face. I thought I saw a look of gratitude written on her countenance. She rattled off several words, a few of which I understood, "*Segundina . . . Naqey . . . chiri . . . Quentibacori Inopi. . . .*" Outside I asked Ardilles what he made of it, and at last we came up with the translation. It meant that if we went to a high, cold place, to a mountain peak (known to us) and to a certain lake which has been guarded by Machiguengas for centuries, we would find great ruins. But she warned us to be careful of the enchantment. Every person that has gone to these two places has coughed blood and died. To reveal the whereabouts of secret places was a strange thing for her to do, probably female defiance to the tribe that had disowned her.

The heavy rains were now coming in force. Sketching the ruins was difficult, and another highland probe was out of the question. We had no porters and a dozen of our bridges over the Chontabamba and Chaupimayo rivers had been washed out. But we did manage to reach a high prominence allowing me to survey with my telescope the towering hill mentioned by the old Machi woman. Through the parting clouds I caught sight of archaeological remains at the summit, the upper ruins of Marcanay; then the mists hid them from view. I marked the spot on my map, determined to come back the following year. We packed up and moved out. The rainy season was upon us in full force and there was no other choice but to bring our explorations to a close.

The Vilcabamba Expeditions had been far more successful than any of us had reason to expect. We had found an ancient Inca metropolis in precisely the spot where legends place the "Lost City." This finding, coupled with the discoveries of two sites answering the description of Marcanay and Mananhuanunca, was substantial proof that we had found the Inca city.

The size and location of the settlement is perhaps as important in itself as the fact that it met the requirements of Vilcabamba the Old. Up to the time of the expedition, indeed, up to the time of this writing, it was not believed possible that Inca civilization had occupied the *montaña* in force. The city was spread over an area of about 500 acres, and could have sustained several thousand inhabitants—an unusually large number for an Inca community outside Cuzco. Vilcabamba was the capital of an Inca state and the center of commerce for the *montaña*. It is doubtful that the Incas had moved here as a quick refuge during the dying days of the empire. From all evidence they had concentrated a rather large population here over a considerable period of time, perhaps a full century or more. The existence of pre-Inca tombs and ceramic fragments of the Tiahuanaco-Huari period shows that the whole valley had been occupied by other cultures long before the coming of the Incas.

The trail back to Cuzco was uneventful, but there was talk of guerrilla bands operating in the jungle. We failed to hire men for the forthcoming expedition and I had some misgivings of being able to return.

Back in Lima my thoughts returned to The Pajatén.

PART III

THE EL DORADO EXPEDITIONS

1965-68

10 · Gran Pajatén, Bird City of the Upper Jungle

Tɪᴛᴜ Cᴜsɪ told the Augustinian friars in Vilcabamba that his father often went to the aid of the Antis people, to whom the Incas were related, during their struggle with the Spanish invaders. The young Inca said he went to "protect his town of Revanto," probably Levanto, the old capital of the Chachapoyas people and today a small highland village in the department of Amazonas. It is most likely from Titu Cusi's testimony that Manco Inca traversed the backbone of the Andes over roads unknown to the Spaniards and extended his domain over a large part of the *montaña*.

I consulted the writings of Garcilaso de la Vega, Pedro Cieza de León, Blas Valera and other chroniclers, and came to the conclusion that the Chachapoyans must have played a vital role in the final days of the Inca. Two old manuscripts, one presently in the possession of a private collector in Lima, the other in the Peruvian National Archives, tell that the Incas brought the Chachapoyans to Cuzco, first as *mitimaes* (workers); but eventually they assumed the role of *alabarderos* or royal guards, and many prominent clans grew up in the Inca capital. Under Huáscar the Chachapoyans were in charge of the Corregidor of Cuzco. Unfortunately Manco alienated them and they sided with the Spanish.

After the Chanca War, 1438 A.D., the surviving Chanca people, old rulers of the Quechua tribes, escaped into the steaming jungles of northeastern Tahuantinsuyo. Their chief, Hancohuallu, sought exile rather than suffer the disgrace of subjection to the Incas. He and his followers, some 8,000 warriors and 50,000 people, the remnants of the tribe, were granted a huge province called Moyobamba (Muyupampa) by the king of Chachapoyas. The Incas under Tupac Yupanqui built a military road from Huanuco to Chachapoyas and marched a large army over it. The Chachapoyans were conquered, but at great cost to the Incas. Twenty or thirty years later the Chachapoyans rebelled and Tupac's son, Huayna Capac, was forced to reconquer them. Inca Tupac Yupanqui spoke of seven great cities (including Levanto) that fell to his armies within the kingdom that was 50 leagues wide by 20 leagues long, roughly 150 miles by 60 miles. Moyobamba was an additional 30 leagues wide.

According to my research, The Pajatén fell into the southernmost extention of this ancient kingdom. This assumption promised fertile new territory for explorations. Not unexpectedly, our Vilcabamba Expedition for 1965 had to be called off due to guerrilla warfare which had erupted in the area, so I decided to explore The Pajatén.

Cieza de León wrote an interesting account of what occurred at Chachapoyas in the year 1550, following its conquest by the Spaniards. Two hundred Indians appeared out of the jungle and presented themselves before Captain Gómez de Alvarado, then mayor of the colonial city. He was told by the unfortunate wanderers that they had been forced to fight many wars during their exile and that the race had all but died out. They spoke of "great lands thickly populated, some rich in gold and silver, that lay to the east."

Pedro Cieza de León referred to this region of the orient to which the Chancas fled as "El Dorado." Cieza thought El Dorado was east of Chachapoyas and so did Antonio de Herrera, a chronicler of the Indies, who wrote that the Incas under Tupac Yupanqui went looking for El Dorado, though they had another name for it, and got as far as Moyobamba. The first recorded search for El Dorado was undertaken by Diego Ordaz in 1531, but ended in tragedy. Antonio de Herrera searched for it in 1535 and failed. In 1538 Pedro Anzures plunged into the wilds of Antisuyo in the Carabaya region east of Lake Titicaca with a large expedition that ended in the deaths of 143 Spaniards, 4,000 Indians and 220 horses, a tragic epic of human suffering in which "they [the survivors] had to eat each other." In 1540 Gonzalo Pizarro, half brother of the conqueror of Peru, set out for El Dorado and the Forests of Cinnamon, but was forced to return to Ecuador. Francisco de Orellana, a member of the ill-fated expedition, went on alone with a small party and, although they never found the fabled El Dorado, they did succeed in naming and navigating the Amazon River, "the great fresh-water sea," and in following it to the Atlantic. In 1541–42 they sailed along the Amazon River until they came to a great city of white houses, stretching for an incredible 250 miles. Machipero, the lord of this mighty city, came out with 50,000 warriors in brightly painted canoes blowing wooden trumpets and beating drums. The Spaniards managed to make their escape, but only after a costly battle. The expedition continued down river to the land of Chief Oniquaque where an engagement was fought and much treasure taken. Many cities were too formidable to be attacked, but on they went, marveling at the wondrous sights. They observed warriors watching their progress, bearing shields and colored emblems, spears, bows and arrows. These were men of "medium stature and of very highly developed manners and customs." They observed public squares, temples and feathered idols. Sometimes they pillaged smaller villages, taking llama meat, fruits, corn, yucca and chicha. They found great highways leading off into the jungle and would have followed them had it not been for the rumors of large populations inhabiting the interior.

Toward the end of their journey the explorers came to the land of the Amazons, a nation of women warriors. The Amazons, who lived in seventy villages with temples dedicated to the Sun, came out to meet them brandishing bows and arrows, filling the sides of two Spanish brigantines with arrows "until both vessels looked like porcupines," records the account of Gaspar de Carvajal. But the intrepid voyagers, taking advantage of favorable winds and a swift current, moved through "a great fleet of canoes" and made their escape. Sometime later, after passing through less civilized regions, they entered the mouth of the Amazon and thence to Nueva Cádiz, a settlement on Cubagua.

The Orellana Expedition is perhaps the most extraordinary of the El Dorado expeditions, but by no means the only one. Philip Von Hutten attempted it without success between 1541–45. In 1558 word reached Lima of an El Dorado sighting. The Crown became interested and undertook an official expedition led by Pedro de Ursúa. The expedition set out on the Huallaga in 1559 with a large body of men and ships but it, too, was ill-fated. Another El Dorado expedition led by Antonio de Berrio failed in 1584. Sir Walter Raleigh traveled some 500 miles up the Orinoco hunting for El Dorado in 1595. Many stories filled the ears of the adventurous. There were tales of the "gilded one," the chief of a nation in the region of Santa Fe de Bogotá, who ceremoniously covered himself with gold and bathed in a sacred lake at sunrise in the legendary city of Manoa or Omoa. (Diego Ordaz actually claimed to have seen the "gilded one.") There were stories of the "magical fountain of health" and of golden temples and sepulchers. Explorations continued, those of Lawrence Kemys, a year following Raleigh's, and another by Robert Harcourt in 1613. These explorations, and others led by French and Dutch explorers, studied the people and the country of the general region of Guiana. The hunt for El Dorado continued in the eighteenth and nineteenth centuries, the expeditions including those of Apolinar Días de Fuente (1760), Sir Robert Hermann Schomburgk (1840), Theodor Koch-Grünberg (1908), Hamilton Rice (1925), and Colonel Percy Fawcett (1925). These explorers were looking in different places but all their efforts centered on the green jungles. The earliest explorations placed El Dorado in the northwest Amazon Basin, in the mountains of Parima in Guiana, the Gran Sabana of Venezuela, or the Mato Grosso of Brazil. Others said it existed in Colombia, Peru, or Bolivia, where Anzures concentrated his efforts with disastrous consequences. Wherever it was supposed to be, it was never found.

I was sure of one thing: Something did exist in the eastern jungles, but no one had managed to find it. I remembered reading about the Inca kings having marched deep into the interior. They had heard rumors of "populous kingdoms" in the jungles, of "double-faced people," and much more in that mysterious region they called Peneca and Hachahacha. Had the eastern *jalcas* and lower jungles not contained large, wealthy populations, the Incas would not have bothered with such a costly enterprise, for it is well known the jungle produces nothing of value on its own. After the Conquest the Spanish heard tales of the "hundred lost cities" of the jungle, the legendary Plateriyayocc, a vast empire never recovered. Following the Spanish victory over Vilcabamba, Alonso de la Cueva passed through the abandoned city and penetrated some 200 leagues into the interior in the regions of the Mañaries Indians in hopes of locating these cities. But the ill-fated expedition was only able to survive at the kindness of the Indians, who, hearing their prayers, recognized them as the same taught them by the martyred Father Ortiz. Assuredly, the Spaniards would not have risked their lives on such adventures had the jungle not promised new wealth.

Rather than plunge wildly into the jungles without something to go on, I chose, as I had done at Vilcabamba, to pick up where others had left off and, most important, to follow the roads. Accepting the premise that Manco II had taken the roads of Antisuyo to Chachapoyas (Revanto), I felt obliged to follow his travels starting from the presently-known Chachapoyas area. Both Tupac Yupanqui and Huayna Capac had testified to the importance of the Chachapoyas Kingdom. Spanish writers substantiated their claim; Pedro Cieza de León even suggested that the El Dorado region of Peru was somewhere between this territory and that of Moyobamba, taken over by the Chancas.

From an explorer's point of view, the area was comparatively unknown, and very little archaeological research had been done. Arturo Wertheman, Antonio Raimondi, Adolph Bandelier, E. W. Middendorf, Kiefer, Villard and General Louis Langlois had made superficial progress. More recently, Hans Horkheimer and Bertrand Flornoy had visited known sites. Paul and Henry Reichlen, a French archaeology-anthropology team, had done the most recent investigation. Henry Reichlen had shown me a copy of the *Bulletin of the Geographical Society* published in Paris in the year 1885. Vidal Senéze, a French botanist, and J. Nortizi had explored the eastern section of Amazonas at Rodriguez de Mendoza and reported scattered archaeological remains. Their description of ruins showed that the area was worth investigating. Though fragmentary, this material gave us a good base for explorations.

August 27, 1965. The Pajatén Expedition; El Dorado I, First Phase

I therefore decided to resume our work in The Pajatén. We elected to call our new expeditions the "El Dorado Expeditions," a rather fanciful name, but one with a long tradition of exploration behind it. We weren't looking for the so-called gilded man and we weren't interested at all in tales of treasure and golden temples. But we *did* hope to throw some light on the whereabouts of the Seven Great Cities of the Chachapoyas conquered by Tupac Yupanqui, and hopefully to press on to Cieza de León's El Dorado— that region taken over by the displaced Chanca Confederation. We knew the exact location of a road and our aerial explorations some three years before had spotted what appeared to be ancient remains on a hilltop of the upper jungle, Evidently these were the same ruins known to a few woodsmen from Huamachuco and Patáz. This seemed to be the best lead. A distance of 100 nautical air miles south from Chachapoyas brings one within the borders of the old Chachapoyas Kingdom. Our chances of success would depend in large part on our ability to find porters and dependable guides— men who knew the backland trails. Our plan was to drive to Trujillo and on up to Huamachuco. From there we hoped to hire men as needed. Then we would cross the Marañón, trek over the sierra and down into the *montaña* over the old road I had sighted from the air in 1962.

I put together a small field party consisting of Doug, Carlos Lopez and two trailsmen from Huamachuco, plus myself. Two archaeologists, one from the National University of Trujillo, the other from the Department of Archaeology, agreed to help us analyze any potsherds found along the way. Lopez had an old truck which would take us down to the Marañón, where mules would be waiting with porters. The 120-mile drive over a dirt road of continual S-bends that came out at 10,200 feet at Huamachuco took the better part of seven hours. We spent the ninth of September with the Augustine monks who extended the hospitality of their mission.

September 10, 1965

We loaded the truck in a pouring rain. The ascent to the pass of Alto Huagil (12,750 feet) was a breathtaking trip past small pueblos and haciendas lined with stately eucalyptus trees. At Huagil we began our climb up to Consuso, gateway to Marañón. The descent to the lower river was a hair-raising journey over a winding dirt road, the rocky precipices on our right dropping off a thousand feet. We spotted eight or nine hilltop remains, probably ancient fortresses, along the summits and picked up several large copper axeheads, one measuring five inches across, some stone knives and other artifacts that were strewn about the ruins. After a harrowing twelve-hour ride we arrived at Chagual. The mules did not come down until late in the afternoon of the next day. The following day we left in the morning darkness at five o'clock and in the emerging daylight came out in the cool uplands. By ten o'clock we were in Patáz, at 8,500 feet altitude, where we picked up a crew of seven porters led by Carlos Torrealva, ex-mayor who had led a group of agriculturists into Pajatén country in 1963. Hours later we entered the outskirts of Los Alisos (9,600 feet) where we stayed the night.

At daylight we were on our way again, steadily ascending a steep, rocky trail to the crests of the cordillera, where we emerged at 12,000 feet. Soon we were riding over the ancient highway. Fairly well preserved, made of broken stone, it measured on the average 9 to 12 feet wide and coursed south to north. The famous Inca road of the highlands ran some forty miles to the west, which suggested this was part of the military road that came up from Huánuco, terminating some miles due north. We rode along under a gray, cold haze and late in the afternoon took a branch road that swung to the east past a series of upland lakes. We camped at the base of a huge outcropping of granite rock and the following morning we were away tramping over the *fango*, the swamplands of the puna country, a freezing sticky morass. It began to rain. We flagged on over the boggy terrain for most of the morning, pushing and tugging the mules who became mired every fifty yards, until we were able to take the old road that had wisely been built above the slough by ancient engineers. No more than six feet wide, the road was constructed in the form of a causeway. I recognized it at once as the same arterial road I had seen from the air three years before. We continued on past a large lake, Empedrada, and then bypassed a second some distance to the east called Braba in order to examine a cluster of scattered ruins on a high peak. From there we moved into a cold, swampy grassland and in the early afternoon reached Puerta del Monte, the gateway to the high jungle. Drenched to the skin, shivering from a piercing wind, we hunched under a rocky ledge out of the rain for a respite.

Into the mossy forest under a pouring rain, cutting the undergrowth with quick sweeps of machetes, we tore down the slushy trail at a furious pace and reached a place called Monte Cristo, 8,800 feet altitude, where we settled for the night.

The camp stirred slowly to life early the next morning. It had stopped raining and a few stars peeped through intermittent clouds of the pre-dawn darkness, which raised our hopes for a good day. I can think of nothing more depressing than traveling in a wet jungle under a pounding rain. But our hopes faded when the mists closed in as we packed up. An hour later it was raining again.

The trail ended at a river and we balanced our way along a slippery log to the other side where we picked up the remains of the stone road. We followed it some distance, hacking away with our machetes, little purple and white orchids cascading about our heads, shaken loose from their fragile hold on the upper branches by our long, steel blades. The men were determined to set a fast pace and I had great difficulty trying to keep up with them. Every so often we would come across walls and I would follow them up the slopes of the hills taking measurements. There were many circular constructions similar to those at Vilcabamba, but the stonework was better. I wanted to climb up to the summits, for the ruins continued in that direction; however, it was best to keep together. Men on the trail think of nothing but reaching its end. Anything in between is of no interest to them—particularly archaeological remains. So I dropped back to the floor of the valley, making a strong effort in the high altitude and damp jungle to keep within calling distance of the main party. We pitched our tents at 8,300 feet at a place called Balcón—a humid, muddy shelf over a nameless river. The rain continued without letup, but we hurriedly put up a lean-to, wolfed down a hot meal, and then fell fast asleep in the deep silence of the inner jungle.

Morning came and we broke camp. Gritting our teeth, we labored a thousand feet up the side of the forested mountain; a difficult climb under heavy packs and a steady downpour that turned the trail to a spongy ooze. At 9,300 feet we hit secondary walls. Fifty feet more and we ran into a twenty-foot stone wall. We snaked around it, hacked a hole in the vegetation and wriggled through only to be confronted by a second wall. This one supported a stone structure. One of the men ambled up and told us there was a big circular ruin at the crest with carvings. We pushed on up the hill toward it.

A quarter of an hour later we were at the summit. My altimeter showed a reading of 9,400 feet above sea level. Eddies of cold air curled down from the misty heights. We dropped our packs like stones, filling our lungs with refreshing dry air—most invigorating after the damp jungle. The men turned to clearing a large space for the equipment which I had forced them to carry with us. A cardinal rule in the jungle: Never get separated from your gear. Twenty minutes and a large clearing was cut out of the primordial setting giving us a view of the river two thousand feet below. It had stopped raining and patches of sunshine broke through billowing, white clouds. A rainbow of splendid colors cheered us and we prayed for good weather. We could see the sierra to the west, the cupped valley over which we had tramped two days before, the brown mountains jetting up on either side, rivers of rainwater streaming down craggy escarpments. Surveying the distant scene through my 9-power glasses, I felt as if I were looking at another planet. We were in an emerald world, a place of wild orchids and bromeliads, fragrant blossoms, tall trees filled with air plants of red, orange and white, thick vines covered with moss, a living world in itself. The naked landscape of the sierra looked dead, empty—a barren stretch of lingering mists and dead grass. What a difference a few miles can make—the highest jungles in the world growing side by side with one of the most barren spots there is.

We opened a long, black, rubber-covered tarpaulin some 15 feet in length and half again as wide and stretched it over two large poles and a length of nylon rope and soon had a comfortable shelter under which we placed our equipment. A fire was started and we enjoyed a leisurely meal— there wasn't much else we could do. A tropical storm had set in with the force of a deluge. Around five-fifteen in the afternoon it stopped raining and we came out of our tent into a brilliant glare of sun reflected from milk-white clouds. We had an hour before darkness so I decided to get to work.

Our camp was no more than twenty feet from a great hulk of vegetation, now steaming from the sun's rays. It was topped by tall trees that reached up seventy feet or more. Blinking in the strong light, we set to work clearing the mess with our machetes. A circular structure of slateblocks was beneath the dense growth. A portion of the curious structure had been cleared by the agriculturists prior to our expedition, exposing part of a stairway and three mosaic-like figures worked in stone. They looked like winged creatures with what had once been human heads tenoned into the walls, though the details had been lost owing to the fact they were made from soft sandstone; rain and wind had worn away the lines over the years. I glanced over my shoulder toward a high vertical sandstone cliff. It loomed up out of the mists towering a full five hundred feet—perhaps a thousand—above us to the south, completely dominating the site. The ruins had been built against it on a flat extension. I recognized it as the same one I had detected from the air.

The following day I put three men to work clearing the big building and the rest of us trudged off into the thicket clearing a path as we went. We dropped down an incline and immediately came upon another circular structure, which was covered with a mound of dense growth. Cutting away with our machetes, we soon discovered winged figures that were half-man and half-bird. How ghostly they looked in the pale, green light! In all, we counted five figures—some of the stone heads were in much better shape than the others we had seen. We found a stairway and on the other side found five similar figures. I went up over the wall and dropped down inside the edifice, pulling off vines and clearing away some of the moss and leaves that clung to the stonework. Geometric stonework patterns of stepped-fret and angular spiral designs came to light. I had observed similar patterns on ceramic pottery and molded patterns on mud walls at Chanchan, but this was the first time I had ever seen them in stone anywhere in Peru. I recalled the rich architectural ornamentation employed in the ruins of Mexico—Chichén Itzá, Labna, Mitla and others. Here was the same idea. Could there be some connection? The surrounding jungle promised more discoveries and we pressed on and soon stumbled upon a small, round building. We seemed to be on a raised platform of some kind. We cut our way down a slope. I had the men peel away a thick blanket of dead vegetation, exposing a descending stairway. We labored on down past two high walls with projecting cornices at the upper levels. We snaked around the upper wall and followed it for some distance. Farther down we approached another series of mounds and found similar circular structures underneath. They were most ornate, of rare architectural elegance boasting intricate motifs of stone mosaic on their upper and lower levels. The buildings were on platforms which followed their contours. Lower down we came out on a level courtyard or plaza and for over a half hour we hacked away at unbelievably dense vegetation. The moss-covered vines were wet and slippery and we found numerous green scorpions that looked like little clumps of moss. I put on my leather gloves. We encountered some rectangular structures, climbed over a high defending wall and reached some terraces that worked down toward the river. We decided to follow the retaining wall on both sides of the plaza, which averaged about 60 feet wide at its narrowest part. It flared up toward the circular structures on higher ground, running up in the direction of the high cliff—a region still unexplored. The wall enclosed the entire site in the upper zone; lower terraces, which were studded with circular, oval and rectangular structures; then dropped down to the south and west. Making our way painfully through the prickly growth, we discovered more ruins, high terraces and raised walls that ran right up to the cliff-face. In the late afternoon we turned back.

At base camp I set up the cameras. The main circular structure had been fairly well cleared, revealing a beautiful circular building around 45 feet in diameter and 12 to 13 feet in height. The ruins were in a very precarious condition due to the tree roots and rattan vines that had found their way inside the ornamental stonework. The façade of the structure was divided in half by a medial molding. The upper sections were rich with friezes, curvilinear angles and step patterns, and there were two rows of fretwork in the form of zigzag lines composed of hundreds of individual elements delicately placed as in a mosaic. Beneath this was a grouping of ten winged, human figures. Some of the heads were crowned with wings, others with rays, like sunbursts. These winged figures faced northwest, five on each side of the stairway, and were made from long, black blocks of slate. (Plate 11.)

While waiting for the sun to come out (it had stopped raining, but heavy, black clouds hung over us like a thick carpet), I spotted a smaller

[PLATE 11] *Large circular building around 45 feet in diameter stands on stone platform. Gran Pajatén.*

circular building about 28 feet in diameter, northeast of the big 45-foot edifice, and put the men to clearing. I wondered who had built these ruins, when and to what purpose these strange architectural specimens of dignity and grace had served. The ruins didn't conform to those of any culture with which I was familiar. Had this site been a city? A fortification? A necropolis? A temple? The plastic decorations suggested a ceremonial center. Two men, painstakingly scraping away handfuls of wet moss, began to expose the upper section of a circular façade. A series of geometric figures and stone carvings came to light. The frieze consisted of step and fret motifs and aquatic representations in bas-relief. This was very original architectural ornamentation. When I saw a large sun-bird with wings spread I became very excited. We smoothed away the mud from the stonework with our fingers. It measured some two feet high by three feet wide and looked like a solar condor! (Plate 12.) The words of Tupac Yupanqui, conqueror of Chachapoyas, came to mind: "The inhabitants *work with stone* as the people of Cuzco . . . I shall never forget their *round houses* built in tiers, their fortresses well situated against the rock and sometimes commanded by a *tower* . . . the monuments which are built on *high cliffs* which appear inaccessible. These are tombs where they enclose the mummified bodies of their chiefs and priests. Their dead have no company but the wind and the *condor which is their god*." (*Italics mine.*)

[PLATE 12] *Condor design in stone wall. The Gran Pajatén ruins, like other cities of the Chachapoyas region, are composed of thousands of individual stone elements fitted together like a puzzle.*

[PLATE 13] *Stone head with headdress design and circular ear decoration. Large foliated nose is characteristic of the sculpture found in the Chachapoyas ruins.*

After a hurried breakfast we continued to clear the ruins and uncovered a large number of circular structures as small as three feet in diameter. I assumed they had had conical roofs at one time. The circular complex suggested an Amazonian link—as it had at Vilcabamba. Both the Chachapoyans and the Cañaris used round or oval buildings, as did the Carib and Arawak tribes of lower Amazonia—the latter made migrations westward some centuries back. The existence of so many stylized buildings and the large complex of circular buildings indicated a new architectural form. What was its origin? It did not appear to have come from the coast or the Andes. Was there an Amazon source? We also uncovered several strange stone stelae, similar in some ways to the Inca *Intihuatani*. What they had been used for I could not determine as they were not carved. The potsherds that came from the surface were typical Marañón-type ceramics with evidence of late Inca occupation, suggesting the ruins had been inhabited at various epochs. We did find evidence that some of the buildings had been reconstructed out of older materials. We also came upon carved heads tenoned into the retaining walls. These carvings were about the size of human heads. (Plate 13.) The cut stones and the stylized patterns reflected a very high civilization. Stone mortars were found in excess. Pottery fragments had zigzag or serpentine designs. I had observed this style on a ceramic pot in the Vilcabamba ruins which lent some strength to the chronicles that gave reference to the Chachapoyans having been in the refuge. The excellent condition of the ruins

141

showed that the Spanish did not reach this site, for they are known to have destroyed all the carvings that they found.

I could not be sure what purpose the buildings had served.

We also found several egg-shaped boulders in the structures. They were not large, about the size of a basketball, pure white, and looked as if they might have been used as pestles. Then I remembered reading from an old manuscript that the people of these mountainous regions used to worship such stones, just as the Incas revered their Huancauri stones.

At dawn the next day I walked over to the eastern section of the ancient city and looked down the deep valley at the river now swollen by rain. Cascading waterfalls dropped down towering mauve peaks, their crests lost in pockets of billowing clouds. Lower down, sheets of vapor burned off the jungle floor giving the promise of a rainless day. The scene appeared out of the dying darkness like a dream. The words of Khalil Gibran rose up in my mind.

> . . . I was free
> As the birds, probing valleys and
> The forests, and flying in the spacious
> Sky. At eventide I rested upon the
> Temples and palaces in the city of the
> Colorful clouds which the Sun builds
> In the morning and destroys before
> Twilight.

The morning was sad but luminous. Carl, Doug and I sat down trying to figure our location. As near as I could tell we were at approximately latitude, 7° 45′ S., longitude, 77° 18′ W. That put us somewhere in the greater Pajatén territory between the Apisoncho and a small stream called Pajatén that empties into the Huayabamba. Wanting to salute the missionaries of times past, we decided to call the ruins Gran Pajatén, and the stream Tumac in its upper reaches and Gran Pajatén below the conjunction of two small affluents that enter it below the ruins, in honor of the famous colonial ruins of Pajatén, an abandoned Franciscan mission some three or four days' hard trail north of our position. A few days later we returned to Lima.

From an explorer's point of view, my work at Gran Pajatén was virtually over. Because of the publicity generated by our find, the Peruvian Government decided to send in a group of specialists. That we had encouraged this was most gratifying. A helicopter pad had been cleared at the summit of the crest and I was asked to serve as guide for the small pilot helicopter that guided in the larger Army Air Force copters transporting members of the expedition, plus a large delegation of the press. Once everyone was in and the work begun, I decided to move on again. We had found remains of a high civilization on the eastern slopes of the Andes, beyond the Chavín area —but my theory that the eastern *montañas* sustained many ruins was not going to be proved by a single, isolated find. Other sites would have to be uncovered.

As it was, we had located an important site on the eastern slopes of the cordilleras. For the moment, no one could be certain that our site was in any way related to Chavín (though I recognized from potsherds a Huaylas influence, a post-Chavín culture). The find was in many ways important because it offered additional material for research and study. The Chachapoyans, whom I thought to be the builders of the ruins, promised to be an exciting new culture of Amazonia. Could they have been indigenous or had they come from the eastern lower jungles? Did they come from the northern Andes to the west? Only further exploration and study could answer these questions. The site appeared to be a ceremonial center or important temple building of a civilization far more advanced than that of the builders of Vilcabamba the Old. The circular buildings, more difficult to construct than rectangular structures, were vastly superior to anything I had seen in the *montañas* of southern Peru. If the ruins did belong to the Chachapoyas civilization, then they certainly had a culture far higher than that of the Incas during the same period.

11 · Gateway to El Dorado

July 7, 1966. El Dorado I, Second Phase

I SPENT THREE WEEKS in Lima preparing our new expedition. Letters and telegrams were dispatched to the interior arranging for guides, porters, lodgings, dugout canoes, crew and other basic needs of an Amazonian expedition. Soon word came back from Juanjuí that the expedition was eagerly awaited and that it would have official support. Messages had been sent up river to all the ports and the local radio station had announced our plans.

Fortunately, I had come into possession of Father Bernardino Izaguirre's account of the Franciscan missionary work in the eastern jungles of Peru, compiled in 1619–21. I had found a later edition of the series, published in Lima in 1923, which included the travels of missionaries during the years 1781–91. Father Álvarez de Villanueva's exploits in the greater Pajatén region was of particular interest. Illustrated with plates and maps, it gave me an insight into the region in which I was interested.

In the month of September, 1788, the Father, in company with three other friars, departed from Valle, a small settlement of 376 inhabitants located on the Huallaga River, and traveled overland to "The Pueblo of the Pajatén Valley," a journey of sixteen leagues which they made in three days. The missionary spoke of crossing the Apisoncho River. He mentions having forded other rivers that do not appear on modern maps. On September 23, he made the preliminary arrangements for the evacuation of 358 residents of Pajatén and other villages in the immediate area, perhaps due to an epidemic of yellow fever. A new village was founded at the mouth of the Huayabamba and named Pachiza.

Guided by these old records, I intended to probe the area known to the Fathers in search of archaeological remains, both colonial and pre-Columbian. Fabrics used by the Hivitos, Indian inhabitants of the Huallaga and its upper tributaries, carried familiar designs—the Greek "T" or key, all of which had been observed on pottery fragments and carvings at the Gran Pajatén ruins. Did this suggest a link with the ancient ornamentation of the Chachapoyas

144

culture? The archaeologist-anthropologist Henry Reichlen, familiar with this culture from his studies in the area, had shown great interest in my work and believed that the area between the Gran Pajatén ruins and Chachapoyas was archaeologically rich and encouraged me to carry on my explorations. Vidal Senéze had hinted at this from his botanical explorations of Rodriquez de Mendoza and the upper Huambo River (a tributary of the Huayabamba) in 1876–77. He reported ruins at Cochamal, Totora, Omia, Anayac and Calca, none of which were known to archaeology.

While the Franciscans had used an old missionary road—now overgrown and lost—I planned to travel by means of the rivers, those highways of the jungle so well liked by the Incas during their lowland probes.

We arrived at Juanjuí, situated on the Huallaga River, and hired a 36-foot boat cut out of *agerano* wood, painted a vivid red. Fitted with a 35-hp outboard motor, it was capable of moving up river against the current at about ten miles per hour, twenty-five miles per hour down current loaded with two and a half tons of cargo, or twenty passengers. With a draft of only two feet when loaded, six inches with a small crew, it was just what we needed to take us as far up river as possible.

The following morning we loaded our gear aboard and moved slowly out past groups of women who had come down to the beach to fill their clay pots with fresh water—which are carried back to the household atop their heads with admirable grace and charm. Occasionally, a balsa raft piled high with green bananas would float past on its way to Iquitos, the crews working poles and paddles to keep them midstream. A fifteen-day journey during the rainy season when the Huallaga is in flood, the men travel by day and night, living and sleeping on board. These huge craft, some measuring 40 by 50 feet, are made from 30 or 40 logs (called *topas*) cut from balsa trees, and carry up to four tons of cargo. An hour later we reached the port of Pachiza, where we picked up a crewman, the lieutenant mayor of the village. Pachiza is a hot, sleepy village of 500 inhabitants built on the banks of the Huayabamba. Their most treasured possessions are the relics of the abandoned missions which have been entrusted to the care of the mayor in perpetuity. These include beautiful embroidered vestments, religious volumes, bells, chalices and a magnificent golden monstrance weighing ten pounds. Unfortunately the church buildings are in ruins.

Continuing up river past the point where the shallow Apisoncho empties into the Huayabamba, we soon came to the first *pongo*, or dangerous ford, where we pulled up to the rocky banks and worked the dugout with ropes over the rapids. We then journeyed to 2 de Mayo, a tiny village of bamboo huts thatched with grass, where we added to our crew. Continuing on we entered the smaller Jelache River. From the outside, the jungle is beautiful; flowering trees dip down to the water's edge, lending a fragrant aroma to the sweet air. Great flocks of parrots sweep overhead, squawking loudly as they go. Our speed supplied a cooling breeze that cut the heat of a burning sun. In many places where the water is shallow we were forced to move carefully over the rocky bottom so as not to damage our propeller. A pointer stood at the bow, looking for shoals. At times we had to use long poles to propel the boat; sometimes we had to take to the water, manhandling the dugout over the rocky, sandy bottom. Before the sun went down we put in at Bendición, a flat pampa below the white sandstone cliffs of Yansenacha. We were given shelter in the hut of a local pioneer farmer who makes a living growing bananas, the major product of these parts. A hectare (2.5 acres) supports 50 to 60 trees. Our host owns ten hectares, 500 to 600 trees, which earns him about 6,000 soles annually when sold at Juanjuí. Bananas bring spending money for salt, cartridges and material for clothing. Corn, sugarcane, yucca, lemons, oranges, avocados and coffee are locally grown. There are also plenty of fish and wild game.

At dawn the men slipped into swimming trunks and went down to the river to fish. Someone lobbed a quarter stick of dynamite into the quiet water. After a muffled explosion a dozen three-pounders, floating belly-up, were hauled in for breakfast. Others used barbasco to poison smaller fish. Our catch cleaned, placed in green banana leaves and thrown into the fire with long, red bananas made delicious fare, delicate and tasty.

At eight o'clock we launched our dugout and moved on. The Jelache averages 200 feet in width hereabouts, but it narrows quickly up river, and we had to work our way slowly with poles over the rushing rapids. Stately palm trees and flowering trees of all kinds line the shore. Great spreading trees thick with epiphytes send aerial roots cascading down like frozen waterfalls through which we cut with machete. Broad-leafed aquatic vegetation float on the water. Four hours later we beached our boat. My altimeter read 1,350 feet above sea level—higher than the Huallaga. Eddies of warm air swirl down from the valley, born in the hot jungles on all sides. We got out and cut our way over an old trail for a quarter of an hour coming to a tiny hut surrounded by banana plants. No one was home, but we went inside knowing we were welcome.

We were seven, including Douglas and myself, and I felt this was as good a time as any to start a conversation with the crew. Our destination was a group of colonial ruins an hour away—the abandoned Pueblo of Pajatén. I spread my map on the dirt floor and the men huddled around. The man from 2 de Mayo had been to the ruins, the only one I had ever spoken to who had. According to my records three pueblos had been abandoned in the region. Pajatén, Tubaibal and Huambo. The first two are known to a few and don't offer much in the way of ruins. Huambo is unknown. I inquired about other ruins. The man from 2 de Mayo, a short, wiry fellow in his early forties, with a reputation for knowing the jungle interior, told us that there are ruins at a place called Golondrina, a towering forested height which we had caught sight of from the river.

There are also rumors of ruins up the Huambo River, northwest of us. But I was quickly told that no man would go into that country. Totally unexplored, known for its giant boas, black panthers, and Hivitos Indians, it is dangerous country. The Satalaya Ruca, not so feared, inhabit the neighboring valley of Sapo. A hostile people, the Hivitos are uncivilized and maintain their isolation by the use of the deadly blowgun. The blowgun (*pucuna*) is a feared jungle weapon which, in expert hands, is accurate and deadly. The Hivitos use poisoned darts (*virotes*) fabricated from palm shoots. The poison is made from a combination of plants. Mirare, curare or ramón (family *Strichnos*), is boiled for twenty-four hours then combined with Pani (*Cocculus toxicoferus*), also boiled for twenty-four hours. From this comes a paste in which the darts are dipped. The Yaguas or Orejones of the lower Amazonian jungles use this same mixture, which can kill a bull.

There was no question that we had to call off any quest into the Hivitos territory. Without men it would be hopeless. Remembering what Henry Reichlen had told me in Lima, I decided to fly to Mendoza and work down into the Huambo River from the uplands, thereby avoiding Hivitos country, an old trick used by Malcolm Burke, another jungle explorer and good friend. "Get up to the high country and work down," he had advised.

After cleaning up our mess, we took to a smaller dugout, canoe-poling our way across the Jelache and up river to the Pajatén tributary, where we beached our boat. We transferred the gear to our backs and cut through the verdant jungle. An hour's pace brought us to the junction of the Ismayacu and Calcache streams that empty into the small Pajatén and here we set up camp at the river's edge.

With daylight we were in the jungle, cutting a path to the Pajatén ruins, ten minutes to the west. It was July 11, exactly two years to the day that we first cut into the Vilcabamba ruins.

The ruins are approached by a six-foot-wide road that goes past the city wall and a cluster of circular constructions made from river stone. Inside, the colonial ruins aren't much to look at. It seemed to me that the city had been burned at one time. A large rectangular plaza, measuring approximately 165 feet with an elevated platform and stairway, makes up the main architectural remain. It is annexed to a long building of stone and adobe some 90 feet long by 26 feet wide, probably the convent. Some distance away we found another ruined plaza, measuring about 57 by 110 feet. The houses were long since gone and nothing more remained of them than clumps of refuse. The old pueblo probably originally covered a square block at its height. The place was infested with *isula*, a huge black ant nearly an inch long whose bite is most painful; *otorongo machaco*, a yellow-and-black-spotted snake whose sting results in death; the deadly jergon; and the *loro machaco*, an emerald-green snake, perhaps the deadliest of the jungle, that lives in the trees and vines. Our man from Juanjuí told of the *mantoña* or *madre del monte* (mother of the jungle) which grows to unbelievable lengths. Related to the boa constrictor, this huge reptile is believed to possess electrical properties (in ancient times it symbolized the life forces and was related to the sun) and draws objects to it like a magnet. Whenever seen it throws fear into all. Admitting that the place did have a mysterious atmosphere—and since there wasn't much in the way of ruins—we dropped back to the river, packed up and took to the trail. Back in the long dugout, we drifted silently downstream without bothering to start the motor, using poles to keep away from the rocks. At five o'clock we were back at Bendición.

Suppertime brought piles of bananas—boiled, roasted and fried—gourds of fish soup and broiled, white fish covered with salt and freshly ground pepper. Sitting around the fire, our faces aglow in the blaze of light, I asked about the roads we had seen at the Pajatén ruins. Measuring on the average 6 to 12 feet in width, I argued that they ran up to the Gran Pajatén ruins. The man from 2 de Mayo agreed and offered to make the trip, saying we could do it in two days. But I explained that there was no time, because I wanted to enter the Huambo territory. At that point, the owner of the house told of having seen an old road across the Jelache. He was hesitant to take us, but a gift from our stores and a double wage for his troubles persuaded him to guide us the next morning. I had heard about this strange jungle road and I wanted to investigate.

The following morning we set out through the jungles, hacking the thickets, until we came upon the road. Six feet wide, built of large stones, it runs north and south. Skirting along the ridges above the floor of the jungle, it is also the lowest pre-Columbian road I have ever found—averaging 1,200 to 1,500 feet altitude. This is proof that the ancients did indeed build a jungle road system. We followed it some distance and came to the junction of the Huayabamba and Jelache. Did the old builders take to the river at this point? Possibly, but I conjectured that it continued on in the direction of the Huambo and the uplands, the southern extention running on up to Gran Pajatén and felt we must fly to Mendoza and look for it.

July 13, 1966

We caught the first plane for Chachapoyas and soon passed over the Blue Mountains of the cordillera. Chachapoyas lies at 7,400 feet above sea level on a high, windy plateau cut by deep river gorges. Its history goes back to 1538 when it was founded by Captain Mariscal Alonso de Alvarado, under the name of San Juan de la Frontera do los Chachapoyas. During Spanish colonial days its gold and silver mines and fertile agricultural lands made it one of His Majesty's richest possessions in the Indies, but when Spain gave up Peru and the missions were abandoned, it fell into decline. Only recently has it begun to boom again with the building of roads connecting it with Cajamarca and Chiclayo. Regularly scheduled airline service has helped to open up commerce, which was neglected for so long. Once linked with the marginal highway and the lower jungle, it will again become a commercial center since it lies at the crossroads between east and west.

Some of the modern buildings seem out of place among the older structures, but Chachapoyas has lost none of its colonial charm: donkeys laden with kindling and sacks of corn or barley trot down its old streets, church bells ring out under an electric blue sky and women dressed in blue and white shawls hurry to answer the call of benediction. I found it the friendliest town of Peru. Perhaps this is because of its proximity to the *montaña* and jungled plains. Peru is really four worlds—coast, sierra, puna and jungle— each with its own distinctive geographical, social and cultural characteristics. The jungle is a special world of its own, a sunny region of happy, industrious citizens who blend the best of the old and the new of this ancient land. Unlike the austere-tempered highlanders, the jungle people are easy-going.

Soon after checking into a local hotel, I went out to meet Carlos Gates, editor of a weekly newspaper, *The Voice of the Amazon,* head of a credit co-op, Catholic priest and amateur archaeologist, and in his own right, an authority on Amazonian cultures who possesses an excellent collection of pottery fragments. We spent the next two days pouring over maps and looking up old documents in the archives.

When the weather allowed, Douglas and I flew to Mendoza, the capital of the province, situated in a lush valley at 5,200 feet. Dotted with herds of livestock, stretches of pineapples, tobacco, cocoa and avocados, groves of orange, lime and lemon trees, it is the heart of eleven tiny villages separated from the rest of the country by high, jungle-covered mountains that reach up ten, eleven thousand feet. Shackled by lack of roads, these communities remain isolated and apart from the rest of Peru. Mendoza is especially known for its large number of tall, blond, Aryan-looking people. If they are the descendants of the Chachapoyas people, it would be proof of the Inca claim that these people were light-skinned.

The problem of finding cargo-bearers hadn't been solved, but the word soon flashed around town that an expedition had arrived. Late the same afternoon, a well-muscled man, about thirty years of age, short, with black wavy hair, bronze skin, humorous brown eyes and a laughing smile, showed up at the hotel with a letter of reference introducing himself as Segundo Honorio Grandez Zumaeta. He was of cheery disposition, tempered with intelligence and wit; I liked him immediately. An expert hunter and agriculturalist, he knew the province well, so I gave him a job. From that time on, he accompanied me on all my El Dorado Expeditions.

The next morning we moved slowly through town with our pack animals, taking the trail toward the Huambo River. Once on the outskirts, we traveled past a high series of white cliffs dotted with caves. Scanning them with my binoculars I found many of these openings walled over with stone, some with doorways. They were ancient tombs. At a place called Mito we found a way up to a huge cave about 60 feet high and 30 yards or so in depth. At the entrance we examined an ancient adobe and stone burial tomb painted a vivid red and white. Some 15 feet high, it contained six rooms, long emptied of their contents. We picked up two or three bags of ceramic fragments for our collection, ducking hordes of bats that flitted in and out of the cave opening.

We journeyed on along the rocky trail past quaint little log cabins that looked like tiny Swiss chalets, the first I had ever seen in Peru. The people here speak a singsong Spanish—a jungle dialect common to the region. Two days later we entered Omia, where we spent the night in the home of Demetrio Chavez, mayor of the sleepy village sheltered in the folds of the jungled hills. The next day we explored some stone ruins and moved on into the interior. A five-hour ascent and we arrived at Yanayaco, a small farm located in an amphitheater-like depression surrounded by high cliffs.

At daybreak we began our explorations. We climbed a high pampa where we examined some stone ruins. The whole area abounded with stone terraces and ancient constructions, both rectangular and the familiar circular style common to the region. The stonework was rough, but we found large Vilca-type stones elevated on platforms.

Days later we found ourselves in the Huambo River area at a settlement known as Achamal. The hills produced some ruins, mostly terraces, so we dropped down into the Huambo River Valley with a parade of porters. We found the road we were looking for some two days down river, at 3,500 feet. Scaling the forests and jungles of the southern bank of the river we found circular and rectangular constructions as far up as 6,000 feet. The ruins went on in seemingly inexhaustable numbers. We explored continually, until pounding rains and shortage of food made us give up. However, we learned that the road we had encountered in the lower Jelache-Huallaga river valleys did run up past these extensive ruins. On the return journey, we crossed the river and discovered that the northern bank was staircased with ruins and agricultural terraces, indicating that the whole river valley might have once been heavily settled.

Most important, we learned that the road went farther on in the direction of Laurel. Rather than hacking our way through unknown country— dangerous in this snake-infested region, and time-consuming—we decided to take another route which would bring us directly to Laurel in two days.

Back at Achamal we marked the maps, giving the name Hivitos to the settlement we had found, and registered it with the lieutenant governor (who had served as head porter). We paid off the men and waited for the sun to come out to dry off the muddy trails. The next day we decided to return to Omia via Milpuc, a small community in a fairyland setting of blue mountain lagoons, green meadows dotted with fragrant wildflowers, orange groves and flowering trees.

Hiring two porters at Omia, we set off with one mule in the direction of Laurel under a falling mist that turned the trail into a muddy quagmire. We camped at Curipampa and the next morning pushed on up over a 7,500-foot crest onto an ancient stone road that leads down into the jungle depths. Access is guarded by a fortress, long in ruins. We continued over a sandy waste until the tall trees closed above us shutting out the sky. We trudged on until darkness overtook us and camped.

At daylight we pushed on through the primitive undergrowth, our clothes soaked from perspiration and the wet leaves and vines. When we came to the edge of Laurel we made camp in an old lean-to used by hunters, at a place called Lajas.

That night the men dined on roasted *maguizapa,* a large black monkey weighing thirty pounds, which they had shot earlier in the day. I settled for boiled *maguncho,* a foot-long banana, yucca bread and wild turkey. Afterward I curled up inside my sleeping bag before the warm fire, listening to the rain fall upon our lean-to and to the cacophonous sounds of jungle life, and fell into a dreamless sleep.

At first light we pushed on into the dense vegetation, cutting a path as we went. For two hours we made our way through a dense forest of tall timber—cedar, *lapuna* and *higrones* that tower up nearly 200 feet, splashed with shafts of light and brilliant wildflowers, and came out onto a grassy pampa at 6,100 feet, surrounded by thick jungle and high cliffs. A rickety shack had been built on an elevated section of the swampy plain as a shelter for woodsmen—this was to be our base camp for the next five days. The afternoon's exploration revealed the pampa to be a central plaza with four entrances. Seven hills, marked by mounds of stone, were connected by a road some ten feet wide with a stone wall measuring three feet in height. The branch roads ran off into the jungle at four points of the compass. We spent the remainder of the day taking measurements and photographs.

The next morning we followed one of the roads to a cluster of stone ruins hidden away in the jungle, composed mostly of rectangular constructions. Pushing on under the persistent screeching of bright papagayos, whose iridescent plumage lent a splash of color to the dark woods, we came to scattered walls and a large series of terraces. Working our way up to the crest of the hill, we found a complex of circular buildings. As soon as we got inside the ruins, hundreds of red-and-black *cotomono* monkeys swept over our heads in waves, frightened by our cutting blades. For three days we explored this ancient city, probing high into the forested mountains until we were stopped by a high series of limestone cliffs. Thunder showers hampered our work and we had to return to the base camp. When the weather cleared again, we followed the other roads which led us to old stone ruins, topped by centuries of decaying vegetable matter. Who built this ancient city? The

Incas? The Chachapoyans? The Chancas? These and other questions could only be answered when I returned to examine the site more carefully. For the moment we were satisfied with having claimed another metropolis from the jungle wastes. We named it Monte Laurel.

August 6, 1966

The sky was clear and we set out to return to Omia. We appeared out of the damp, clinging rain forest into the open air with a tremendous sense of freedom. It was like coming out of a hole in the ground. Gone were the black shadows, the semi-darkness of the dull jungle. We were enveloped by a kaleidoscope of color: vivid green palms, purple and red and yellow blooms of all kinds.

The weather favored our explorations and justified a trek over the highlands between Omia ond Yanayaco. After exploring agricultural terraces and ruins at Cortadera, we struck out for the heights and following the backbones of the ridges, went from peak to peak, uncovering ten little temple layouts dominating the crests—circular buildings on platforms approached by stairways. Several large, conical-shaped jars of stone, weighing approximately twenty-five pounds, dyed brick-red, were photographed. At Chontapampa, we investigated numerous cave-like dwellings and subterranean tombs. Back at Yanayaco, we walked to a hill known as Estoraque, where we found a rather extensive series of circular and ovaloid ruins built into the sides of the hills. We penetrated the forested heights and seeing that the ruins stretched on endlessly, gave up the quest for lack of porters. It was too much territory to explore in one season. Besides, we kept hearing about a place called Purun Llacta which was on the road to Cheto. Muleteers carrying cargo from the lowlands said that "well-built ruins" had been observed along the sides of the trail, but no one ever went inside for fear of the forest spirits.

At Cochomal, a beautiful city-type remain known as Carbon Pata was found at the top of a mountain overlooking the village. Circular buildings of two and three levels stood protected by imposing stone walls. The largest buildings measured 35 feet in diameter and 25 feet in height. We explored many caves within the city which suggested that the ancient builders may have been a cave sect. Curious stone carvings in the form of a human phallus were found in the ruins. Phallus carvings are found in the Mayan horizon and are represented by a sun-serpent in the Tiahuanaco culture.

From there we tramped to Huamanpata over an ancient road, past a large lake to the jungled pampas of Arenal, where we were surprised to find an extensive city of stone which we named Monte Arenal. Some of the rectangular constructions measured 60 feet in length, and there were a large number of circular structures with niches averaging about 20 feet in diameter. Though Arenal gave promise of additional ruins, we cut our search short because of the weather and the shortage of cargo-bearers and cutters, and flew back to Chachapoyas.

Our explorations had uncovered a vast, new archaeological zone and stone roads that penetrated deep into the jungle interior toward the Ecuadorian frontier and the upper watershed of the Amazon River. There could be no question that ancient peoples had inhabited these regions in large numbers—a fact which would, I believed, alter current ideas about ancient man having occupied the *montaña*.

August 22, 1966

Chachapoyas received the news of our jungle penetration with great excitement. During our two days there we re-outfitted the expedition (our clothes were badly torn, our boots barely holding together), purchased provisions, carefully packaged the film for flight to Lima and attended to correspondence. A local student of archaeology, Dr. Humberto Arce Burga, who had accompanied General Langlois' explorations some years before, invited me to his home where I examined his collection of antiquities. One particular piece caught my eye—a stone carving with twin figures very similar in design to those at Gran Pajatén. (Plate 14.) He said a farmer from Mito had found it on the trail, dragged it to town and given it to him for his collection.

[PLATE 14] *Twin figure with phallic design, common motif of the Chachapoyas civilization. Stone slab stands about three feet in height. (Courtesy Dr. Humberto Arce, Chachapoyas.)*

Victor Zubiate, the local archaeological inspector, also showed me a stone carving picked up from La Jalca, a small village to the south. The characteristics were Pajatén-style. (Plate 15.) There was no doubt that there existed a link between the ruins of Chachapoyas and those farther to the south in Pajatén country. I was certain that there were many unreported ruins in the area. According to Middendorf, Chachapoyas was a word from the Aymara language meaning "cloud people." We had proven that the lower jungles had been inhabited by these people at one time in history. And roads ran up to the uplands. Inca Tupac Yupanqui recorded that these people lived in the upper heights. I decided to start exploring the towering peaks of the cordillera.

We took a truck to Pipos, at the end of the dirt road, then walked to Cheto, 6,700 feet, and went on in the face of a cold wind to Huacapampa, a tiny pueblo of eighteen inhabitants. Seven or eight houses made up the community. Livestock—cattle, horses, mules, sheep, pigs and poultry—grazed on a small, grassy square. We were told that the surrounding *monte viejo* (old forest) was known to contain ruins of the ancients, but was enchanted. A half dozen sites in the Cheto-Huacapampa zone and in the neighboring village of Soloco were vaguely known to the populace. None had been studied to my knowledge. What wasn't known was the existence of at least thirty-five

[PLATE 15] *Stone figure from La Jalca ruins. Note inverted "T" at crown and beard similar to those of Egyptian pharaohs, long ears and foliated nose. (Courtesy Victor Zubiate, Chachapoyas.)*

or forty hills, higher up the trail. These hills had names but were strictly taboo. Here lived the spirits of the deceased, who inhabited the *iglesias* (churches). When darkness fell over the villages, people stayed at home and listened to the spirits ringing bells or blowing conch shells.

When the sun rose, we set out on a path through the undergrowth. Almost immediately we hit upon the first ruins—circular and rectangular constructions, they were the best I had seen during the expedition. The place was called Mito. An hour later we came to the forests of Purun Llacta. We had been tramping over a stone stairway which was walled in on either side. I stepped over the stone construction and cut into the thickets, and found myself standing next to a high wall of white stone. Following it I came out to a large plaza, surrounded on all sides by big buildings. We moved farther along to a large rectangular building some 55 feet long, 30 feet wide and 8 feet tall, graced with windows and annexed to an oval structure with a large stone doorway. Taking a long stairway up a hill for 300 yards, we came to an elevated and platformed ovaloid structure 130 feet in length. Two circular structures, the largest 24 feet in diameter, were built on top. They were corniced like the Gran Pajatén buildings, 90 miles to the south. A third building, rectangular with windows, was at the far end. Dropping down a long stairway past scattered remains, we reached a two-storied building—a beautiful structure of white limestone blocks about 36 feet long with a medial molding running around it. Encouraged by these finds, we explored the surrounding hills and found the whole area littered with broken remains of very sophisticated architecture of circular, ovaloid and rectangular design. Numerous plazas and squares came to light, including many curved terraced levels with stones tenoned in the walls. Situated at the crests of the 8,000-foot hills, all the groups were linked by inter-city roads and avenues, showing that it was an urban center of large size. Climbing the highest peak over a broken stairway, I took out my powerful telescope and studied the hills beyond. They were littered with ancient terraces that worked their way up to the summits. Often a building would show through the vegetation, glimmering white in the wintry sun that burned above our heads.

Back at Huacapampa we told the townsfolk about the ruins. They had no idea that they were so extensive, and talked excitedly in their musical Amazonian accent about the enchantments, amazed that we were not afraid. Next morning a woodsman and hunter from Dauguas showed up. He agreed to take us to a big *iglesia* on the Soloco side of the mountain, not known to the men from Huacapampa.

We climbed the long, difficult trail up over the mountain and dropped down to Soloco, an out-of-the-way village of tiled houses with a large plaza and church. The mayor lodged and fed us and the following day we hurriedly climbed over an ancient road past terraces and old ruins to the upper crests and cut a trail to the right. The man from Dauguas pointed to a long wall and began clearing away the green vegetation with his machete, revealing excellent stonework. With more cutting and searching we soon found the area to be rich with circular buildings. We then pushed up into the sharp rattan burrs, cleaving away with our blades. For hours we climbed to an altitude of approximately 10,000 feet, passing all the while a continuous string of circular buildings of all sizes and shapes looming up out of the dark woods like haunted castles. On one trail a group of tall buildings reached far above our heads and we spent the rest of the afternoon making a plan of it for the records. It was a ninety-by-seventy-foot ribbon-shaped platform group with twelve circular houses on the upper level, the largest measuring 40 feet in diameter, niched and tenoned with stones, none of which were carved, however. Afterward, we hiked back to Soloco.

For several more days we explored this ancient sanctuary that stretched for many miles across the mountains. Sometimes we walked over grasslands that forested blue lakes and climbed up crests only to find more ruins. The numerous groups, each a little city in itself, revealed this to be a great metropolis, perhaps the largest in South America. A year later when we continued our explorations of the city in the forested pampas of Olia and Tinas, a virgin jungle area around the 6,000-foot level, several days' journey over an ancient stone road with a cut stairway that runs nearly a half mile over the mountain summits, we found additional ruins. Checking our findings carefully with engineers in Chachapoyas, the size of the colossus was determined to be some 60 square miles—70,000 acres of continuous ruins. Its influence must have been felt over a much larger area that spread far down into the lower jungles. The architecture reflected a high civilization with advanced technical skills. The buildings were fairly well-worked, though the ornamentation was not as elaborate as that of the Gran Pajatén ruins. We did not have time to clear the ruins, partly because of their immense size, partly because they were covered by centuries of rotting vegetation which, I conjectured, hid many designs. We did find evidence of stone carvings, suggesting that the better part of the city was beneath our feet. The rough walls of some of the buildings had been covered by lime plaster at one time, similar to the technique employed by the Mayas.

Because of the large size of the jungle metropolis and the many, many sites (some groups being larger than the whole of Gran Pajatén), some named, others not, we christened the city Monte Peruvia, for it had no name of its own. I theorized that this area was probably a capital city of the Chachapoyas culture, certainly one of the seven cities conquered by Tupac Yupanqui.

September 3, 1966

A few days later we went to Shipasbamba, a small, lonely community north of Chachapoyas in the direction of the Ecuadorian frontier. The townspeople helped us explore the neighboring hills, in which many ruins and roads were found, though inferior in quality to those with which we were previously familiar. Nevertheless, we did find new research material.

A copy of an old manuscript in the Municipal Archives (No. 109), prepared by Judge Juan De La Cruz Anguilar, of His Majesty's City of Kings, Chachapoyas, mentions the traditions and folklore of the area. He made mention of an ancient city, Pueblo de Tiapollo, located somewhere off in the jungle interior at a site known as Villunca, beyond the gorge of Alba. We did search this area and found ruins above Lake Pomacocha; rectangular, 36-foot-diameter buildings and many terraces broken by time and the jungle, which appeared to be the outer works of this fabled lost city.

According to the legend, a snake was hatched from an egg laid by a chicken or condor (or a cock). The serpent grew feathers and had the power to kill with its eyes. Its head was shaped like that of a lion and water poured out of its mouth. Sometimes this mythological creature is likened to *solpemachaco*, a coiled, feathered reptile that inhabits subterranean places, especially caves, and falls upon intruders, coiling about them like a net. It is believed to have seven heads. The mythological account says that the serpent finally flew away to the west over the highlands of Cajamarca and Santiago de Chuco where it was killed by a ray from the sun, and fell to the "pampa of serpents."

It is very interesting to note that the word *tiapollo* or *tiapolo* is a Polynesian word for "devil-god." The idea of the flying snake is very similar to the basilisk or cockatrice of the Middle Ages of Europe, a deadly creature incubated by a toad (the egg also came from a cock), which had a long tail, flew on wings and killed with its eyes. Inca mythology told of Anti-Viracocha, the dragon-serpent or Lord of the Andes, a feared creature of darkness that held the power of life and death over the people. The Mochicas often pictured this terrible reptile in their mythological art, which, in many ways, was similar to the Aztec interpretation of Quetzalcoatl. Quetzalcoatl was the Lord of Light and Wind, a dragon-headed serpent with feathers, often pictured as a coiled rattlesnake with the mouth shaped like a trumpet, a divine creature who was the god of fertility.

I had explored the highlands south of Cajamarca some time before at an old temple site called Yaume, near Santiago de Chuco, where I uncovered carved stone heads and a huge monolith some eight and a half feet in length and weighing over a ton. A black basalt block, originally painted red and white, showed two very well-carved double-headed serpents. The heads were dragon-like, with characteristics of a dog or fox, a trumpet-shaped mouth with protruding tongue, feline ears, weeping eyes and a tail-rattle. It was pictured with solar designs and bars in place of feathers, a common feature on portraits of the Mexican Huizilopochtli, and suggested a Tiahuanaco or Mochica origin. This unusual sculpture appeared to me to be a Peruvian interpretation of a feathered serpent deity. (Plate 16.) The Incas often pictured Viracocha, whom they inherited from pre-Inca cultures, as a divine personage with arm raised in salute to the Sun. He always carried a book and staff and was accompanied during his travels by a fox, a serpent and a lion.

[PLATE 16] *Stone monolith photographed by the author in the Santiago de Chuco area. Weighing over a ton and measuring eight and a half feet in length, stone represents double-headed serpent.*

He was Lord of Light, Wind and Rain, and, like Quetzalcoatl, wore a long, flowing beard. His skin was white, and he was reputed to be foreign to Peruvian shores.

The ancient chronicle also referred to a small village to the south known as Santo Tomás. We drove down and talked with the parish priest who enlightened us still more concerning this legend. The story is mentioned in the writings of Torres Saldmando in his *Los Antiguos Jesuítas del Perú* and in *Vida de Santo Toribio*, written by Father García Irogoyen. It seems that a long time ago a very holy man named Didimo came to the peoples of these parts in the first century of the Christian era. He taught among the people who were known as the tribes of Calinapos de Quillay. After this he sailed away over the ocean. During the colonial epoch around 1597, St. Toribio Alonso de Mogrovejo awakened the spirit of these teachings in the people, which were in many ways similar to the Christian message. He found a huge rock with the foot and knee-prints of Didimo in the old city of Quillay and brought it to the present village of Santo Tomás where it exists today under the altar of the church. With the aid of the priest we did in fact find a stone buried under the church answering this description and explored the heights coming across many ruined cities west of the village of Yeso, though we did not identify the legendary city. We also came across a small carved head with aquiline nose and flowing beard reported to be from the ruins of Kuelap. St. Toribio, and many other missionaries, attempted to link the New World cultures with those of Israel, saying St. Thomas had come to America. These legends purport that an ancient teacher going back to the first century of the Christian era or earlier taught in the Amazon, was bearded and fair-skinned and had much in common with the legendary figure known as Viracocha among the Incas and pre-Inca peoples of southern Peru. Was there a connection? No scientific evidence is available.

The cyclopean monument of Kuelap, the supposed capital of an ancient culture that goes back 1,000 years or more, is described by Mateo Paz Soldan in the work published in Paris in 1862. The notes of Juan Crisóstomo Nieto, who came across the ancient site in 1843 (it was then called Quelap or

Quelape), record a tremendous structure of concentric walls towering nearly 60 feet in height. In my estimation it is far more impressive than the famous fortress of Sacsayhuaman at Cuzco. Situated at around 9,400 feet on the top of a high prominence above the valley floor, its gigantic walls stretch for 700 yards. It is one of the most imposing relics of ancient man and assuredly one of the great wonders of the world. (Plate 17.) Its massive white stones were originally described as soaring up 150 feet(?) high, long since fallen, and etched with fine carvings of serpents and geometric figures, many having been defaced over the years. Access is gained through various high doorways which lead to inner sepulchers, crypts and circular towers. The architecture at Kuelap is similar to that of Monte Peruvia and Gran Pajatén on the other side of the valley to the east.

In the middle of September the rains came in force and I returned to Lima for a long overdue rest hoping to return to the field during the second dry season, two months away. The Chachapoyas explorations were far from completed. I had not as yet identified the principal lost cities of the Chachapoyas Kingdom, those great cities stormed by Tupac Yupanqui and his son Huayna Capac. On the other hand, we had located the remains of an important upper Amazon people, which would undoubtedly prove to be that of the Chachapoyas, conquered by the Incas in the fifteenth century. Most scientists doubted that the jungles, high or low, could have been the home of a culture as advanced as those of the coast and sierra. My findings were solid arguments to the contrary: The existence of the metropolis of Monte Peruvia was evidence of a population center of considerable size in the *montaña*, with vast agricultural settlements and access roads spreading into the lower zones. This finding suggested that a very advanced people (their monumental buildings rivaled anything I had ever seen on the coast or highlands) had made the high jungle their home.

[PLATE 17] *The monument of Kuelap. Walls tower upward of 60 feet in height.*

12 · Lost Cities of the Chachapoyas Kingdom

November 14, 1966. El Dorado II

WE LANDED at the Chachapoyas airport fully prepared to move higher up to the summits and the upland jungles (according to my new theory this was the best place to look for the remains of the Chacha people). At sunup we drove to Magdalena, and thence to the Hacienda Calpilon by mule, where we spent the night. The next morning we moved up into the dirty-green-and-brown covered forests, two machete men clearing the way. An hour later we came upon some colonial ruins (probably a mission). Two hours later, at 8,900 feet, we approached the first pre-Columbian remains—typical circular buildings that ran to the crests of the hills. I sent six men off with Douglas. Two of his men later reported having seen carvings in the shape of birds and zigzag lines on the façades of some upper buildings near the 10,000-foot level. I carried on with my own cutters and with the owner of the hacienda, Don José Ruiz Tenorio, 72 years of age, who had agreed to accompany our expedition. We explored a number of ruins which showed the area had been heavily populated in ancient times.

The following day we started exploring the upper green forests above the village of Montevideo. The townspeople had told us before leaving that the hilltops were enchanted (nobody would go up with us), and that they believed we would find ruins. They told us that the only ruins previously visited by the local archaeological inspector and other visitors were those lower down. No one had ever gone higher up. That was good news. I was hoping to find a building with a façade on the order of Gran Pajatén—some definite link with those ruins far to the south.

Making our way through poppy-studded fields and prickly growth we soon entered the forest. At first I wasn't impressed with the small walls—badly overgrown and broken—and prepared myself for a disappointment.

At 9,200 feet, however, we came to a spot known as Monja Tranca. What I saw amazed me—a big circular building with carefully structured fretwork. And there were many more such buildings. Wanting to see how far they extended, we tramped along through the sharp thorns and thick vegetation for many hours. There seemed to be no end to them. In all, we explored thirteen different sites, all containing important ruins; old sites with old names—Pilca Cunga, Moras, Olan, Cruz Pata, Inga Pirca, Monja Tranca, Rumichaca, Monja, Queshol, Balconcito, Shucsho, Santa Cruz, Vecerro, Pucapirco and many, many others—hundreds of finely-built structures with marvelous ornamentation. I ran my trembling hand over intricate designs that were laborously put together from many individual stones like pieces of a mosaic—diamond patterns, stepped-fret, zigzag, double zigzag. (Plates 18, 19.) These were well-worked buildings, constructed with great care, an ancient city of white stone hidden away for centuries in the cloud-covered forests and jungles. The exterior walls were graced by medial moldings that jutted out nearly two and a half feet. Here were the kind of ruins I had been looking for; the first genuine link with the Gran Pajatén ruins. This find seemed to prove that the Pajatén ruins were no isolated phenomenon. Here was proof that the earlier ruins we had cut our way to a year before were part of a continuous chain of ruins strung out along the high forested peaks of Amazonia! And they fell into that territory occupied by the Chachapoyas Kingdom.

[PLATE 18] *The author before circular building with double zigzag design. Building is part of complex of Muyok Viejo in high jungled mountains south of Chachapoyas. (Andean Explorers Club photo.)*

[PLATE 19] *Diamond design on façade of jungle-topped building in Muyok Viejo.*

The next day we took a snaking mountain trail toward the village of San Pedro, a tiny hamlet of red tile roofs, tall eucalyptus trees and shy people. The local church had been built of stones taken from the surrounding ruins, as is often the case in these isolated villages. The elevated pueblo afforded a magnificent view of the lower Utcubamba River and the jungle highlands to the west. We rested a few minutes, exploring the golden brown and green hills with our binoculars, marking everything on our expedition map. Noticing a string of circular buildings, we studied the decorative motifs. Had the ancient Chachapoyas people used decoration for their residences? Or only for their temples? Or were these elaborate buildings used as tombs? It would require the work of archaeologists to solve this mystery—but that would have to wait. . . .

Inca Tupac Yupanqui, during his conquest of the territory, went to Cajamarca with 40,000 imperial troops and from there went down to Huacrachuco and made war against these vigorous people who dwelt in a high, dry mountainous country. The men wore headdresses topped by a deer's horn, and had put up many defensive strongholds to resist the Inca troops.

162

But the battle-wise Tupac Yupanqui split his forces into three parts and captured so many fortresses that the Huacrachucos were forced to surrender. The following dry season, for the area was very rainy, the Inca brought up an additional 20,000 soldiers in order to make war on the Chachas of the Chachapoyas Kingdom. It is said that he crossed the Marañón River (it will be remembered from his account mentioned earlier in the book) and stormed the first city. It was named Pias or the Questa of Pias, built atop a hill two and a half leagues in length. It was easily overcome since it was inhabited largely by old men, women and children, the Chacha troops having withdrawn to a stronger defensive fortification.

The ruins I had named Gran Pajatén would appear to fit the description of Pias, being located inland between the modern villages of Patáz and Pias. In 1961, agriculturists from Pias had penetrated for two days down a river valley (which the farmers from Patáz call Santa Cruz) and come upon funeral monuments containing mummies, textiles, ceramic vessels and other artifacts, and scattered ruins along the river valley. I knew from my aerial flights that the Gran Pajatén ruins, in addition to the principal cluster which received so much publicity, ran along the mountain summits in that direction, which offered fairly substantial proof that these old ruins were probably those first conquered by Tupac Yupanqui.

The old conqueror treated the people kindly, then marched north through the "bad gate" (a snowy pass now called Nevado de Cajamarquilla) near the modern pueblo of Bolívar, and then plunged into the jungle interior. After many days of fighting, he succeeded in taking the second city, Contur Marca.

The Inca took several highland fortifications to protect his flanks and rear (Chirmac Cassa is mentioned), then penetrated into the jungle interior again where he captured many lesser cities. He continued north and after a long, difficult struggle, captured a third large city called Cajamarquilla, eight leagues from Pias. This very large city later revolted and was reconquered by Huayna Capac. Tupac treated his prisoners very favorably, hoping to impress the Chachapoyas and bring about their surrender without undue fighting.

Some of the fortified cities did lay down their arms, but others continued to resist even stronger than before. The fourth large city to fall was Papamarca. The fifth (whose original name is not recorded in Garcilaso de la Vega's account of the Inca's conquest of Chachapoyas, though Father Valera called it Pumachaca) was re-named Raimipampa, because the Incas entered it during the Sun Festival of Raimi. It was eight leagues north of Papamarca.

Three leagues farther along, the Inca took the sixth city called Suta. The Seventh, the former capital of the Chachapoyas Kingdom, Llauantu (Levanto), capitulated without struggle. From there the Inca sent an army to Moyobamba. The Chancas, learning of the defeat of the Chachapoyas, also capitulated.

163

I was fairly certain that our explorations had succeeded in re-discovering two of these seven cities conquered by the Incas, the first and seventh. The Gran Pajatén ruins fit the description of Pias; the metropolis of Monte Peruvia seemed likely to be the ancient capital of the Chachapoyas, Llauantu. But I was not certain. The job now confronting us would be to find the missing five cities and to identify the present ruins definitely.

Hearing of ruins stretching far to the south toward La Jalca and of a road leading off toward the valley of Chilchos and the eastern jungles, we set out to explore. La Jalca, the original site of Spanish Chachapoyas before it was moved to Levanto and finally to its present site some miles to the north, is a populated village situated at 9,200 feet. I counted some three or four hundred houses, topped by thatch or red-orange tile. It reminded me in many ways of Spanish Vilcabamba, except for the very green fields and the surrounding *montaña*.

After asking around we were taken to the home of a local farmer where we discovered to our amazement a magnificent carved stone head tenoned into the adobe and rock wall. With a kingly face, an inverted "T" at the crown, Gran Pajatén-style earrings and round eyes, it wore a very dignified expression and measured about 16 inches in height. The nose was foliated, as were all such carvings of the Chachapoyas culture. It is an interesting point that a large, foliated nose is a common characteristic of the Aztec god of Quetzalcoatl and the Mayan Kukulcan—which suggests some association with the Chachapoyas god pictured on their ancient temples, who, for the moment, must go unnamed, though we can assume that he was a forerunner of the Inca Viracocha and may have been called Didimo. The "T" figure, always found in Chachapoyas carvings, presents another interesting comparison with northern cultures. The Rain-god Chac had a T-shaped eye in the Mayan glyphs—a supposed symbol of rain or tears. The T-figure is the main element in the hieroglyph *ik*, one of the twenty day signs, and stands for air, movement, life and spirit, being related to the Sun-god.

Encouraged by these finds—which had to come from ancient remains nearby—we began a systematic search of the nearby hills over the next four days. Ollape was the first ancient site we visited. Quite close to the village, the ruins represent extraordinary examples of stone fretwork, duplicating designs often seen painted on ceramic ware—the common zigzag motif, quadrilaterals, triangles, hooks and concentric diamonds. From Ollape we moved to the highlands.

For four days we explored some eight major archaeological sites consisting of circular and rectangular constructions with which we had become so familiar—all covered by a thick mantle of growth. The better part of the buildings were not visible, but we knew from the quality of the stonework that the buildings had stone carvings plus the fact that we had seen so many on the walls of the village homes (Plate 20). We gave the name Muyok

[PLATE 20] *Monkey carving at La Jalca. Many such carvings are found about the village and in the surrounding ruins.*

Viejo to this highland city that stretched for 12 miles across the mountain crests. *Muyok* is the name of a flowering tree that grows in all of the ruins; *viejo* means old in Spanish. There is a old site of ruins above the modern pueblo of Zuta called Muyok Viejo and we thought this a fitting name for the whole, for it seemed that this was the sixth city conquered by Tupac Yupanqui, old Suta. We also found an ancient road leading off into the jungle that some said led to a city. I had an account in my notes from a chronicle by Alejandro Hernández who wrote that, "Antonio de Herrera, chronicler of the Indies, records that the Incas during the time of Tupac Yupanqui made an excursion into 'El Dorado' through Chachapoyas, land of the Chachas." It was evident from this and many other accounts, that El Dorado was not a single city, but a vast jungle empire which lay in that green world of Anti-suyo. And it was evident that Chachapoyas was the gateway to it.

I was anxious to explore the heights between La Jalca and Tacta, a mountain range averaging 9,000–10,000 feet altitude with many unexplored forest regions. To begin our journey we explored the mountain ranges past the place called Alcalde Urco, where we came upon a group of very fine circular buildings with architectural decoration. Higher still we found ruins that spread along the forested summits to the next village, Duraznopampa, proving that the ruins were a continuation of the large city we had named Muyok Viejo, which ran along an unbroken chain of jungled mountains for 12 miles. We also found a road, showing that this old city had been connected to the Cochamal ruins of Rodriguez de Mendoza. To the western side of the Utcubamba we explored Talape, Baute and Lindaje, ancient remains covered by thick jungle, but inferior in quality to those to the east. We found evidence of many circular constructions, the largest measuring 25 feet in diameter, and a good number of rectangular structures with doorways —one measured nearly 120 feet in length. Built of irregular stones cemented with mud, they had no ornamentation of any kind. Those found at Obisbo were of the same type. Diosan was equally disappointing, but in the vicinity of Quinjalca we found several stone monoliths, carved heads and large amounts of ceramic fragments decorated with a bat motif.

I returned to Chachapoyas on the fifth of December. Some weeks before we had attempted to reach a cave dwelling but a landslide had dammed up the waters of the lower Utcubamba causing a huge artificial lake on a three-mile stretch of road that linked Chachapoyas with Chiclayo. The towering overhangs above the road were known to hold a cluster of anthropomorphic mummy-casings perched in the hollows of the cliffs. I wanted to explore the area because it might prove to be the largest of its kind anywhere in Amazonas. Reichlen had studied similar sites in the Aispachaca and Chipuric valleys, and dated the remains about A.D. 1250. Since the new site was located in the northern tip of the Province of Luya, and archaeologically unreported, it sounded to me to be more than worthy of an investigation.

We took a twelve-foot rowboat propelled by an outboard motor and puttered away from the shore. Several miles of road were under 50 or 60 feet of water. We headed toward the middle of the lake, away from falling gravel that showered down from the high cliffs. At the northern tip of the lake we got out and hiked up a slippery, muddy trail that led over a 600-foot hill and down the other side. It started to rain. We hugged the sides of the mountain to avoid being struck by falling boulders that whistled past our ears and plunged into the raging torrent below. Long files of cargo-bearers, stripped to the waist, labored past carrying crates bound for Chachapoyas, now isolated and cut off from direct contact with Chiclayo. They came padding by, grunting and groaning under fifty-pound loads. They represented the sole means of transportation between the two points of the road now permanently submerged. A dozen trucks were backed up at either side of the lake, waiting their turn to unload cargo. We walked to Tingorbamba.

Lugging our gear up the scrub and cactus, we made a 3,000-foot climb that required the better part of three hours. At the 8,000-foot level we approached a series of hanging cliffs that jutted several thousand feet above our heads. Andres and Fortunato, our bearer-guides, pointed to a ledge some 100 yards to my right. I took out my glasses and examined the cliff-face. Four anthropomorphic figures were perched on an overhang, about 50 feet above the ledge upon which we were standing. I estimated the tallest to be about four feet in height. Made of mud mixed with vegetable fiber, the figures were shaped like huge cigars and painted vivid purple and white with

166

geometric designs in black. Each was crowned with a representation of a human head decorated with painted stylized designs. Two of the figures had a top piece, one a single, small human head, the other was twin-headed. While the designs were of typical Chachapoyas zigzags, the noses were strangely different and reminded me of those found on stone carvings in Melanesia. I looked at my watch and decided against climbing up to them; I wanted to push on since the porters said there were many more ahead.

Farther along we sighted other funerary monuments. We continued on along the ledge, hacking the scrub and thorns with our machetes. We rounded a bend in the cliff, roped up to a large overhang, and I was stunned to find some forty anthropomorphic figures—a regular pantheon of the dead. (Plate 21.) Several had been toppled over, probably by marauding tomb robbers long before our arrival. They lay there on a flat ledge like tenpins in a bowling alley. The figures were of all shapes and sizes. The larger ones weighed

[PLATE 21] *Cliff necropolis of Pueblo de los Muertos (City of the Dead). Funerary casings are in foreground, village built for the dead in center background.*

167

anywhere from 200 to 300 pounds and were five feet tall. We could see that the casings were hollow and had contained mummies wrapped in grave nets. Yet some of the casings were stuffed with white bones. Many shards found in the broken ruins had a distinctly Amazon quality, and I noted the cruciform design which is also used among the Shipibas of the Amazon forests. Others had designs similar to the pottery of the Cajamarca region and the Vicus culture.

The mud-sarcophagi carried the nose style of the smaller group we had examined earlier, as well as the broad, foliated type similar to those seen on Easter Island. Even the designs were similar, down to the neck pendant, though the long ears were missing. This is interesting in view of the old legend about Polynesians or Easter Islanders having landed on Peruvian shores during a remote period in history.

After photographing the find and taking measurements, we dropped down to a lower ledge and a second group of mud figures clustered together before a huge mound of mud. One or two of the conical forms had been broken into and the contents removed, but many were unopened. I discouraged the men from tampering with them, hoping to return someday with specialists so they could be studied. The mound appeared to be a sepulcher and I conjectured that it covered an inner cave, undoubtedly filled with mummies and artifacts.

Working our way along the overhanging cliffs we came out on a shelf. The two bearers pointed to a high sandstone cliff straight ahead. We saw structures built on the cliffs, which reminded me of the Indian cliff dwellings at Mesa Verde, Colorado, except that this was, properly speaking, a place for the dead. The larger part of the pueblo ran about 150 yards and was situated atop an artificial ledge built of stone blocks cemented with mud. In all, the shelf must have run for 500 yards or so. It had been preserved from ruin by a natural overhang of rock that protected it from the heavy seasonal rains.

We formed a rope, went up the craggy bluff and reached the platform in a half hour, a flat ridge over 2,500 feet above the valley floor. We explored a dozen circular mud buildings. Although badly broken by falling stones, they gave us a good idea of what the site must have been like in its original form. The walls were incised with cruciform designs, snakes and odd hieroglyph designs which I had never seen before, looking like loops or bars with F-designs. (Plate 22.) To my way of thinking this was one of the most fascinating archaeological sites I had examined. I couldn't resist naming the site Pueblo de los Muertos (City of the Dead), as it came to be known following our expedition. The rains came at last and brought our El Dorado II Expedition to a close. Leaving Chachapoyas until the following dry season, we returned to Trujillo.*

* Shortly thereafter Douglas Sharon, who had been my field assistant for a number of years, left Peru to undertake anthropological studies in California. I hated to lose him, but was pleased that he had decided on a career in anthropology.

The first phase of the El Dorado III Expedition took place during August 1967, in the lower jungles of Rioja, Moyobamba and Tarapoto. Among these scattered ruins of poor quality (not much building stone is found in the jungle plains) we picked up ceramic specimens and axeheads, studied portions of road that disappeared off to the east, and made some anthropological studies.

At the village of Lamas, a small Indian settlement built on the summit of a 2,500-foot truncated hill overlooking Tarapoto we witnessed an Indian ceremony celebrated annually each August 25–30. A thriving community of 7,000 inhabitants, Lamas goes back to colonial times when it was settled in the year 1554 by Pedro de Ursua. In 1650, Captain Martín de la Riva incorporated it into Chachapoyas, and in 1857 it became part of the Department of San Martín. It is a curious ethnological riddle that the Indian

[PLATE 22] Incised designs in the walls at Pueblo de los Muertos. Cliff ruins stretch for hundreds of yards some 2,500 feet above Utcubamba River.

169

population (estimated to number about 5,000) speaks a highland Quechua mixed with Cahuapana, a language spoken by a tribe after the same name near Moyobamba.

Legend says that they are descendents of the Chanca people who fled from the invading Incas, though there is no scientific proof to support this. Whatever their origin, these isolated people cling to their ancient customs and live apart from the mestizos in their *caserío*. The women of the village wear bright-colored, richly embroidered clothing, long ribbons entwined in their hair and numerous strings of beads about their necks. (Plate 23.) During

[PLATE 23] *Indian women from the jungle village of Lamas.*

170

the ceremonial dances the menfolk hang rows of stuffed tropical birds, hunted down in the nearby jungles, across their shoulders—the beautiful *huacamayos* with their red plumage, black and yellow toucans and pinshas, emerald-green loros—which give them the appearance of birdmen trying to take flight. I watched one of these ceremonies for the better part of two hours, and couldn't help thinking there might be some connection between their costume and the ornamentation of the birdmen found on the Gran Pajatén ruins.

The old men of the village speak of ruins in the jungles. An old witchdoctor with a string of *huayruro* beads draped around his neck, a chain of *shacapa* nuts over his shoulder and a bright headdress made of brilliant black and red bird feathers, confirmed this. But he refused to give any details, though we did pick up the name Pastasa, and a place called Angaisa where ruins are believed to exist. We were told that the Indians use an herb named *ayahuasca*, which produces visions and sends the taker off on a trip to the underworld, where he speaks with Chullachaqui, the devil-spirit. Only the witchdoctor is allowed to administer this potent herb, and anyone who wishes to take it must observe a strict diet of bananas for thirty days beforehand—a religious experience not without its dangers, because the person sometimes has difficulty in returning so that his soul remains with the devil while the body sleeps in a trance-like condition in the physical world.

The Indians also told me about a giant snake of the jungle that grows to tremendous size. One said he had seen one of these "mothers of the forest" some years before; as long and as thick as a cedar. It had ears and was covered with dead leaves and twigs, which made it look like a dead tree. A schoolteacher at Tarapoto said later that he himself had seen one of these huge snakes crossing a trail. He stood petrified, watching it move slowly into the jungle. It required fifteen minutes for the massive reptile to reach the other side. He showed me a book on jungle animals which gave reference to this reptile. It is called *Sachamama*, a boa of the forest that lives in isolated parts of the *montaña*. Very rare, it is said to reach 80 feet in length. I didn't believe it myself. I asked how long he thought the one he had seen was and he answered that it must have been 40 meters (132 feet) and a meter thick. Many hunters of the area testified that 15–30 meters was not an uncommon size for this monster. P. H. Fawcett killed an anaconda 62 feet long, and Brazilians claim to have seen them as long as 80 feet. I imagine the boa of the *montaña* is as long, but I have never seen one myself. But because I know the jungle holds many mysteries which cannot be rejected until further study and exploration is made, I choose to withhold judgment and take the words of the people who live in the interior. (I was skeptical of many stories which later proved to be true.) One old tribesman told me that he saw a 100-footer and swore that it hypnotized small animals and drew them to it by some electrical or magnetic force (ancient pottery vessels often depict this snake which represented lightning and thunder and was related to the sun). No hunter of the jungle harms this reptile, for it is believed to be bad luck to kill it. It is said that whenever one is killed the earth dries up and nothing will grow for years. The bushmaster abounds, some reaching 10, even 15 feet in length. The Indians, who learned the trick from the Hivitos, masticate a stick of the piripiri bush like a wad of tobacco and spit the juice at poisonous snakes and kill them. Such legends and mysteries are common to the deep jungle and are a part of its powerful fascination.

The Indians have been content to live at Lamas—the village nearest to civilization—while remaining apart in their little settlement of *chozas*, eking out a living by selling animal skins and growing coffee, corn, bananas and yucca; but with the coming of the marginal Andean Jungle Highway and the increased prosperity which commerce is bringing, the Indians are returning to the interior, back to Sisa and beyond. They say their customs are dying out, that education is taking the young away from the tribe. Wanting to preserve their traditions and their own way of life, they are seeking refuge in the jungle.

I thought it strange that they would reject the advantages of modern society, but after a careful study of their habits, I can understand their reasons. Naturally shy and timid, mechanized society confuses and frightens them. There are other reasons—they love the freedom the jungle gives. Being natural-born hunters and fishermen, the deep forests and rushing streams provide them with meat, wild game, hides, feathers, fish and medicinal herbs to cure their illnesses. The city gives them nothing—on the contrary, it takes away their liberties and imposes a way of life completely alien to their ancient traditions. The Lamas Indians believe themselves to be free men, part of a way of life that goes back to primitive times; so long as they live it, they will remain a strong and vigorous people If they give it up, they will die out as have so many other tribes that have been absorbed into civilization.

Late in September we were back at Chachapoyas. I was eager to identify the missing four cities conquered by Tupac Yupanqui, which we now believed lay between Muyok Viejo and Gran Pajatén. While arranging for mule transportation to the southern highlands, we went down to Tinas in an effort to reach a mountain height upon which a temple area was believed to exist. But we were turned back when our camp was overrun by *loro muchacuy*, a green serpent, highly poisonous and very difficult to detect in the greenery. We found them by the score, on the trail and clinging to the overhanging vines. Our snake-bite serum had expired past the thirty-day limit—the yellow contents of the glass tubes turned a milkish-white in the humidity of the low jungle. Not wanting to risk the lives of my men, I gave up the search. Archaeologically, the exploration was successful, for we came across miles of high walls tenoned with stones and many circular buildings. The "temple" would wait for another day.

From Tinas we went over to Mito and explored the heights again, coming across a dozen new sites—showing that Monte Peruvia extended in that direction. While the people were most hospitable, we were continually bothered by *garrapatas* (ticks) that attached themselves to our legs and arms as if we were the first living creatures to enter their world. We would drop down to Mito and burn them off with cigarettes, putting the lit end at their tails until they pulled their heads out of our flesh. But even the village was infested with them. It is said that they transmit uta (a kind of leprosy from which a large percentage of the population suffers), so we were glad to leave.

October 13, 1967

One wet, rainy morning I went with Segundo to Leimibamba, a small community at 6,800 feet, several hours south. From there we took our caravan of men and beasts up a stone road that led to the source of the Atuen River, a place called Churu Churu, a plot of land with a small hut at 10,700 feet above sea level, where we explored the city of platforms and circular buildings. While cutting through the thorny bush and soft ferns, we stumbled upon a cylindrical stone that looked as if it were part of a column, or possibly a center stone. I had seen the latter at the Gran Pajatén ruins, but this find was of far better workmanship. The find excited me because if it were a column it suggested a link with the Chavín culture. Not wanting to jump to any premature conclusions I thought it could also have been used as a pestle or some kind of stone for crushing or grinding. I made a sketch of it, took measurements (it measured about 50 centimeters wide, the standard width of Chavín columns) and recorded it on film. (Plate 24.)

[PLATE 24] *Circular stone carving, possibly used as a column or grinding stone. Found at Cochabamba, it is typical of the type of stones found in all major ruins of the area.*

173

The next morning we found another city of imposing circular buildings at a place called Bobeda, a grassy highland. That afternoon we dropped down to Tajopampa, a flat grassland of broken ruins in a poor state of preservation. The surrounding hills were cut with agricultural terraces (surcos). The pampa was dominated by a high, sandstone prominence called La Petaca. Upon examining the cliff-face with my binoculars, I observed a large number of ancient tombs in the rocks. It was one of the largest sites of its kind I had seen anywhere and I made plans to explore it. One of the porters told me that farther down the river, at a spot known as Diablo Huasi (Devil's House), similar ruins existed, but that it was taboo.

Examining the broken ruins at Tajopampa, we uncovered several cylindrical stones of uniform size, which suggested they were parts of pillars (similar to the style I had seen at Chichén Itzá) that had originally been placed together. A little later we found two cylindrical stones with incised designs and serpentine lines, decidedly Chavín in feeling.

Late in the afternoon we forced our tired mounts up a steep incline to La Joya, a high prominence at 11,000 feet that overlooked an Indian community in the lower valley. On the way to a small hut we observed scattered remains on the northern tip of the mountain. The buildings were circular and rectangular, some of three levels, and decorated with fretwork. During dinner we were told by the owner of the house that a large number of ruins existed at the southern end of the peak, where the forest was thickest, but that nobody had ever explored them. Like so many other residents of Amazonas, he was not interested in anything that did not directly affect him.

At first light we sharpened our machetes on a large rock outside the door and started out to explore the forests. We had barely cut into the upper jungle when we came to a stone wall. On the other side we found a group of circular buildings. Beyond that we saw a long, rectangular structure with a zigzag motif. Then I saw a white mass built up against the forest-clad mountain and dispatched the men to clear it. As the green vegetation was cut off the white limestone blocks my heart skipped a beat. "There it is!" I shouted. "The key! The link we have been looking for!" The rectangular base (about 13 feet high) supported an oval building with stone doorway and frieze of step spirals, the same kind that we had found at Gran Pajatén. But the dressed stonework here was far superior. The two-story structure measured 20 feet tall. Anyone familiar with the architecture of American cultures would have seen that the society responsible for these sophisticated buildings and art work was highly advanced.

Encouraged by the find and hoping to uncover more, I split the men into two groups and sent them into the high woods to the south. I slithered through the tunnel-like trail and came to a long, white-walled building with several niches. Upon examination I found it to be a huge rectangular construction. It was adjoined to a circular edifice with rectangular tower. We went on up through the thickets, past a score of imposing well-worked stone buildings, glimmering white against the green jungle. Not far away, a two-leveled building with a high cornice and circular tower graced with niches and windows and covered by brilliant wild flowers met our eyes. On another trail we discovered scores of stone buildings that stretched on and on—big rectangular and circular bases supporting ovaloid buildings and projecting cornices, some with ornamented façades displaying the familiar stepped-fret, concentric diamond and zigzag designs. Farther along we came to the summit. We were out of the jungle now and approached a series of step-plazas, running up the slope of green grass and scrub like happy children returning to the playground after a lengthy confinement in a closed schoolroom. The fresh, dry air filled our lungs, eddies of cold air whipped about our feet. We could hear the soft rumbling of the Atuen River far below, but could not see it because of the hanging clouds. We worked our way carefully along the edge of the precipice over broken walls and white turrets. A slip meant a fall of 1,500 feet down a steep precipice. It was then that I realized La Joya was an impregnable mountain citadel on a Machu Picchu-like setting. Several hundred yards farther along we attained the north peak. We stood amidst a dozen fine buildings. There was no woodland here and the structures were crumbling, not having been protected by the heavy growth.

The lower slopes of La Joya were stacked with ruins; and it was there that we found evidence of more carved cylindrical and tenoned sculptures—small human heads and a sculpture with a feline mouth and interlocking teeth and fangs—unquestionable Chavín features. (Plate 25.) We picked up many ceramic specimens with typical Chachapoyas zigzag designs and broken bits of pottery figures, one shaped like a parrot.

[PLATE 25] *Feline figure carved in stone is examined by the author. Interlocking teeth suggest Chavín link. Sculpture was found at La Joya ruins. (Andean Explorers Club photo.)*

The early sun promised a clear day and I went up to the north peak lugging cameras, telephoto lenses and film chest. I wanted to get a good look at the surrounding peaks. Most of the ruins followed a pattern: rolling mountains were etched with hundreds of small agricultural terraces, showing that the region had supported a large population. These uplands, averaging 11,000 feet in altitude, were grasslands, the summits topped by thick forests. So far the expedition had discovered important archaeological remains in the forested jungle growth—first at Churu Churu, Bobeda and now La Joya. Woodlands grow where there is water, so I reasoned that where there was forest, ruins would be found.

I attained the summit and sat down to rest. A marvelous view spread out before me. There wasn't a cloud in the sky. The Atuen rushed far below, cutting a deep gorge through the fertile hills. La Joya means "the jewel" in Spanish—a name well-suited to the place. I had marveled at the scenic splendor at Machu Picchu, which many think more imposing than the ruins themselves. La Joya was, in many ways, more spectacular. As opposed to the Inca setting with its sharp, tight precipices on all sides, the hill upon which the Chachapoyas city of La Joya is situated rises up out of the rolling, green-clad hills like an island. (Plate 26.) It affords a magnificent view. To the north, east and west great ridges of 12,000 and 13,000 feet loom up like an encircling defensive wall. The rushing Atuen, fed by numerous tributaries, winds along below, fighting to reach the Amazon. To the north a craggy, purple sentinel, its jagged granite slopes streaked with white, towers up 14,000 feet to meet the royal-blue sky—a snowless pyramid. It was one of the most beautiful sights I had seen in my travels.

To the east, on the first ridge across the Atuen, my eyes fell on the crowning heights—treeless, windswept puna, some 500 feet higher than La Joya. I squinted in the yellow sunlight and saw a glimmer of white stone. I quickly took out my binoculars from their leather case and focused them for a closer look. Ruined buildings stretched all along the summit in a northerly direction and disappeared into the forests of a high summit. Upon closer examination with the telescope, I could see the circular and rectangular buildings very clearly, topped by green and brown tufts of bunch grass. I learned from my men that the lower part of the mountain height was named Tambillo and the upper part Londres.

Farther to the northeast, on a second range of mountains, I picked up another cluster of ruined buildings, Pavillon. Beyond that to the east lay the great forests of Lajasbamba, where, I was told by my principal guide, Mamerto Hidalgo, lay an enchanted city. The people also spoke of a large body of water, an uncharted lake, that does not appear on any map.

I surveyed other mountain peaks with my glasses—Timbambo, Gentil Loma, Monte Bravo, Monte Paula, Teaven, Torrera, Torre Pampa, Checko, Chanchillo, Checko Pukro, Orno Punto and others. On each I could distinguish white buildings protruding out of the green forests. Leagues and

leagues of ruins. These heights, which were anywhere from a half- to two days' travel away, had to be explored. Each promised a new city.

The sun shone brightly, but shreds of clouds were starting to form around it, so I hurriedly took out my big telephoto lenses, attached them to my cameras and went to work documenting my finds. An hour later big black clouds rolled over us and a fine mist began to fall, but it soon grew in intensity and became a thunder shower. I threw on my poncho and returned to

[PLATE 26] *Four-story building overlooking Atuen and Timbamba river valleys south of Leimibamba. Ruins are part of La Joya.*

177

the house. I was afraid that the rains would come in force and bring the expedition to an abrupt close before the other ruins could be explored.

The following morning we took the mules up the trail to the crest of mountains overlooking Bobeda. Rags of dirty clouds filled a bleak, sunless sky. We rode past massive white cliffs and reached the summit. Then we dismounted and made our way along the mountain slopes and hours later entered the Petaca Valley. Making our way along perilous ridges we soon reached the river and went across the rushing stream over slippery boulders. On the other side we scaled the heights and came out before a series of dwellings built into the face of a sandstone cliff hundreds of feet high. (Plate 27.) A phantasmagoria of stone tombs, great red pictographs, sealed caves and hanging pueblos dotted the steep bluff. How the ancients were able to

178

build these structures in the precarious cliffs I did not know. My telephoto lens showed they were 200 meters away, others much farther, for they worked their way up to the green-streaked summit a thousand feet above our heads. The stone structures had doorways and were decorated with zigzag fretwork and Greek "T's". One cluster of ruins was built above a series of caves, some with doorways. Another was plastered, painted red and white. Below I saw a splotch of red. With the aid of my binoculars I distinguished a human figure with a solar crown, rays streaking out from its head. (Plate 28.) Several huge condors circled overhead. They had made these ancient tombs their home. We had discovered a sanctuary of condors.

We tramped along in wondrous awe for the better part of the morning, thunder rumbling overhead. Hours later we reached Diablo Huasi (Devil's House), and stared up in disbelief at the burial tombs hanging like beehives in the rocky clefts. Sheets of rain drove us to an overhanging rock. We did not observe mummy casings like those we had seen at the City of the Dead near Tingorbamba, but I had no doubts that this was a necropolis. I could see human skeletons and mummies inside some of the tombs where the stone coverings had fallen away. (Plate 29.) I wanted to climb up to these ruins but the rain made that too dangerous.

When the rain let up we crossed the Petaca and climbed the opposite bank. At the summit the rain caught us again and we put up in an abandoned hut. It rained until the sun went down. In the fading light we made for home over a slushy, muddy trail—the rains had set in for good. The expedition had

[PLATE 28] *Pictographs of human figure with crown and frog etch cliffs at La Petaca in the heart of the City of the Dead.*

come to an end. We would have to wait until the following season to explore the many ruins we had spotted by telescope.

On the morning of our departure, I climbed up to the north peak of La Joya to take a last look at the forested mountain peaks that hid a dozen or more nameless ancient cities still to be explored. Which of these citadels had carried the name Raimipampa, Papamarca, Cajamarquilla, Contur Marca? Surely we had found one of the four missing cities stormed by Inca Tupac Yupanqui and later by Huayna Capac. At that moment a great king condor swept overhead, dipped its wings and flew on toward the south. (Plate 30.) I followed it with my glasses and watched it soar past the sun and disappear into the mists. I could understand why the Chachapoyans had such a deep reverence for this giant bird. With a flick of its huge wings it cruised effortlessly high above, drifting from one mountain to another. Each mountain of the Chachapoyas is separated by many thousands of feet of descent and climb over scraggy brush and rock. To the Chachapoyans, the "cloud people" who built their ancient shrines and cities on the uppermost crests, the condor must have seemed a magic being, and perhaps this is why they pictured it on their ancient temples and placed the remains of their dead high in its nesting grounds.

The major result of our expedition was that we had stumbled into an ancient sanctuary consisting of a dozen or more mountain citadels. Other than the names of the mountains upon which they are located, the cities had no names of their own, but we felt these names would serve, since nobody knew what they had been called in ancient times. As a name for the group as a whole I chose "The Cities of the Condors," and so marked it in my notes and maps. A fitting name, I thought.

[PLATE 29] *Hanging stone tombs in the high cliffs of Diablo Huasi. Niches in the shape of crosses crown doorway. Note human skeleton inside the tomb.*

[PLATE 30] *King condor takes to air in neighborhood of The Cities of the Condors, a sanctuary for these rare birds worshiped by the ancient Chachapoyas people.*

It was imperative that we return to explore these ruined settlements for two reasons. First, it was important to determine their size and importance. Second, we had to identify them as Chachapoyas remains, not an easy thing to do since very little is known about these mysterious people who, for the most part, belong to legend and myth. But I felt that radiocarbon dating could be done. If the remains were dated to the period during which the Chachapoyans were conquered by the Incas, it would be conclusive proof that they were indeed Chachapoyas cities.

In the first weeks of May 1968, I carried on my El Dorado IV Explorations in the company of Mr. Carl Landegger, a prominent New York industrialist and a member of both the Explorers Club of New York and the Andean Explorers Club of Lima, who had arranged to make radiocarbon tests of our findings in behalf of the Smithsonian Institution of Washington, D.C. When the tests were made available to me in Lima I was overjoyed to find that the dates reinforced my theories about the ruins belonging to the Chachapoyas culture.

We were able to return to the Cities of the Condors and explore several of them. Our first find was made at Lajasbamba, where we claimed from the dense jungle a spread of circular and rectangular ruins that covered an extensive area, which we estimated to be about two square miles. These ancient remains of typical Chachapoyas stonework with medial moldings were situated in the upper jungle at an altitude of 10,400 feet above sea level. We also found specimens of very finely-worked stone bowls with a linked-diamond design in relief, weighing some forty or fifty pounds apiece. (Plate 31.) They littered the floor of the ruins. Near this city we found an uncharted lake at approximately 10,000 feet, surrounded by green jungle. We

[PLATE 31] *Stone Chachapoyas dish with nested-diamond design similar to that found on the buildings. Dish, weighing nearly fifty pounds, was found at Lajasbamba jungles in vicinity of ancient metropolis.*

182

[PLATE 32] *Lake of the Condors, explored during El Dorado IV Expedition.*

calculated it to be about two miles in length. Giant king condors came out of the towering cliffs upon our intrusion into their domain and we fittingly called the nameless lake, "Lake of the Condors." (Plate 32.) Not far away, at the base of a cliff known as Achupa, we took our first radiocarbon specimen from the wooden rafter on a cliff tomb that had a zigzag motif in stone, a typical characteristic of the ruins in Amazonas.

From there we worked our mules over soggy swamplands dotted with quicksand pits, climbed up the heights and explored Pavillon (which I had seen the previous season by means of my field glasses), a small citadel of sixty to seventy buildings at 11,500 feet altitude. At Embovedo we came across several cylindrical stones with raised knobs lying inside the fallen buildings. Beyond these ruins tower the broken remains of Tambillo and Londres,

183

about 150 ruins that work their way up the slope from 11,000 to 11,500 feet altitude for nearly a mile. Here we discovered the remnants of spiral stairways.

Dropping down to the stone highway that skirts the river Atuen (Plate 33.) we made our way to Monte Bravo, and there we discovered a beautiful hanging citadel built atop a steep, 10,800-foot elevation facing La Joya and La Petaca. We partially cleared one building, a two-storied structure made of two circular levels separated by a cornice. (Plate 34.) A spiral stairway led to the upper section, which was decorated with a stepped-fret design. Other buildings partially cleared of jungle growth were found to be ornamented with the double zigzag motif. Some contained human heads tenoned into the outer wall. We also came across one building with tenoned stones in the interior, which seemed to have served no practical purpose. Some might have been used as hinges, since they were found beside a doorway; but others were stuck at odd places and reminded me of similar stones used in the Inca Sun Temple at Cuzco. We took bone samples from these for radio-carbon tests.

[PLATE 33] *Ancient Chachapoyas jungle road in Atuen Valley which leads to Cities of the Condors.*

A week later I was back at the ruins with a German film crew. Ingo and Eckart Grill, brothers and professional film-makers, had recently joined the Andean Explorers Club and decided to make a colored motion-picture documentary of my jungle explorations. While they were fundamentally interested in filming the Club's work over the past seasons, they were particularly eager to record on film a new discovery. A lost city had never been filmed while actually being cut out of the jungle and this, they thought, would be of great interest to viewers and a graphic historical document. Thus we launched the El Dorado V Expedition, underwritten by the Club and in collaboration with the municipality of Chachapoyas.

Returning to the Atuen Valley and the Cities of the Condors, we re-explored many of the sites covered in previous expeditions. With the aid of mountain-climbing equipment we scaled the high cliffs of La Petaca and Diablo Huasi, thus gaining access to the otherwise inaccessible tombs. Only previously disturbed tombs violated in ages past were studied and photo-

185

graphed; the contents were left undisturbed. Pushing on up the Timbambo and Chanchillo quebradas we discovered numerous other cliff tombs hanging on the scraggy heights, and in the grassy pampas above we visited many fortified hilltops, now lying waste under the naked Andean sky. At a place called Torrera we examined a cluster of ruins and a lonely chullpa (Torre Pukro) perched on a windswept pampa. (Plate 35.) The surrounding hills were cut with thousands of agricultural terraces and scattered remains. On the southern side of the Atuen we noted a large number of well-made chullpas clinging to the mountainsides, some of which reached four stories high and were graced with doors and windows. (Plate 36.) In many ways they reminded me of Tiahuanaco-type monuments. Had the religious-militant Tiahuanaco culture left its imprint on this area when it spread from the Huari region sometime around A.D. 1000? Winged figures, the zigzag motif, frets, T-shaped designs, step patterns and curvilinear angles, all examples of Chachapoyas art, were also used by this southern culture.

Explorations of the surrounding forests brought interesting remains to light, but it was on the upper heights, above Teaven, that we found one of

[PLATE 35] *Inside a stone funerary chullpa. Ancient Chachapoyans, like Incas and Tiahuanacos, buried the remains of their dead in these vaults.*

[PLATE 36] *Chachapoyas burial chullpa of four stories in Teaven Valley. Discovered during El Dorado V Expedition.*

the more important sites in the area. On a 10,500-foot elevation known as Monte Paula, we found an extensive area teeming with circular buildings atop stone platforms. (Plate 37.) The walls were tenoned with deer horns and carved heads similar to those found at Gran Pajatén. In addition, we found spiral stairways of the caracole style found in Mayan ruins (von Hagen had noted this similarity at nearby Choquillo). We also noted architectural ornamentation of zigzag and fret design. There were hundreds of buildings and there seemed no doubt that this had been one of the large cities of the greater valley complex. We would have continued to explore the high jungles had not a heavy rain forced us to move on (the rain forests know no dry season).

Time did not permit further explorations to the south where we picked up roads running off into the sunny pampas. A helicopter, which we had contracted to help us trace these roads, failed to arrive, due to heavy overcast. Still eager to track down some of the missing Chachapoyas cities, I decided to look for Manco's fortress city of Revanto (Levanto) which had been the old capital city of the Chachapoyans. Originally I thought that the Monte Peruvia ruins were an extension of old Levanto, but on second thought I felt obliged to explore the Levanto area to make sure.

We lugged our cameras by foot up the towering mountains above the town of Chachapoyas to the tiny village of Levanto (a good three hours' climb and 8,300 feet above sea level) and the next day, in company with

187

[PLATE 37] *Round buildings at Monte Paula above Teaven. Ancient city is composed of hundreds of circular buildings built atop stone platforms. Structures are decorated with carved human heads and friezes. Stairways give access to buildings.*

local machetemen, visited the known sites: Huallpa, Collacruz, Pamal, Rosurco, Llui, among others. But I was not impressed with the extent of these ruins. Father Gates had been the parish priest of the village for some years and he had heard rumors of additional ruins in the upper jungles, a few of which he had visited in quest of pottery fragments. On the strength of this and from what I could learn from the villagers, I led the men up into the highland forests to the 9,000–10,000-foot level. Here we found some remarkable architectural specimens under the foliage-enveloped heights at Navarch, Yautapina, Lancoqunga and Puyan, and a magnificent monument at Yalap, whose walls stretched for hundreds of yards and boasted the finest stonework known in Amazonas. (Plate 38.) The concentric diamond friezes found on the stone walls were very reminiscent of similar designs found on Imperial Inca pottery vessels, which suggested an Inca influence—or possibly the Incas had borrowed these designs from the Chachapoyans. At Congona Pampa we found ovaloid buildings with corbeled or false-vaulted stone roofs, an extensive aqueduct and large agricultural works. There were extensive residential areas and cemeteries, as well as temples and ceremonial centers—all signs of a metropolis. From the immense amount of pottery fragments found on the floor of the jungle (typically Chachapoyas with its zigzag and serpentine

188

motif, and Inca design) I concluded that we had located a former capital city of the Chachapoyans, probably the Revanto fortress of Manco—a surprising find considering our close proximity to Chachapoyas. Possibly the Monte Peruvia ruins were an extension of this site or an earlier capital.

The middle of November to the middle of December saw me once more in the field where El Dorado VI was committed to a CBS production for television. In addition to the camera crew, with David Burke as director, we were joined by Charles Kuralt, CBS correspondent; Dr. George O'Neill, Professor of Anthropology and Archaeology of The City College of New York; Father John Schiff, a Maryknoll missionary and linguistic expert; and about a dozen other people.

We were able to put together a filmed document of our activities which included a re-examination of major archaeological sites uncovered during previous explorations in Amazonas; but we were also able to reach inaccessible cave sites where important samples were taken for carbon-14 testing (Plate 39.). Our climbing efforts were aided by the German Alpinist Frank Hentschel, who had brought over the latest mountain-climbing equipment. We felt that a climbing specialist was indispensable to the success of our expedition, which later proved to be correct. He assisted O'Neill and myself up the sheer cliffs to tomb sites which could not have been reached without the assistance of an expert. While selected samples of wood and bone were removed for carbon-14 purposes, and selected ceramic and textile pieces turned over to the proposed museum in Chachapoyas, the tombs were left

[PLATE 38] *Magnificent stone monument with complex diamond frieze at Yalap above Levanto. Wall stretches for hundreds of yards through jungle.*

[PLATE 39] *Archaeologist O'Neill brushes dust from mummy casings in cliff sites above Utcubamba River.*

[PLATE 40] *String of cargo-bearers and explorers trek over grasslands of upper Amazonas on way to the Lake of the Condors during El Dorado VI.*

intact for future study. We also succeeded in exploring the Lake of the Condors (Plate 40.), first sighted by Carl Landegger and myself in May, and other lakes of the region. We used scuba-diving gear (Plate 41.) for underwater exploration and discovered a new road leading off into the jungle interior. O'Neill's reaction to what he saw is summed up in the following quote: "These new discoveries in the *ceja de la montaña* reveal the remains of a vast civilization that built cities, mountaintop citadels, cliff tombs, and extensive areas of contoured agricultural terracing which undoubtedly maintained a very large population. With further work and reconstruction of the cultural history of the Chachapoyas area, these discoveries should fill the void in the archaeological record in the Northern Andes and resolve some of the many questions that remain concerning regional growth and cultural influences in northern Peru during pre-Inca times."

For the first time ceramic shards were analyzed and classified, not only the many samples picked up from the surface of the ruins studied, but those I had been collecting over the years from other sites. In this respect, O'Neill's contribution to the expedition was paramount (Plate 42.).

[PLATE 41] *Scuba divers attached to El Dorado Expedition probe the highland lakes for specimens. Local porter watches as member of party photographs the efforts.*

[PLATE 42] *Pottery fragments found in ruins of Chachapoyas. Serpentine or zigzag design is typical of Chachapoyas pottery.*

January 4, 1969. Leimebamba

Our mule train had come in from another highland probe into a new area and boxes of gear and equipment lay piled on the floor of our field headquarters awaiting transit to Chachapoyas. Three weeks of exploration had served to clear up some of the unanswered questions about the southern regions between the Cities of the Condors and the Bolívar-Cochabamba territory. Helen McKenna and Dr. Ollie Backus, both members of the Andean Explorers Club, had written from California that they would be interested in financing an expedition with the understanding that they be allowed to participate. McKenna had trekked up to the Monastery of Tyhamboche on the trail to Mt. Everest two years before, and Backus had a deep interest in archaeology. It was the first time I had ever considered taking women on an expedition, but because of their qualifications and the fact that I wanted to explore unknown territory I agreed to take them along. So it was that El Dorado VII came into being.

We took our mounts up the familiar Chachapoyas road, past rolling hills cut by thousands of agricultural terraces, to the tiny village of Atuen, a lonely mountain settlement of sixty souls, seemingly as forgotten as the dead cities to be found hanging up on the rocky heights. One looks down at the water splashing from old Inca fountains and wonders where the original inhabitants went. Time seems to stand still up here. We spent Christmas Eve in a grotto at 11,600 feet altitude (brightened up with boxes of candles taken from our stores), and next day pushed on through a 13,000-foot pass coming out to the little community of Quiñuas. From there we rode up to Uchumarca under the shadows of the Nevado of Cajamarquilla, a 15,800-foot peak over an old roadway that had probably been taken by Tupac Yupanqui during his conquest of the region.

At a grassy plain whipped by strong, cold winds we made our way over the rubble of broken, circular buildings to a place called Llamac Tambo, and at the crest of a 12,000-foot peak discovered to our amazement a huge temple building built of great stone blocks (Plate 43.). Its walls towered up thirty feet or more. It reminded me of the construction used at Chavín de Huántar to the west. It was odd seeing such a large rectangular structure amidst so many circular constructions. The first such building to be found in Chachapoyas, it suggested the first real link with the Chavín culture. We found many stone monoliths in the surrounding ruins decorated with llama and feline figures. The whole region abounded with ancient remains—temple buildings, residential units, chullpas, and there was evidence of agricultural terracing. We named the site Gran Chivani from a local tambo after the same name. Because of its close proximity to the Cajamarquilla peak, I conjectured that it more than likely was the ancient city of the same name taken by the Inca Yupanqui in A.D. 1480. It was close to where the advance guard of the conquering king was supposed to have lost 300 troops in a blizzard at the place called "bad gate."

From there we trudged over to the Tajopampa-Pomio area, and making our way blindly through low clouds, came to two mountain heights supporting an ancient city of circular buildings littered with fallen sculptures of both human and feline figures. (Plate 44.) Farther along we came to another city known as Pueblo Viejo (Old Town) and more ancient remains.

At Chuquibamba we explored scattered remains and rode over the mountains to Cochabamba, where we visited the fine Inca ruins still standing within the village proper. The fine stonework found in Inca baths and doorways was Cuzco-style—mute testimony that the Incas had considered the site important. (Plate 45.) At Achil, a mountain crest overlooking the settlement, we examined a few typical Chachapoyas edifices. The better ruins were at San Isidro, another height, where we found circular and rectangular buildings graced with stone head sculptures. It was here that we ran into one of the typical snow blizzards that strike unannounced. We were at 11,500 feet, when suddenly we found ourselves enveloped in clouds. It began to rain

193

and a strong wind came up. Then it began to hail violently. Despite the protection of rubber ponchos, we were soon soaked to the skin. We pushed our reluctant mounts down the trail as fast as they would go, but wound up walking them down the muddy slopes, slipping and sliding in the slush. We arrived hours later at Cochabamba, drenched and half-frozen, fortunate enough to have escaped the fate that had befallen the advance guard of the Incas caught in a similar storm.

The area in which we had been working appeared to be the place to which the Incas had gone following their conquest of Cajamarquilla; and one of the cities may very well have been Papamarca, the fourth city conquered by Yupanqui. He had driven eighteen leagues from the point where he crossed the frontier and from there went to Pias, which I conjectured was the ancient city now known as Gran Pajatén. As for Contur Marca, the second city conquered, I had not succeeded in identifying it, but felt it lay somewhere over toward Bolívar, probably to the south in the Condormarca-Bombamarca area—still unexplored. Gran Chivani, one of the major sites in the vicinity, answered the description of Cajamarquilla, the third city to fall to the Inca. Raimipampa, the fifth city, fell somewhere in the area of the Cities of the Condors because of its proximity to Leimebamba (Raimebamba). The sixth and seventh cities, Suta (Muyok Viejo) and Llauantu, or Levanto (the Levanto-Monte Peruvia complex), also seem to have been located. (Map VI.) The rains were coming and I was satisfied to have tracked down what I believed to be six of the seven lost Chachapoyas cities. The seventh would have to await a new expedition (and by this time I had a good idea of where it would be found owing to the fact we had uncovered a stone road that led down into the jungles from the Gran Chivani ruins).

From what has been written the reader will be able to deduce that the Peruvian *montaña*, believed to have been inhospitable to ancient cultures, was in reality the center of a vigorous civilization in ancient times. Indeed, the monumental remains are as imposing if not superior to anything found on the coast or sierra.

While my explorations have not succeeded in proving that ancient man in Peru came up from the tropical rain forests, they have shown that high civilizations flourished in the eastern *montaña*. This in itself is important since it shows that large populations existed there, and more important, may have developed there.

The vestiges of the Chachapoyas culture show evidence of a highly advanced and sophisticated people. The first carbon-14 tests show dates of A.D. 1430 ($\pm$ 120 years) and A.D. 800 ($\pm$ 100 years). The samples tested were recovered from superficial grave sites (undoubtedly test pits would render older specimens). The first date puts the ruins into the period during which the Chachapoyas were conquered by the Incas, *i.e.*, A.D. 1480-1511.

[PLATE 43] *Huge stone building at Gran Chivani ruins. Large stone blocks used in construction weigh several tons.*

194

The earlier carbon-14 date, going back to A.D. 800, is significant because it is contemporary with the classic period of the Tiahuanaco and Maya cultures —which may show that all three cultures were experiencing a golden age at about the same time. Stratigraphic studies will throw more light on the age and history of these cultures.

I think I have been able to show that the Chachapoyas occupied the territory lying between the Marañón and Huallaga rivers, extending south to the Apisoncho. They could have experienced an expansionist period, for we find similar designs to the east in the Cajamarca region, particularly in the Chota-Vicus area. The next logical questions are: Where did the Chachapoyas originate, and who were their forerunners?

It has been shown that man was present in the greater Amazon basin for millenniums, and I personally believe that it was the cradle of primitive man in Peru. The pottery fragments I have studied from the Chachapoyas area display a style strongly influenced by the Amazon as opposed to those styles from the Andes. The circular buildings and art forms reflect contact with the eastern jungles. Almost every great Peruvian culture shows this intimacy with the tropics, from the Chavín right down to the Inca. Just what contact these cultures had with Mesoamerica remains to be seen, but again there are certain similarities to be studied. The mystery will only be cleared up with additional explorations and careful archaeological studies of these and other sites.

196

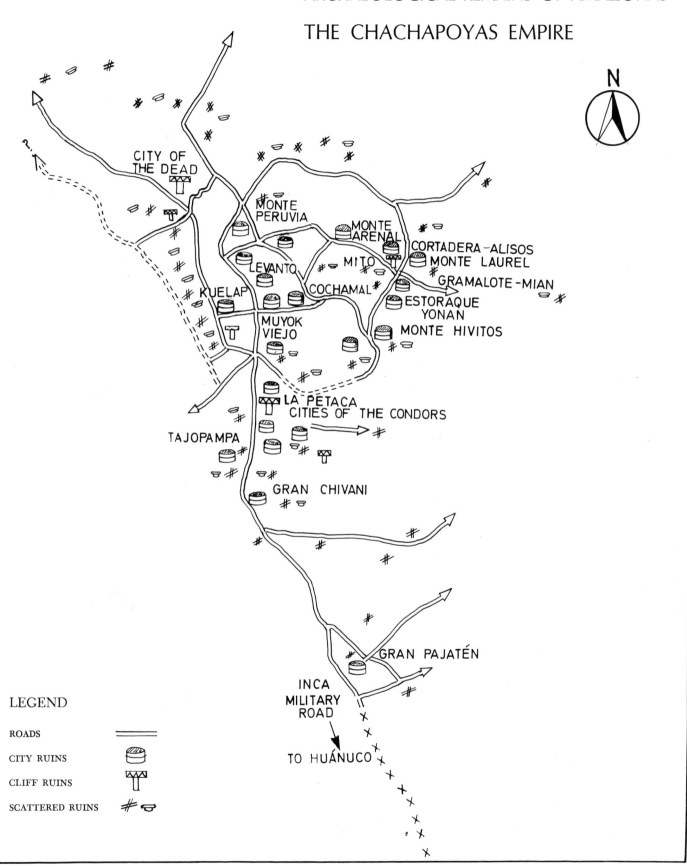

ARCHAEOLOGICAL REMAINS OF AMAZONAS

THE CHACHAPOYAS EMPIRE

N

CITY OF
THE DEAD

MONTE
PERUVIA

MONTE
ARENAL

CORTADERA – ALISOS
MONTE LAUREL

LEVANTO

MITO

GRAMALOTE – MIAN

KUELAP

COCHAMAL

ESTORAQUE
YONAN

MUYOK
VIEJO

MONTE HIVITOS

LA PETACA
CITIES OF THE CONDORS

TAJOPAMPA

GRAN CHIVANI

GRAN PAJATÉN

INCA
MILITARY
ROAD

TO HUÁNUCO

LEGEND

ROADS

CITY RUINS

CLIFF RUINS

SCATTERED RUINS

[PLATE 45] *Imperial Inca stonework at modern village of Cochabamba. Ruins indicate handwork of the Incas who conquered the Chachapoyas civilization between A.D. 1480-1511.*

EPILOGUE · New Horizons

The explorations of the coast and sierra regions of central and northern Peru show the large number of archaeological remains still to be studied and identified. Use of the airplane has helped locate these remains. But it goes without saying that a large number of important sites remain covered by centuries of drifting sand or the accumulation of rocks and slide. These are not visible to the naked eye, but the ever-developing technical aids upon which archaeology grows more dependent, such as infrared film, can and should be employed for their recovery. Indiscriminate tomb robbing, which has been going on ever since the Conquest, reminds us of the priceless objects being lost to scientific study. In addition to the treasures which are lost, the destruction of archaeological remains and the pillaging for stone carvings and building materials are gradually destroying the great ruins.

The destruction of pre-historic remains is by no means confined to the coast and sierra. As pioneer farmers are encouraged to colonize the *montaña*, forests are burned off, lands cleared and ancient monuments razed forever. Unless the Peruvian government recognizes the need for the legislation and control of her national heritage in the *montaña*, innumerable historical and archaeological monuments will be lost forever. What treasure, if any, is still to be recovered from many sites of the *montaña*, remains to be seen. The lost treasure of the Incas was not fully recovered at Vilcabamba. Huáscar's chain—700 feet of solid gold, with links the size of a man's first—is still missing. So is the balance of Atahualpa's ransom that never reached Caja-marca. And what of the large stores of gold, silver and jewels taken from the temples soon after the loss of Cuzco, sent over the Andes to be guarded by the Amautas? All this is fascinating speculation, but not as exciting as the possibility of finding lost civilizations.

The Vilcabamba Expeditions have reclaimed the old legendary city of the Incas after many years of searching. This does not, in the least, dimin-ish the achievement of Hiram Bingham, who thought Machu Picchu was the Lost City of the Incas. His early explorations of the region were thorough and informative. As a youth I lionized Bingham and had it not been for his book on the "Lost City," I might not have started looking for Vilcabamba. His preliminary, though unsuccessful, exploration at Espíritu Pampa, and his tracings of the Inca road into that area, all were instrumental in my own success.

Our El Dorado Expeditions have so far uncovered forty cities and temples from the forested slopes of the eastern Andes. From an explorer's point of view, the work has only just begun—with more than three million square miles of tropical Amazon forest still to be archaeologically explored, one hardly knows where to begin. I believe that tropical Amazonia holds the vestige of ancient cultures of which we know nothing—perhaps a civilization of far greater magnitude than we suspect (the size of the Chachapoyas ruins, which surpass those of Cuzco, hint at such a possibility). This culture might prove to be the forerunner of other known cultures. If found, it would shed new light on man's cultural development in the Americas.

It is imperative that foundations and universities undertake scientific studies of the archaeological and historical monuments uncovered to date. Furthermore, the Peruvian government must take measures to restore and preserve these sites and see that they are opened to the general public. We of the Andean Explorers Club will carry on further explorations of the inner Amazon. We have traced roads in that direction and our files are thick with reports from the Indians about other ruins. At the time of this writing plans are being made for a Grand Amazon Expedition, something far more ambitious than anything undertaken to date.

Amazonia presents the greatest challenge to explorers since the discovery and the promise of new horizons in archaeology. I for one do not believe that exploration is dead on this planet—in South America it has only just begun.

BIBLIOGRAPHY

My historical research involved many sources, including unpublished works, periodicals, published works of limited circulation, and oral tradition. A list of the principal works follows which may be of interest to researcher and student alike.

There is a large number of manuscripts not found in print and many more that, though published, have very limited circulation. These are to be found in private collections, the National Archives in Lima, in monasteries, and the General Archive of the Indies at Seville, Spain. In this respect I am very grateful to Mr. Malcolm Burke, who researched the Seville files for nearly three years. I am grateful to him for his kindness in sharing his material with me. I am also indebted to many librarians and custodians of the manuscripts in question for their kindness and advice.

Unpublished Manuscripts, Periodicals, and Published Works of Limited Circulation:

Alaya, Luis, and Soldan, Paz, *Mi País, En Las Breñas del Perú*, Vol. IV.

Alvarado, Captain Alonso de, *Los Primeros Descubrimientos y Conquistas de Los Chachapoyas por el Capitán Alonso de Alvarado, Vol. IV, Los Relaciones Geográficas de Indios, Historia General*, Vol. II. 1535.

Bandelier, Adolfo F., *Chaski*, Vol. I, No. 2. Lima, 1940.

Calancha, Antonio de la, *Crónica Moralizada del Orden de San Agustín en Perú*.

Gamboa, *History of the Incas*, English translation. London, 1907.

Genares, Gerónimo de, *Procedimientos Civiles Contra Diego Lopez de Olivares por los Derechos a Las Tierras de Amaybamba*, Archivo Histórico de Lima, Real Audiencia, Legajo 20, año 1579, Hojas utiles 88.

Horkheimer, Hans, "Algunas Consideraciones acerca de la Arqueología en la Valle del Utcubamba," *Actos del II Congreso Nacional de Historia del Perú*. Lima, 1959.

Langlois, General Louis, *Publicaciones del Museo Nacional*, Lima, 1939.

Las Casas, Bartolomé de, *Antiguas Gentes del Perú*. Madrid, 1892.

Llaysa, Diego, *Testamento Hecho por Diego Llaysa Principal del Pueblo de San Miguel de Amaybamba por Unas Tierras en el Valle de Quillabamba, Lima*, Archivo personal del Pedro Terry García, 1590, Hojas utiles 25.

Maurtua, Victor, *Juicio de Límites entre Perú y Bolivia*, Vol. VII. Barcelona, 1906.

Navarro y Lamarca, Carlos, *Historia General de América*, Vol. II. Buenos Aires, 1913.

Pachacuti, Santa Cruz, *Relación de Antigüedades del Perú*.

Reichlen, Henry and Paul, "Recherches Archéologiques dans Les Andes du Haut Utcubamba," *Journal de la Société des Américanistes*, 1950.

Santiago Vela, P. Gregorio de, *Cartas del Inca Titu Cusi Yupanqui*; Códice 3,040, Biblioteca Nacional, Vol. V. Madrid, 1916.

Torres, Bernardo de, *Crónica de la Provincia Peruana del Orden de San Agustín*. Lima, 1657.

Ugarte, Ruben Vargas, *Historia General del Perú*, Virreinato, Vol II. Lima, 1966.

Urteaga Collection, *Descripción y Sucesos Históricos de la Provincia de Vilcabamba*, Vol. I, Baltazar de Ocampo Conegeros, Colección de Libros y Documentos Referentes a la Historia del Perú, Second Series.

Yupanqui, Titu Cusi, *Relación de la Conquista de Perú Hechos del Inca Manco II*.

Published Works:

Beals, Carleton, *Nomads and Empire Builders: Native Peoples and Cultures of South America*. Philadelphia, Chilton Book Company, 1961.

Bennett, Wendell C., and Bird, Julian B., *Andean Culture History*, 2nd rev. ed. Garden City, New York, The Natural History Press, 1964.

Bingham, Hiram, *Lost City of the Incas*. New York, Duell, Sloan & Pearce, 1948.

Brundage, Burr Cartwright, *Empire of the Inca*. Norman, Oklahoma, University of Oklahoma Press, 1963.

Bushnell, G. H. S., *Ancient Arts of the Americas*. London, Thames and Hudson, 1965.
———— *Peru*. London, Thames and Hudson, 1956.

Cieza de León, Pedro de, *The Incas*, Victor W. von Hagen, ed. Norman, Oklahoma, University of Oklahoma Press, 1963.

Dietrich Disselhoff, Hans, and Linne, Sigvald, *Ancient America*. London, Methuen, 1961.

Fawcett, Colonel P. H., *Exploration Fawcett* (Arranged by Brian Fawcett). London, Hutchinson & Company, 1953.

von Hagen, Victor W., *The Ancient Sun Kingdoms of the Americas*. Cleveland, The World Publishing Company, 1957.

Lanning, Edward, *Peru Before the Incas*. Englewood Cliffs, New Jersey, Prentice-Hall, Inc., 1967.

Prescott, William H., *History of the Conquest of Mexico* and *History of the Conquest of Peru*. New York, The Modern Library, Random House.

Rostworowski de Diez Canseco, María, *Dos Manuscritos Inéditos con Datos sobre Manco II, Tierras Personales de Los Incas y Mitimaes*. Lima, Facultad de Letras; Universidad de San Marcos, 1963.

Sejourne, Laurette, *Burning Water, Thought and Religion in Ancient Mexico*. New York, Grove Press, Inc., 1960.

Vega, Garcilaso de la, *The Incas*. New York, Avon Books, 1961.

Villarejo, Avencio, *Los Agustinos en el Perú y Bolivia*. Lima, Editorial Ausonia, S. A.. 1965.

Zarate, Agustín de, *The Discovery and Conquest of Peru* (translated by J. M. Cohen). Baltimore, Penguin Books, Inc., 1968.

GLOSSARY OF NAMES, TERMS AND LOCATIONS

Abra-Puncuyoc—Pass in Vilcabamba that links Quillabamba with Lucma.

Aguardiente—Alcoholic beverage made from sugarcane.

Alabardero—Halberdier.

Alforja—Woven double satchel for carrying articles; saddlebag.

Altiplano—Highland plateaus, particularly around the Lake Titicaca Basin.

Amauta—Inca wise man or teacher.

Amazonas—A department of northeastern Peru.

Amazon Basin—Largest rain forest in the world, covering approximately 2.5 million square miles.

Ancash—Department of north-central Peru.

Antimonia—A supposed disease of spitting blood caused by deleterious emanations from excavations in the archaeological remains.

Antis—Inca term for jungle Indians living east of the Andes.

Antisuyo—One of the four quarters of Tahuantinsuyo of the Inca Empire consisting of that vast region of high and low jungle east of the Andes.

Apisoncho—River of San Martín in eastern Peru.

Apurímac—River of southern Peru.

Arawak—Tropical people of Amazon rain forest.

Aryballus—Inca pottery vessel for carrying liquids.

Atahualpa—Inca ruler (A.D. 1532–33) who took the crown by force from Huáscar. Recognized as the thirteenth Inca. Son of Huayna Capac and his concubine, a Chachapoyas or Quito princess.

Ayahuasca—Herb that produces visions.

Aymara—Name and language of people living in Lake Titicaca region.

Barbasco—A plant used as fish poison.

Bildebuyo—Highland village of the Department of La Libertad in province of Patáz, Peru.

Cahuapana—An Indian tribe near Moyobamba, Peru.

Cajamarquilla—Ancient city of the Chachapoyans conquered by Tupac Yupanqui.

Callejón de Huaylas—Valley formed by the upper Santa River between the Cordilleras Blanca and Negra, Peru.

Campa—Indian tribe of the Amazon forests.

Campesinos—Peasants.

Cañaris—Tribe of southern Ecuador conquered by the Incas.

Candonga—Reptile of Amazonas forests.

Carbon-14—A process of determining the age of radioactive isotope of carbon in organic materials.

Ccolpa Casa—12,000-foot pass at inner Vilcabamba.

Ceja de la Montaña—Eyebrow of the Mountain. (*see Montaña*)

Chachapoyas—An ancient kingdom of northeastern Peru (the general region between the Marañón and the Huallaga rivers) occupied by the Chacha people (among other peoples) who were conquered by the Incas in 1480 and again in A.D. 1500–11. Carbon-14 tests of artifacts taken from the surface of archaeological remains in the region give dates of A.D. 800 and 1430. The large monuments, cities, metropolises, ceremonial centers and extensive agricultural works indicate the Chachapoyas had been a highly advanced civilization who may have had their origins in the eastern jungles. Modern Chachapoyas is the capital of the Department of Amazonas.

Chacra—Small farm.

Chancaca—Raw sugar in blocks.

Chancas—A fierce warrior race northwest of Cuzco who dominated the Quechua tribes until finally defeated by the Incas. They escaped into the *montañas* east of Chachapoyas and there built a neo-empire.

Chanchan—Large mud-walled metropolis of Peruvian north coast covering some 11 square miles.

Chasqui—Inca runner or messenger.

Chaupimayo—River of Vilcabamba.

Chavín—An ancient civilization of north-central Peru which is believed to have developed sometime between 1800–400 B.C. Most noted remains are those of Chavín de Huantar on the eastern slopes of the Andes in the Department of Ancash. Chavín ruins are found throughout Peru—*montaña*, highlands, coast.

Chibcha—A confederation of tribes in the highland basins of Bogotá, Colombia.

Chicha—Peruvian beer made from fermented corn.

Chichén Itzá—Stone remains of Yucatán, Mexico.

Chicotillo—Aggressive reptile of Amazon forests.

Chimbote—Industrial and fishing center of north-central Peru.

Chimu—An advanced civilization of north Peruvian coast whose cultural center appears to have been Chanchan. The Chimu dominated the coastal valleys of the north sometime between A.D. 1100–1400 until defeated by the Incas in 1466.

Chimuco—Bushmaster snake.

Chinchaysuyo—One of the four quarters of the Inca Empire, it included the region from Chincha Valley to Quito, Ecuador.

Chirihuanes—Name of Indian tribe of Amazon forest.

Chirmac Cassa—Ancient city of the Chachapoyas conquered by Tupac Yupanqui.

Choclo—Peruvian corn.

Chonta—Hardwood palm tree.

Chontapampa—River of Vilcabamba.

Choquequirau—Inca city of Cuzco.

Chuclla—Indian hut used by highlanders.

Chullachaqui—Small devil-spirit of Amazon forest.

Chullpa—Funerary monument.

Chunchos—Savage Indian tribes of eastern forests.

Chuquichaca—Inca bridge over the Urubamba River (possibly Vilcabamba) near Chaullay.

Chuquipalpa—A town of Vilcabamba, site of Yarak-Rumi stone.

Cloud Forest—Tropical forest between 6,000–10,000 feet.

Cloud People—Refers to the Chacha people.

Coca—Shrub which yields narcotic leaf chewed by Indians.

Coishco—Fishing center north of Chimbote, Peru.

Concevidayoc—River of Vilcabamba, source of Cosireni River.

Condor, Cities of the—A dozen or more hanging cities on the lower Atuen River.

Condor, Lake of the—Lake of Amazonas, Peru.

Condur Marca—Ancient city of the Chachapoyas mentioned by Blas Valera.

Copa—Drinking glass. To have a "copa," to have a drink.

Corbeled arch—False arch formed by overlapping stones.

Cordillera Blanca—Snowy peaks of the Cordillera Occidental which average 18,000–20,000 feet in altitude, north-central Peru.

Cordillera Negra—Chain of snowless mountains averaging 15,000 feet in altitude, north-central Peru.

Cosireni—a tributary of the Urubamba.

Coya—Matrons of the Inca.

Cuntisuyo—Fourth quarter of the Inca Empire; the sierras around Cuzco, Peru.

Curandero—Witchdoctor or healer.

Curare (Mirare)—Family *Strichnos*, a poison used by Hivitos and other Amazon tribes for blowgun darts.

Cuy—Guinea pig.

Demonio del agua—A demon of the water, half-fish and half-man, who wears a snakeskin belt and captivates his victims with luminous eyes and drags them into the depths.

Didimo—Chachapoyas version of Viracocha, the culture hero.

Duende—A forest spirit.

El Jobo—Pottery style in Venezuela.

Eromboni (Erombori)—A group of ruins near Espíritu Pampa.

Espíritu Pampa—An old Machiguenga camp, presently a small farm clearing of the low *montaña*.

Fango—Swamplands.

Garrapatas—Ticks.

Gran Chivani—Imposing archaeological remains on 12,000-foot peak near village of Uchumarca.

Gran Pajatén—Archaeological remains located east of Marañón in the Department of San Martín, Peru.

Guarancalla (Huarancalla)—Inca community in Vilcabamba where Fray Ortiz had his mission, hospital and school.

Hechicero—One who bewitches.

Huaca—Pre-historic site or tomb venerated by ancients.

Huacamayo—Macaw.

Huaco—Pre-historic object.

Huacrachucos—Ancient people believed to have occupied the upper banks of the Marañón.

Huallaga—Tributary of the Marañón.

Huamachuco—Highland community in the Department of La Libertad, Peru.

Huamachucos—Ancient people of the central highlands.

Huancauri—Sacred stone or boulder of the Incas.

Huánuco—Highland community of central Peru.

Huaqueros—Grave robbers.

Huasachugo—Remains of unknown civilization in highlands near Santiago de Chuco, Peru.

Huáscar—Twelfth Inca, Huana Capac's heir. Half-brother of Atahualpa (rule: A.D. 1526–1532).

Huascarán—High peak of the Cordillera Blanca (22,198 feet), Peru.

Huaylas—(see Recuay)

Huayna Capac—Eleventh Inca (rule: A.D. 1493–1525).

Huayna Pucara—Young fortress; stormed by Spaniards when they attacked Incas in Vilcabamba.

Iccma Ccolla—Sacred peak of Markacocha-Pichqacocha range in Vilcabamba.

Ichu—Bunch grass used as roofing.

Ik—Maya glyph for day.

Illapa—A divine spirit of light or sun. A thunder god.

Inca—A ruling class of Quechua people that founded Cuzco (A.D. 1100–1200) under Manco Capac. About 1350 they began to expand and by 1527 reached their apex of rule. (*see* Tahuantinsuyo)

Inti—The physical sun according to Incas.

Intihuatani—Sun calendar.

Ita—Vermin of the jungle.

Jalcas—High grasslands of sierra or puna.

Jergon (Bothrops pictus)—Poisonous reptile of Amazon forests. The fer-de-lance is known by many names in greater Amazonia.

Jívaro—Savage tribe of Ecuadorian forests.

Jornada—One day's journey.

Kilineris—Amazon tribe northeast of Vilcabamba.

Kollasuyo—Fourth quarter of the Inca Empire comprising the highlands of Titicaca region of Peru, Bolivia, Chile and Argentina.

Kon Tiki Viracocha—The Inca Supreme Creator.

Kotosh—Pottery style of central *montaña* dating as early as 1800 B.C.

Kuelap—Ancient Chachapoyas monument discovered by Juan Crisóstomo Nieto in 1843.

Ladrillo—Brick.

La Horca del Inca (Mananhuanunca)—Site of martyrdom of Fray Ortiz.

Lajasbamba—Forest regions south of Leimibamba in the Department of Amazonas. Site of archaeological remains of same name.

La Libertad—Department of north Peru.

League—A Spanish league is the distance covered in one hour or about three miles. An Inca league was somewhat longer.

Levantu (Llavanto, Levanto, Revanto, Rebanto)—Ancient city of Chachapoyas (their old capital city) conquered by Tupac Yupanqui.

Loro Muchacuy (Cobra Papagayo)—Poisonous reptile of the jungles in Amazonia. A vivid green color, thin and up to six feet in length, it is difficult to see until it falls upon its victim.

Lucma—Capital of the District of Vilcabamba, Cuzco.

Lucuma—A tropical tree with leathery leaves and small axillary flowers that yields an eggfruit.

Machiguenga—Tribe of Amazon forests. Linguistically related to the Campas.

Machu Picchu—Archaeological remains above Urubamba River northwest of Cuzco, discovered by Hiram Bingham in 1911.

Mananhuanunca—Site of Fray Ortiz' martyrdom in Vilcabamba.

Mañaries—Indian tribe of lower Urubamba.

Manco Capac—First Inca king; founded Cuzco.

Manco II (Inca Manco II)—First Inca king of neo-Inca state of Vilcabamba (rule: A.D. 1534–45). Son of Huayna Capac and Mama Runtu.

Maquizapa—A black monkey; food source of inhabitants of the jungle.

Marañón—A large river of Peru; source of the Amazon.

Marca Huamachuco—Remains of ancient city near modern community of Huamachuco.

Marcanay—Inca town or temple near Vilcabamba.

Markacocha—A mountain range of Vilcabamba.

Maskaypacha—Inca crown of gold and feathers.

Mayas—An ancient civilization of Mexico and Central America that flourished from A.D. 400–900, after which they began to abandon their cities.

Mestizo—Half-breed.

Miradores—Inca watchtowers. *see* Tukuy Rikuqs.

Mitimaes—Conquered people put to work under the Incas.

Moche—Small community of the Department of La Libertad. A river valley formerly occupied by the so-called Mochica civilization. Site of Pyramids of Sun and Moon.

Mochicas (or Moche)—A civilization of north Peruvian coast that flourished between A.D. 200–800 who were absorbed by a highland tribe around A.D. 800–1000. The forerunners of the Mochica go back as far as 200 B.C. or earlier.

Mojos—Pottery style of eastern Bolivia.

Montaña—The upper rain forests which grow on the eastern slopes of the Andes at altitudes ranging from 3,000–10,000 feet or more.

Monte Bravo—Archaeological remains south of Leimibamba, Amazonas.

Monte Peruvia—Name of ancient Chachapoyas metropolis comprising some forty major archaeological groups covering an area estimated to be 60 square miles.

Mucha—A kiss.

Muyok Viejo—Ancient Chachapoyas metropolis in highland east of Utcubamba River.

Nahuatl—Race of Mexico and Mesoamerica, including Aztecs.

Naymlap—Founder of Lambayeque (Chimu?) culture.

Neotropica—South America as a zoographic area.

Ñusta—Inca virgin. Mountain of Vilcabamba.

Ñusta Hispana—An Inca site in Vilcabamba.

Ollantaytambo—Terraced Inca city above banks of Urubamba River near Cuzco, Peru.

Orejones—Inca wise men. Guardians of Inca history. Curacas or long-eared ones.

Pachacutec—Ninth Inca (rule: A.D. 1438–71).

Pachamama—The Inca Blessed Virgin; earth goddess.

Paititi—Legendary Inca city.

Paja—Dried grass; straw.

Pajatén—Abandoned Franciscan mission near river of same name in the Department of San Martín, northeastern Peru.

Pampa—A plain or flat land.

Pampaconas—Highland pueblo in District of Vilcabamba, Department of Cuzco, Peru. A river, source of Concevidayoc.

Pani (Cocculus toxicoferus)—A poison combined with curare, ramón or mirare by tribes of the lower Amazon for blowgun darts.

Patasinos—Men from Patáz.

Patáz—Highland community in province of same name, Department of La Libertad, Peru.

Petaca, La—Cliff tomb site in Department of Amazonas.

Petroglyph—Rock carving.

Pias (Questa of Pias)—Ancient city of the Chachapoyas conquered by Tupac Yupanqui.

Pichqacocha—A mountain range of Vilcabamba.

206

Pictograph—Rock painting.

Pilcosones—Tribe of eastern forests.

Piraña—Amazon cannibal fish.

Piripiri—Stick or bark chewed by Indians of the Amazon, used to kill or maim poisonous snakes.

Pisco—Peruvian white brandy made from grapes.

Pucuna—Blowgun.

Pucyura (Puquiura)—Modern village of Vilcabamba. Site of Fray Marcos García's mission. Place where Inca Manco maintained his armies.

Pueblo de los Muertos (City of the Dead)—A cliff necropolis of Amazonas.

Pumachaca (Papamarca or Raimipampa)—Ancient city of Chachapoyas conquered by Tupac Yupanqui.

Puna—High grasslands around 11,000 feet.

Punchao—An Inca idol of the Sun; the Golden Disk of the Sun.

Puncuyoc—Mountain of Vilcabamba upon which ancient Inca remains are located.

Purun Machu—Indian name for a supposed affliction or illness caused from evil spirits that frequent ancient ruins.

Quebrada—Dry river gorge.

Quechua—Name of one or more tribes of Inca Empire. They are believed to have originated in the Urubamba-Apurímac watershed of the southern *montañas* of Peru. A language spoken by these people.

Quetzalcoatl—Ancient god or culture hero of old Mexico believed to be symbolized by a plumed serpent. Creator of man; god of water, air, spirit.

Quillabamba—Community on Urubamba River, Peru.

Quito—Northern capital of Tahuantinsuyo. Presently capital of Ecuador. The ancient kingdom of Quito conquered by the Incas.

Ranrahirca—Community of Callejón de Huaylas destroyed by avalanche in 1962.

Rebanto or Revanto—Fortified city ruled by the Incas up to the time of Inca Manco. Believed to be the Levanto of Chachapoyas.

Recuay—A post-Chavín culture sometimes called the Huaylas culture which was widespread throughout the north-central highlands.

Relámpago—Lightning.

Rodriguez de Mendoza—Province of the Department of Amazonas, Peru, east of the capital of Chachapoyas and laden with archaeological remains.

Rosas Pata—An Inca site in Vilcabamba.

Sacha mama—Boa of *montaña*.

Sacsayhuaman—Cyclopean Inca fortress above Cuzco, Peru.

Salcantay—A 20,000-foot peak of the cordillera of Vilcabamba.

San Martín—Department of northeastern Peru.

San Miguel—Valley of inner Vilcabamba.

Sayri Tupac—Second king of neo-Inca state of Vilcabamba (rule A.D. 1545-60).

Selva—Jungled plains at the foot of the eastern Andes below 3,000 feet altitude.

Shapingo—A forest spirit.

Shushupe (Lachesis mutus)—The Peruvian bushmaster snake; the most poisonous and ferocious reptile in the Amazon.

Sierra—The highlands.

Solpemachaco—Mythical seven-headed serpent that lives in caves.

Stratigraphy—The arrangement of strata used in geology and archaeology for relative dating of deposits.

Surcos—Small agricultural terraces.

Tahuantinsuyo—Ancient name of Inca Empire. It consisted of four different worlds or quarters, Cuzco being the center. These four worlds had great climatical and cultural extremes. Cuntisuyo was the temperate area around Cuzco that included the Quechua or Cuntis tribes. Kollasuyo consisted of the old altiplano inhabited by the Kollas or Aymara people of the Titicaca region, and included parts of Bolivia, Argentina and Chile. Chinchaysuyo was the warm coastal areas of the central coast that spread as far north as Quito. Here lived the Chinchas or Yungas peoples. Antisuyo was formed of all the tropical forest areas east of the Andes (Antis) mountains occupied by the Antis People. Inca Pachacutec is believed to have established the division.

Tamputocco—Legendary cave of origin of the Incas.

Tapajo—Amazon pottery style.

Teja—Roofing tile.

Tenon-head—A carved head of stone with an extension to be inserted in walls.

Tiahuanaco—Ancient high civilization from Lake Titicaca region that flourished at one time between A.D. 500–1000. It spread to north Peru and coastal areas sometime around A.D. 900–1000, after which it collapsed.

Tiapollo—A legendary city of Amazonas, Peru.

Titicaca, Lake—A high navigable lake shared by modern Peru and Bolivia situated at 12,500 feet above sea level.

Titu Cusi—Third king of the neo-Inca state of Vilcabamba (rule: A.D. 1560–71).

Trujillo—Capital of the Department of La Libertad, Peru.

Tukuy Rikuqs—Inca Watchtower. An Inca official meaning one who sees all.

Tunchi—A spirit devil of Amazonian forests.

Tupac Amaru—Fourth and last king of the neo-Inca state of Vilcabamba (rule: A.D. 1571–72); judicially murdered by Spaniards at Cuzco in 1572.

Tupac Yupanqui—Tenth Inca (rule: A.D. 1471–93).

Ungacacha (Yunkakasa)—Lake or swamp which Frays García and Ortiz had to traverse on their way to Vilcabamba the Old.

Urubamba—River of southern Peru.

Usnuyoc—Mountain height in Vilcabamba.

Utcubamba—River of Amazonas, Peru.

Vilca—An old name for the sun.

Vilcabamba (Willcapampa)—Territory of Inca Empire northwest of Cuzco occupied by Manco II and his host following his revolt against the Spanish in 1537.

Vilcabamba, San Francisco de la Victoria de—Vilcabamba the New, a city built by the Spaniards in 1572 shortly following the capture of Tupac Amaru. It was peopled by the survivors of the Inca Army.

Vilcabamba Cordillera—A mountain chain of high peaks in the Department of Cuzco.

Vilcabamba Lakes—A cluster of lakes in the Markacocha range.

Vilcabamba the Old—Capital of the Province of Vilcabamba and the main city of Manco II. It was abandoned by Tupac Amaru in 1572 and set to the torch. The Spaniards occupied it soon after.

Viracocha—An Inca king of the fourteenth century. Also the name of a religious teacher of Inca legend who taught arts and sciences. Loosely applied, Viracocha applies to any fair-skinned person. (*see* Kon Tiki Viracocha)

Vista Alegre—A small farm on Vilcabamba trail.

Vitcos—A fortified city of the province after the same name that defended against invasion of Vilcabamba.

Willka (see Vilca)

Yalap—Ancient Chachapoyas monument of imposing size in high forests above pueblo of La Jalca.

Yucca—Manioc; a tuberous root used as basic food of the *montaña*.

Yurak-Rumi—A sacred stone in the Temple of the Sun revered by the neo-Incas.

Zuta (Suta)—Ancient city of Chachapoyas conquered by Tupac Yupanqui.

CHRONOLOGY OF EVENTS
AND EXPLORATIONS*

A.D. 1437 Chancas attack Cuzco.
    1438 Chancas defeated by Inca Pachacutec.
    1440 Antisuyo campaigns undertaken by Incas.
    1466 Incas conquer Chimu.
    1471 Death of Inca Pachacutec; Tupac Yupanqui assumes Inca Crown.
    1480 Tupac Yupanqui conquers Chachapoyas.
    1492 Columbus discovers America.
    1493 Death of Inca Tupac Yupanqui; Huayna Capac assumes Inca Crown.
    1500 Brazil discovered by Pedro Álvarez Cabral; mouth of Amazon discovered and explored by Vicente Yáñez Pinzón.
  1500–11 Huayna Capac puts down Chachapoyas rebellion.
  1518–20 Huayna Capac conquers Quito.
    1522 Cortez conquers Mexico.
    1526 Death of Inca Huayna Capac; Huáscar assumes Inca Crown at Cuzco; Portuguese launch expedition to colonize Brazil.
    1527 Inca Empire reaches its zenith; Pizarro off coast of Peru; civil war begins between Huáscar and Atahualpa.
    1530 Spaniards first hear rumors of El Dorado in Ecuador.
    1531 Diego Ordaz looks for El Dorado; Pizarro launches full-scale expedition of conquest of Peru.
    1532 Pizarro lands at Tumbes, marches to Cajamarca.
    1533 Death of Huáscar by order of Atahualpa; Pizarro executes Atahualpa, marches on Cuzco; Sebastian Belalcazar conquers Quito.
    1534 Manco II crowned Inca at Cuzco with approval of Francisco Pizarro.
    1535 Antonio de Herrera looks for El Dorado; Pedro de Candia sent by Hernando Pizarro to investigate the Kingdom of Ambaya, eastern Bolivia.
    1536 Manco revolts against Spanish, lays siege to Cuzco.
    1537 Manco forces Chachapoyas from Amaybamba to Vilcabamba and beheads their chief at Urubamba; Manco retires into *montañas* of Vilcabamba with large host.

* Modern and Spanish dates used in the Chronology are as accurate as research permits. Inca dates must be considered tentative.

1538 Manco aids Antis Indians, visits Revanto; Spaniards found San Juan de la Frontera at Chachapoyas; Pedro Anzures leads expedition into Antisuyo east of Titicaca; civil war among conquistadores.

1539 Pedro Anzures contacts the Maguire nation on plains of Mojos and hears of a lost empire in the interior; Gonzalo Ximenes de Quesada fails to find El Dorado.

1540 Gonzalo Pizarro sets out for El Dorado and Forests of Cinnamon.

1541 Francisco Pizarro assassinated.

1541–42 Francisco de Orellana navigates the Amazon River.

1541–45 Philip Von Hutten hunts for El Dorado.

1542 Almagrists seek refuge with Manco in Vilcabamba.

1544 New Laws for the Indies issued by Spanish Crown.

1545 Manco assassinated in Vilcabamba; Sayri Tupac assumes crown of Vilcabamba line.

1550 Two hundred refugee Indians appear out of the forest at Chachapoyas.

1554 Huallaga region settled by Pedro de Ursúa.

1558 Lima receives word of El Dorado sighting.

1559 Spanish Crown sponsors El Dorado expedition under Pedro de Ursúa.

1560 Death of Sayri Tupac; Titu Cusi crowned Inca at Vilcabamba.

1565 Diego Rodriguez de Figueroa visits Titu Cusi in Vilcabamba.

1566 Marcos García enters Vilcabamba.

1568 Fray Diego Ortiz enters Vilcabamba.

1569 Viceroy Don Francisco de Toledo arrives in Peru.

1571 Death of Titu Cusi; Tupac Amaru crowned with Scarlet Fringe at Vilcabamba; Fray Ortiz martyred at Marcanay.

1572 Spanish army invades Vilcabamba under General Martín Hurtado de Arbieto; Vilcabamba the Old occupied by Spanish troops; San Francisco de la Victoria de Vilcabamba (Vilcabamba the New) founded by victorious Spanish; Tupac Amaru, last of the Vilcabamba kings, executed at Cuzco.

1581 Viceroy Toledo returns to Spain.

1584 Antonio de Berrio looks for El Dorado.

1595 Remains of Fray Diego Ortiz removed from Vilcabamba to Cuzco; Sir Walter Raleigh hunts for El Dorado, explores Orinoco.

1596 Lawrence Kemys sets out for El Dorado.

1597 Toribio Alonso de Mogrovejo missionizes Amazonas, Peru.

1613 Robert Harcourt looks for El Dorado in Guiana.

1619–21 Franciscans missionize jungles of eastern Peru.

1654 Fray Tomás Chavez claims to have contacted the Empire of the Musus after a 33-day journey from plains of Mojos. Paititi is said to be more densely populated than Peru and richer in gold than all the Indies.

1760 Apolinar Días de Fuente launches El Dorado expedition.

1764 Bodavilla expedition makes futile search for El Dorado.

1788 Fray Álvarez de Villanueva traverses The Pajatén.

1824 Eugene de Sartiques discovers Choquequirau.

1840 Sir Robert Hermann Schomburgk looks for El Dorado.

1843 Juan Crisóstomo Nieto discovers Kuelap.

1860 Arturo Wertheman explores Amazonas.

1865 Antonio Raimondi visits Spanish Vilcabamba in quest of Inca city.

1875 Charles Wiener travels over Pass of Panticalla, hears rumors of existence of Machu Picchu.

1877 Vidal Senéze reports existence of scattered remains in Rodriguez de Mendoza, Amazonas.

1892 Arturo Wertheman visits Kuelap.

1893 Adolph Bandelier explores Amazonas.

1895 Rubber planters explore fringe areas of Espíritu Pampa.

1901–07 Agriculturists first cultivate terraces of Machu Picchu.

1908 Theodor Koch-Grünberg looks for El Dorado.

1911 Hiram Bingham discovers Machu Picchu; makes unsuccessful attempt to explore Espíritu Pampa.

1916–28 Christian Bues maps Vilcabamba highlands.

1919 Augusto Weberbauer discovers scattered remains, roads leading to Pajatén country.

1925 Hamilton Rice looks for El Dorado; Colonel Percy H. Fawcett disappears in the Brazilian Mato Grosso.

1931–32 Shippee-Johnson Aerial Expedition discovers Santa Wall.

1933 General Louis Langlois explores Amazonas.

1942 Bertrand Flornoy explores upper Marañón.

1947 Arquimedes Toulier explores lower Urubamba.

1950–55 Henry Reichlen studies remains of Utcubamba.

1953 Malcolm Burke rafts down Urubamba, sights Inca terraces at Yavero; Victor von Hagen traces Inca roads of Peru; Julian Tennant explores for ruins in lower Urubamba.

1963 Brooks Baekeland and Peter Gimbel make first recorded traverse of Apurímac-Urubamba region; agriculturists from Huamachuco, Patáz and Pias observe archaeological remains in Pajatén territory.

1964 Carlos Neueschwander explores Pantiacolla for ancient remains; F. K. Paddock probes Urubamba.

INDEX